THE NEXT CHINA IS STILL CHINA

THE NEXT CHINA IS STILL CHINA

An Insider's Playbook for Winning in the New Era

JOE NGAI AND **NICK LEUNG**

First published in the USA by Scribner in 2026
An Imprint of Simon & Schuster, LLC

First published in Great Britain by John Murray Business in 2026
An imprint of John Murray Publishing Group

1

A CIP catalogue record for this title is available from the British Library

Hardback ISBN 9781399839853
ebook ISBN 9781399839860

Typeset in Warnock Pro

Printed and bound in Great Britain by Clays Ltd, Elcograf S.p.A.

John Murray Publishing Group policy is to use papers that are natural, renewable and recyclable products and made from wood grown in sustainable forests. The logging and manufacturing processes are expected to conform to the environmental regulations of the country of origin.

John Murray Publishing Group
Carmelite House
50 Victoria Embankment
London EC4Y 0DZ

John Murray Business
Hachette Book Group
123 South Broad Street
Ste 2750
Philadelphia, PA 19109, USA

www.johnmurraybusiness.com

John Murray Publishing Group, part of Hodder & Stoughton Limited
An Hachette UK company

The authorised representative in the EEA is Hachette Ireland,
8 Castlecourt Centre, Dublin 15, D15 XTP3, Ireland (email: info@hbgi.ie)

For our families

Contents

PART III WHAT'S NEXT, CHINA?

Prologue

In January 2023, at the World Economic Forum—the annual, invitation-only gathering of global business and political leaders in Davos, Switzerland—several dozen Asia-focused CEOs and senior executives of the world's largest companies gathered for a private dinner. The topic of the evening: China.

The gathering was hosted by McKinsey & Company and moderated by Joe Ngai, the Firm's Greater China chairman and one of this book's co-authors. He'd led dozens of similar discussions over the years, but the mood that night was different. The executives in the room were leaders who'd invested heavily in—and benefited from—China's rise of the past two decades. Collectively, they commanded operations employing tens of thousands, supply chains spanning dozens of provinces, brands recognized globally from Shanghai to London to Abu Dhabi. And yet, for the first time in memory, the conversation wasn't about growth targets or market expansion; it was about whether their China strategies still worked at all. Questions came quickly, circling what we'd titled the evening's discussion: "unprecedented headwinds"—or the collision of economic uncertainty, geopolitical tension, and rapid technological change: *When would China's housing downturn stabilize? Should our board be anxious about the slowdown in consumer confidence? Do we expand India operations as a hedge to China?*

Beneath each question lay the same unease: whether China's role as the engine of global growth—the foundation upon which so much progress had been built—was coming to an end. After guests stepped back out into the snow, a journalist lingered in the hallway and asked Joe what had become a recurrent boardroom query: "If this is the reality now," he said, "where does the next opportunity lie?" The question followed naturally: "What's the next China?"

The query, of course, wasn't philosophical but practical. Which country—or combination of countries—would replace China as the world's next engine of growth, profits, and scale? Throughout the week at Davos, the notion "China + 1" dominated private conversations—the imperative of finding alternatives to China as the country labored through geopolitical challenges, overcapacity, weakening sentiment from consumers and investors alike, and rapid technological change.

While Joe fielded questions in Davos, Nick Leung—his predecessor as McKinsey's China head and this book's other co-author—was halfway around the world in Shenzhen, the glass-and-steel city at the heart of China's manufacturing ecosystem. He was leading a procurement workshop for a multinational client whose China footprint was foundational to its competitive advantage—dense supplier networks, specialized tooling clusters, production lines calibrated for speed and precision, and a labor force that could scale up or down by the hour. The stakes were high enough to draw the global CEO into the room.

The directive from headquarters was clear: find an alternative. Costs were rising. Policy risk felt harder to navigate. The company needed options, and it needed them now. Nick and his teams had spent months stress-testing scenarios. Yet every alternative led to the same judgment: "There are no great substitutes—we must choose the least bad option." In other countries, the promise of stability and efficiency proved fragile. Rising wages and input costs eroded gains. The frictions of "friend-shoring"—logistical delays, substandard infrastructure, quality inconsistencies, a lack of institutional knowledge—piled up. Finally, the CEO voiced what everyone in the room was thinking: "We're starting to realize how much we've taken China's ecosystem for granted."

No other country pairs the world's most advanced supply chains with its largest consumer base. In China, companies can launch faster, adjust in real time, and iterate—refining and improving with each repetition—inside of a digitally connected, highly competitive marketplace in which innovation is a condition of survival. Is it any wonder, then, that this combination of scale, speed, and depth has proven so hard to find elsewhere?

Against this backdrop, a pattern began to emerge. In Davos, executives were asking "What's the next China?" In Shenzhen, Nick was watching a client discover there were no good answers. Across dozens of similar conversations, in boardrooms, forums, workshops, the same reality kept surfacing. The companies searching hardest for alternatives were having trouble finding the answers they wanted—not because China was getting easier, but because replicating what China has to offer proved impossible anywhere else.

The realization crystallized six weeks after Davos, on a flight over the South China Sea. The conclusion felt almost too simple: The next China is China.

Joe posted it on LinkedIn, expecting a ripple. Instead, it exploded. The phrase had circulated before, rolled out whenever an obstacle had emerged or a sector lulled. This time, it landed differently, generating more than twenty-eight thousand mentions across Chinese and global media, from the *China Daily* to CNBC to Bloomberg. Over the months that followed, multinational and Chinese clients alike began asking us to take the idea into board and investor meetings. A consumer goods CEO asked us to brief the board on whether the "consumer depression" headlines were real. A private equity founder invited us to his limited partners investor day to discuss which segments remain investable. An entrepreneur asked, over lunch, how to reorganize his company for overseas growth.

We've been careful—then and now—to be precise about what we're saying. Growth in China is slowing. The economy is maturing. Competition is intense, corporate debt has climbed, and weaker consumer confidence has struggled to offset the economic drag from a prolonged property downturn. This isn't the China of 2010 or even 2019. It's a reset, and the contrast with the past two decades of breakneck growth feels jarring.

But the numbers tell a more durable story. At just 2 percent annual growth, China would add output over the next decade equivalent to today's entire Indian economy; at 5 percent—the government's target—it would be like adding an India, Japan, and Indonesia combined. Already the world's second biggest economy and the largest by purchasing power parity (PPP), China is the top trading partner for more than 120 countries—far more than any other single economy—and accounts for about 30 percent of global growth.

No collection of "speedboats" can displace the same water moved by a supertanker. In terms of raw growth, beyond its former quantitative role, China is likely to play a larger role qualitatively—increasingly shaping the technologies, business models, and industries of the future. Its companies are among the leaders in sixteen of the eighteen high-growth "arenas of competition" that McKinsey identifies as future engines of global value—from AI software and cloud infrastructure to electric vehicles, e-commerce, and consumer internet.

We're not suggesting competing in the next China will be easy—if anything, it'll be harder. The bar for success has risen, outcomes will diverge more sharply, and only companies willing to fundamentally rethink how they compete will endure. This transition to the next China will be both macroeconomic—from hard manufacturing toward services and IP creation—and microeconomic, demanding new capabilities: operating across borders, building and defending global footprints and brands, managing IP at scale, and embedding AI and robotics. For Chinese firms, it means extending global reach and organizational sophistication; for foreign multinationals, it means moving beyond merely selling into China toward partnering and building within its innovative ecosystems. For both, the rewards remain significant for those that can continue to adapt.

We don't believe in one-size-fits-all playbooks. Consider this book a navigator's chart—drawn from decades of experience in

China—which maps long-running currents as well as hidden risks. The forces we describe will persist, but tactics, timing, and execution must constantly evolve.

We hope you'll come along for the ride. As we will show, understanding how to compete and win in China will equip you to succeed anywhere. The next China is *still* China; the real question is whether it's for you.

PART I

HOW WE GOT HERE

McKinsey's Early Days in China

The next China can't be understood without first appreciating how the current one came to be. What now feels inevitable—the scale, the speed, the sheer audacity—was once a fragile experiment. A rural country of bicycles and ration books dared to reinvent itself, and in a single generation, it did. Villages were folded into mega-cities, factories became innovation hubs, and hundreds of millions surged into the middle class while the world began not just watching China but also learning from it.

Like many business tales, this one begins with a virtually blank slate on which a few pioneers were willing to scrawl a new vision for how things should work.

A "Business Doctor" Lands in China

"Mai-ken-xi, not Mai-dang-lao." The year was 1995. In Mandarin, McKinsey's name shares its opening syllable with McDonald's, and more than once we were mistaken for the American golden arches that had landed in Beijing just a few years earlier. The Firm's first attempt at explaining who it was—and what it did—was met with polite confusion. "What exactly do you sell?"

At the press conference announcing McKinsey's first mainland China offices, the headline wasn't our arrival; it was that one of our lead partners, Tony Perkins, a fluent Mandarin-speaking Mormon, had six children. In the land of the one-child policy, a large family was bigger news than the advent of an unknown firm whose name sounded vaguely like a fast-food chain's.

The other McKinsey lead, Gordon Orr, was an electrical engineer turned strategist who'd become one of the youngest partners in the Firm's posh London office in St. James's. Restless, he had volunteered for Hong Kong and, soon restless again, pushed on to Beijing. "But if we were serious about building in this part of the world," Gordon says, "the real adventure would be in mainland China." In China's capital city in the mid-1990s, it might take two years just to get a landline installed. By the time Gordon retired three decades later to join the boards of Lenovo, Swire Pacific, EQT, and Meituan, the country had become the world's largest smartphone market, home to 1.3 billion mobile users.

Most multinationals were still years away from entering China—McDonald's had been one of the first—and parachuting into a business culture that understood products better than services was a bold move. Back then, "advice for a price" didn't even exist in China's legal code: you could register a factory or an import-export firm but not a consultancy. A district halfway to Tianjin agreed to classify McKinsey as a "wholly owned foreign enterprise" in commercial services—a bureaucratic workaround that created the Firm's first China foothold with offices in Shanghai and Beijing.

Gordon spent the first weeks positioning himself. After a few clumsy attempts to explain management consulting, he tried a new line, portraying himself as a business doctor for companies that needed to get healthy—or if that failed, a coach who trained average athletes into gold medalists. It wasn't quite poetry, but he'd learned that mentioning McKinsey drew blank stares; alluding to his Harvard and Oxford degrees earned a dinner invitation.

Looking out across the city from McKinsey's glass tower in today's Beijing, population twenty-two million, it's easy to forget how tenuous those beginnings were and also how far the Firm—and China—have come. In the mid-1990s, Beijing was a low-rise city of twelve million, its wide roads packed with bicycles, dust, and scaffolding. Foreign hotels were few. Only one in twenty Beijingers owned a car. Office space was easy to find; phone lines weren't. The Firm's first deal was securing the vacant office of a departing Canadian telecom company: "We'll take your lease if you leave the phones." The city buzzed with anticipation and hope for the future.

The First Generation of Business Talent

The next big challenge was people. With no alumni to tap, not a single senior Chinese colleague at McKinsey anywhere, and few Chinese returnees from Western business schools, the Firm had to create its own pipeline. So we went to Beijing's elite schools: Tsinghua University and Peking University. One evening at Peking University in 1995, the two-hundred-seat hall overflowed while another two hundred would-be attendees pressed outside the doors. "We didn't know if anyone would show up—we were a foreign company with no product," Gordon admits. "But the word was out that we were hiring, and success meant a ticket to a US business school."

The aspirants were rocket smart. Their résumés reflected the hunger of the times: top in economics at Tsinghua, highest scorer on Sichuan's national entrance exam. Two women from that group would form the backbone of the Beijing office. One, Sha Sha, gravitated toward Gordon because he'd announced that McKinsey believed in mentoring "local talent and together creating impact."

Sha dove into global-mining work just as Chinese steel became the world's volume leader, spending weeks inside China's steel towns. "The frontline mill workers were very kind and hardworking— I began to realize how marvelous Chinese manufacturing was," Sha says. She then went to Harvard for an MBA, returned to the Firm, and by the late 2000s was hosting CNBC China's *Boss Town*, interviewing entrepreneurs and CEOs on their professional and personal arcs. Commerce had officially entered the Chinese zeitgeist—vaulting in just a few years from Gordon's "business doctor" days to prime-time TV.

The Firm's first multinational projects were more detective work than strategy. Rémy Martin, for instance, had no legal presence in China, yet its cognac flowed freely into the mainland through Hong Kong. "If you believed the numbers," Gordon recalls, "Hong Kong's per capita consumption would have left everyone permanently drunk." McKinsey analysts counted bottles in Beijing nightclubs and trucks at the Shenzhen border to estimate sales of cognac and Nokia phones. It was consulting stripped to its core: look, count, report—among the Firm's first experiments in data gathering in 1990s China.

In those days, McKinsey's work was as much about language as analysis. Concepts like "discounted cash flow" didn't exist in Chinese business vocabulary, so the Firm created an "Introduction to Consulting" glossary for clients. Kickoffs began, quite literally, with "Hi—this is the language we're going to use in meetings." To build relationships, the Firm gave talks at conferences and published a Chinese-language edition of *The McKinsey Quarterly*.

Every client meeting felt like a threshold moment—enterprise leaders grappling with the idea of governance, entrepreneurs confronting "return on investment" as a quantifiable metric. We weren't alone. Accountants, bankers, and consultants were fanning out across Beijing. Goldman Sachs, Morgan Stanley, and Ernst & Young were all knocking on the same doors. Another first: in the mid-1990s, Wangfujing Department Store hired away one of our star retail consultants, Todd Anderson, who'd been staffed from the Firm's Minneapolis office. He stayed at the Beijing retailer only a few months—but it foreshadowed a McKinsey-to-client talent conduit that would become routine.

Then came the first local Chinese clients—raw, unsophisticated, but eager to learn how modern companies worked. A paging company run by underworld figures approached us after its founder picked up a street-side copy of *The McKinsey Quarterly*. We politely declined their business. A few months later, four rice farmers from Guangdong with a $100 million bottled water business signed on. When the farmers took offense at a critical progress review—those biweekly project check-ins—they staged a protest lunch. Every dish crawled with worms—sea, earth, big, small. "Our Hong Kong team would've had a heart attack," Gordon says. "I knew it was a test. I'm British. I eat anything." We helped the company grow into a $200 million Nestlé acquisition target.

In those early days, Gordon and his tiny team—your authors' predecessors—weren't just serving clients. Along with many other professional services firms, they were helping to bring modern business thinking, techniques, and tools to China. In the 1990s, "consulting" hadn't been classified as a category in China, but by 2024, about half a million people worked in the industry, generating revenues of about $39 billion. McKinsey had front-row seats to a country inventing itself, and each day felt as if the foundations were being poured.

The Global Ambition of Lenovo—an Early Reference Case

"To get rich is glorious." Deng Xiaoping's phrase, uttered in the early 1980s, gave license to a generation of Chinese villagers and entrepreneurs to take risks and imagine a life beyond farming. The village and family enterprises that began to sprout in unlikely places—metal parts in Zhejiang, furniture in Guangdong, textiles in Jiangsu—were the seedlings for what would eventually become one of the world's most dynamic private sectors.

By the 1990s, private Chinese firms were no longer operating in the shadows, and by the mid-2000s, companies such as Huawei, Alibaba, and Legend were no longer a sideshow but a main act: by 2005, private companies were accounting for more than one-third of GDP, more than 75 percent of new urban jobs, and half of total social investment.

The story of Lenovo shows the roots of this Chinese ambition. Started by a handful of ex-academics out of an office at the Chinese Academy of Sciences, Lenovo, an offshoot of Legend Group, had become China's top PC maker by the early 2000s. It moved about five million desktop PCs in China in 2005, accounting for roughly a third of the market. Yet Dell and HP were moving aggressively into China, and Lenovo faced stark choices: diversify, defend the PC market at home, or go abroad.

When IBM's PC division came up for sale, Lenovo faced a defining choice. None of Lenovo's leadership team had ever worked outside China, and most spoke little to no English. International expansion meant betting the company—and possibly losing it—while the government offered no safety net if the gamble failed.

In an energized Beijing meeting, Chairman Liu Chuanzhi asked each executive for their view. As is normal in meetings of Chinese executives, the most senior leader speaks last. One by one, they said: "Buy IBM!" They'd witnessed the remarkable rise of their own company, of the domestic PC industry, of Beijing now full of cars, and the Chinese economy over the last decade in a trajectory beyond their most ambitious dreams. This had wired them for growth and expansion. Liu delivered his verdict: Lenovo would try to buy IBM. It would go international.

The $1.25 billion deal closed in 2005, and the integration of IBM PCs into Lenovo proved to be complex with issues big and small.

Lenovo's China-based team and IBM's leadership brought different business instincts to the table, for example. At the first annual planning meeting, members of Lenovo's sales organization proposed aggressive growth targets, shaped by years of competing for survival in a fast-moving market. By contrast, IBM's executives favored goals that could be met with greater certainty; after decades of industry dominance, caution came more naturally. Other discussions similarly grappled over the balance between speed and restraint. Early meetings could be testy. Lenovo owned IBM's PC division but endeavored to maintain a fifty-fifty split among senior leaders. Executives began counting heads, and if the room leaned one way, the other side would joke about a takeover.

These integration-related issues didn't resolve overnight, but they gradually subsided as decision-making structures and leadership roles were formalized. Lenovo would emerge as a distinctive global brand, and one of China's few true multinationals.

Bridging East and West

By 1997, Nick had returned to China from Zurich, drawn by what the Firm's multinational clients were calling China's "insane growth." Half Chinese and half Swiss, he'd grown up in Hong Kong, the product of a family history in the region that stretched back a century: his grandfather had built a trading firm in 1920s Hong Kong and raised twelve children. After university at the London School of Economics and a few years working in Europe, Nick was back walking the streets of his youth.

China seemed the polar opposite of sometimes too predictable European stability. As a young engagement manager in Zurich, Nick would work on Swiss projects that ran for years, with careful optimizations of a few basis points on a giant insurer's investment portfolio paying out for decades. "You could spend eighteen months aiming—because the target didn't move," he recalls. In China, shuttling between Hong Kong and Beijing, Nick jumped into projects that, comparatively, felt like they were running at warp speed. Hong Kong's handover loomed amid China's booming 1990s: the targets were shifting every week.

Speed was everything. In the 1990s, China's growth defied historical norms for a large economy—surging past 13 percent in the early years and averaging about 10 percent across the decade—and some clients were doubling revenue every three years. No one wanted long strategy debates. For one fast-growing consumer credit client, Nick had prepared a classic McKinsey strategy: size the market, formulate a strategy, define the choices, prepare for implementation. The client cut in: "No time! Bring Saturday whatever data you have—implementation will be Monday."

McKinsey's early market data came from improvisation, such as deploying hundreds of temporary staff to survey pedestrians as a way of tracking consumption trends. That kind of creativity marked consulting in China in the early 2000s, when China's entry into the World Trade Organization (WTO) cut tariffs, opened markets, and set Beijing and Shanghai as boardroom priorities.

"Second Home Market"

China's WTO entry in 2001 was the invitation that multinationals had waited decades to receive. But the China they found was unfinished and opaque—like America's Wild West, raw, promising, and lacking in rules. Glassmaker Corning, chasing the telecom boom, was like many multinationals at the time so fearful of intellectual property (IP) theft that McKinsey flew to Corning, New York, for every single meeting.

Despite the opacity, the size of the prize was irresistible. Between 2000 and 2010, foreign direct investment into China nearly tripled to north of $1 billion. By the end of the decade, foreign-invested enterprises were generating 28 percent of China's industrial output and 22 percent of its tax revenues. Executives who'd grown used to eking out single-digit growth in the West were thrilled to see China deliver double-digit revenue growth year after year. We told clients to treat China as "your second home market."

Autos led the way. Volkswagen formed a joint venture with SAIC in 1984; General Motors followed in 1997. By 2002, Chinese buyers were purchasing 3 million vehicles a year. Seven years later, China overtook the US to become the world's largest auto market—more than 13.6 million vehicles sold in China versus more than 10.4 million in the US and 3.8 million in Germany.

Consumer goods followed as well. Coca-Cola and Procter & Gamble were already entrenched, but the 2000s brought a retail and fast-food explosion. Walmart and Carrefour rolled out hypermarkets, McDonald's propagated from city to city, and KFC, owned by Yum! Brands, moved fastest; by 2011, it had more restaurants in China than in the United States, serving congee and soy milk alongside fried chicken. For urban families, these brands became symbols of modern life.

No sector embodied both risk and promise more vividly than pharmaceuticals. Foreign drugmakers faced vast unmet patient needs, primitive diagnostic capabilities, and a drug distribution chain riddled with opacity and stunningly high markups. For Pfizer,

AstraZeneca, and Johnson & Johnson, China's healthcare system was both commercial opportunity and moral imperative.

Corporatization accelerated when the reforming Premier Zhu Rongji allowed state giants to be listed overseas. By the mid-1990s, the first Chinese state-owned enterprises (SOEs) were floating shares in Hong Kong, with China International Capital Corporation (CICC)—Morgan Stanley's joint venture with China Construction Bank—at the center. "To be listed, bankers told SOEs they needed a strategy—and McKinsey was where to get it," Nick recalls. Investment banks, accountants, lawyers, private equity—everyone had a role as China plugged into global capital.

China's 1.3 billion people were rapidly becoming an economic force. By the mid-2010s, no global CEO could present a growth strategy without a China chapter; by the COVID era, multinationals were drawing a good portion of their global revenue from China.

The market's sheer speed and scale were reshaping entire industries. Over the past fifteen years, the pharma market jumped nearly three-fold to north of $110 billion in 2024. GM was selling more cars in China than in the US by 2010; Volkswagen and BMW crossed that threshold relative to Germany in 2009 and 2013. L'Oréal was booking tens of billions of RMB in China by the late 2010s, while Western markets remained flat. Wall Street reaped windfalls, too. Goldman's $2.5 billion stake in the Industrial and Commercial Bank of China (ICBC) returned more than $10 billion, and more than forty Chinese firms went public in the US in 2010.

Growth has since slowed for many of these firms, but their legacy endures. These companies brought billions in capital, modernized supply chains, and set new benchmarks for management, R&D, and compliance.

China Charts Its Own Path

Joe joined McKinsey in 2002, returning to China, like Nick, after a childhood in Hong Kong and years of study abroad. A native Cantonese speaker, Joe attended boarding school at Phillips Exeter Academy in New Hampshire and ironically began studying Mandarin only as an undergraduate at Harvard.

In one of his earliest entrepreneurial adventures, Joe and a group of fellow undergraduates from Hong Kong convinced university administration to offer a new language class—Mandarin Chinese for Cantonese speakers. Everyone mastered pinyin—the Romanized representation of Chinese characters—aced the class, and unknowingly prepared for what came next: little did Joe expect to be working with mainland Chinese clients every day, drafting PowerPoint slides, documents, and emails in simplified Chinese, strokes streamlined for speed and scale.

After law school at Harvard, Joe co-founded an internet company that took him back home to Hong Kong. Following the dot-com crash, he joined McKinsey as an associate, initially in financial services, before expanding into large-scale transformations for China's fast-growing private enterprises. A classically trained cellist and an avid trail runner, Joe drove transformation work with the same persistence required by the concert hall and endurance sport.

In the early reform years, McKinsey's work was largely focused on importing Western best practices. China's leaders were hungry to learn. Reform-minded officials and executives asked: How does JPMorgan manage a global portfolio? How does GE motivate managers? How do European telecoms run networks? Chairman Levin Zhu of CICC, one of Joe's first clients, aimed literally to become "the Goldman Sachs of China." In other industries, Western icons such as GE and Citibank became templates for Chinese firms, models for how to structure, govern, and manage risk.

By the mid-2000s, homegrown "Lenovos" were sprouting across nearly every industry. The private sector became the growth engine—its share of GDP rose from about 40 percent in 2000 to more than 60 percent by the late 2010s—driven by market reforms, WTO entry, and pro-growth policies.

Financial services offered both promise and peril. In the early 2000s, global banks and asset managers saw China as the next great frontier—vast, underbanked, and ready to open. Joe's widely read paper "The One Trillion Dollar Opportunity in Asset Management" became a rallying cry. Yet efforts to transplant New York–style risk models—built on deep credit histories and audited disclosures—quickly collapsed in China's fast-evolving, data-poor financial system. Credit bureaus had little information; the stock market ran on speculation. Still the money came in: from Goldman into ICBC, from Bank of America into China Construction Bank, from Temasek into multiple lenders, and from Carlyle into China Pacific Insurance.

McKinsey's job, as Joe recalls, was to translate and bridge—helping Western institutions adapt global frameworks to local realities while teaching Chinese clients the language of modern finance and partnership. But even as capital poured in, the limits became clear. "We watched Nike thrive in China's consumer market," Joe says, "but we argued whether a Western bank could ever truly win here. Would Chinese banks' home-field advantage in a renminbi system always prevail?"

Two decades later, the verdict is in. China's banking ecosystem stayed Chinese. Foreign firms earned solid returns as investors, but their market share today is only around 1 percent. The constraint wasn't ambition but structure: a renminbi-based system, limited access to local funding, and regulations that kept foreign banks at the margin.

Throughout, Chinese companies absorbed Western ideas—and then reshaped them. In a landscape of fierce competition, fast-moving consumers, and rapid digital change, they developed scale-first models driven by iteration that more stable markets couldn't have produced. By the 2010s, McKinsey teams could feel the shift: China was no longer following global frameworks but redefining them.

The Chinese Leapfrog

Soon enough, private Chinese firms weren't just catching up—they were vaulting ahead. Village clusters that began in the 1980s making metal parts, furniture, and textiles had become global suppliers to

Mercedes, IKEA, Nike, and more. By the 2000s, Chinese companies were acquiring firms overseas and launching their own brands. Global expansion wasn't easy—weak global brand recognition abroad, public relations mishaps, regulatory hurdles, and cultural pushback—but Lenovo, Ping An, Midea, and others were no longer looking to Western examples. They were writing their own playbook.

If Lenovo's story was about global expansion, Ping An's was about reinventing finance at home. Founded in 1988 in Shenzhen, it grew from a small insurer into a diversified financial group. Ping An founder Peter Ma studied global peers like AIG and Allianz, brought in foreign executives, professionalized governance, and managed performance and risk. That foundation powered Ping An's leap into the digital age, and by 2010, its income from insurance premiums neared $32 billion. Today Ping An sits at the forefront of AI-driven finance, serving more than 240 million retail customers across insurance, healthcare, and wealth management. Its 118-story Shenzhen headquarters is a pilgrimage site for global financial executives who want to partner with or learn from this $1.9 trillion financial giant, now one of the world's largest and most technologically advanced financial institutions.

Digital services marked another inflection point. By the mid-2010s, China's mobile internet had rewired daily life. Two super-apps—Alibaba's Alipay and Tencent's WeChat Pay—turned the smartphone into a place where all transactions happen. Even wet-market stalls ran entirely on mobile payments—no terminals required. By the end of 2024, mobile payments had reached 86 percent of the population, the highest penetration in the world.

These systems became economic infrastructure: slashing transaction costs, pulling millions of merchants into the formal economy, and generating data loops that powered new innovations in logistics, retail, credit scoring, and lending. The ripple effects spread across the economy, enabling everything from one-hour food delivery to connected cars.

Alibaba founder Jack Ma captured in 2019 why mobile payments took off: "From the very beginning, credit cards were designed for the wealthy, and now their influence is fading. Mobile payment, on the other hand, was designed for the poor from day one." Elon Musk has repeatedly pointed to WeChat as the benchmark for scale: "It does everything—sort of like Twitter, plus PayPal, plus a whole bunch of things, and all rolled into one."

Joe recalls bringing thirty foreign banking executives to China in 2017—the first time McKinsey had invited global clients to learn from Chinese fintech. They were stunned. In Shanghai cafés, customers ordered on WeChat, paid with a scan, and picked up drinks without waiting; at Alipay, algorithms spat out credit scores and approved loans within seconds.

Joe saw the contrast clearly: "In London, people still talked about 'digital transformation.' In China, we were already living it. You didn't *go* online; you just *were* online."

We saw the same leapfrog in electric vehicles. By 2020, Shanghai's green-plated EVs outnumbered petrol cars, and Shenzhen was running fully electric bus fleets. BYD and Geely—once dismissed as budget brands—turned Chinese EVs into a global success story. In the first seven months of 2025, BYD sold 2.5 million electric vehicles, surpassing Tesla. German executives soon found themselves flying to Shenzhen to study China's EV ecosystem. Meanwhile, Chinese suppliers became Apple's largest manufacturing partners, powering the global iPhone and iPad boom.

The flow of expertise had flipped. In the early 2000s, McKinsey sent German consultants to teach Ping An about insurance. A decade later, European insurers dispatched digital teams to Shenzhen to decode Ping An's finance-plus-healthcare machine.

Chinese companies are no longer students; they have become peers. They're now leading across major technology sectors: in 2024, 70 percent of the world's new EVs were sold in China. Its express delivery volume ranked first globally for the eleventh year, surpassing 180 billion packages, with year-on-year increases of 21 percent or more. China installed half the world's industrial robots and registered more World Health Organization–tracked clinical drug trials than the US—roughly 21,500 to the US's nearly 12,000.

Pushing the Next Frontier

Understanding how China built its business landscape—from make-shift phone lines to advanced digital ecosystems—is central to navigating "the next China."

We'd like to say a word about perspective. China's transformation has been extraordinary, but visitors to Shenzhen, Shanghai, or Hangzhou are seeing the showcase version of the country: high-tech campuses, financial tower skylines, and globally recognized digital giants. Behind these cities lies a vast country still profoundly uneven in its development.

Four decades of reform pushed hundreds of millions to lift themselves out of poverty and built the world's largest middle class, yet GDP per capita remains only about a sixth that of the US and a third of the EU. A third of Chinese remain in rural areas, where life feels shaped by a different pace and set of possibilities. Even within China, millions travel to Shanghai or Beijing not for leisure but to witness what they call the "economic miracle."

At the top end, ambition hasn't slowed—it's intensified. Each entrepreneurial generation pushes closer to the technological frontier. In the 1990s, China entered the PC era a decade behind Silicon Valley; by the 2000s and 2010s, internet firms followed Western models on a short lag. Today, innovation spreads almost instantly—and often emerges more sophisticated.

"McKinsey's had more than a thirty-year history in China, and we've been the first in many dimensions," says Bob Sternfels, McKinsey's global managing partner. "We think it's time for a next set of firsts—focused on an evolving playbook for how organizations thrive in today's context."

We're eager to see what the next wave holds.

CHAPTER 2

A Market Like No Other

Everyone believes their market is special; exceptionalism is, ironically, a near-universal affliction. China's case stands apart—because of structure, not sentiment. No other market harnesses the following five forces with comparable intensity: sheer scale and growth; blistering speed; adventurous young consumers; unmatched supply chain efficiency and depth; and a culture of relentless, sometimes ruthless, competition. Only in China do they interact at this magnitude. Together, they form not just a market but a singular ecosystem—one that reshapes every company that enters it. We return to these characteristics not because they're new but because they're enduring phenomena. They're systemic, defining, and decisive in shaping China's economy—and are increasingly felt worldwide.

The Story of Chinese Violins

By coincidence we both play string instruments—and our childhood experience of "trading up" to obtain better and better musical gear captures the essence of how China innovates. Nick remembers visiting Zurich's Jecklin shop as a boy for a rite of passage: graduating from the half- and three-quarter-size Chinese student violins that he'd started on to a "proper" full-size French violin.

As a teenager, Joe—far more accomplished on the cello than Nick ever was on the violin—played in the Tanglewood Institute Summer Orchestra when Yo-Yo Ma dropped in to perform a Shostakovich concerto. By then, Joe had also moved on from a Chinese cello to a French instrument; of course, Yo-Yo played his priceless Stradivarius, and Joe still displays in his living room a photo of him standing alongside the cello master.

Where did these instruments originate? We're familiar with the old world: Cremona, Italy, famous for nurturing a dense cluster of master luthiers stretching back to the sixteenth century. This quaint river town's cobblestone streets have witnessed centuries of devotion to the singular craft of violin-making. Antonio Stradivari emerged from this tradition, before his death in 1737 producing about 1,100 violins, violas, cellos, and guitars using "only the wood of trees on which nightingales sang," as a violin virtuoso would famously say. Centuries later, Stradivari's violins command the highest prices, such as a $15.3 million sale in 2022.

And yet, the story of violins didn't remain anchored to the cobblestones of Cremona; the evocative image of seasoned woods and varnish also applies to a very different town in Jiangsu province, China, where nearly every child studies music and factories produce almost 40 percent of the world's violins.

In the city of Huangqiao, the rise of China's violin-making industry took mere decades, starting with factory-like low-cost workshops in the 1980s supplying beginner instruments to eager Chinese families; the workshops then scaled rapidly through the 1990s as foreign buyers flocked to violins a fraction of the Western price. By 2007, a low-end Huangqiao violin cost around 200 RMB (about $30), a quarter the Western price and a level that still holds today.

Competition drove relentless specialization. Production was broken into as many as 208 steps, explains Xiaofeng Xu, the Italian-trained former chief technician at the town's largest producer. Workers, many new to violin-making, were trained for narrow tasks from rough cutting to fine carving, varnishing, and painting. One might carve components for a thousand instruments a year—only his or her specific part. No one built a full instrument, but together they achieved a scale that the Cremona handcrafters never could. Today, the Huangqiao industrial cluster produces more than a million violins, cellos, and guitars annually.

As skills improved, production for mid-range violins (about $300) compressed to just fifty to sixty steps, a niche that the Chinese now dominate. "For the same quality in Europe, you pay ten times more," says Inneo Group president Junjian Qian. "Many brands just import ours and put their own labels on. They don't even bother to try anymore." At the high end, luthier Xiaofeng describes training teams of five Chinese masters who handcraft violins using imported Italian spruce and Bosnian maple.

Quality has followed. Chinese violins have earned awards at the Violin Society of America's biennial competition, and in 2024, Chinese luthier Liu Zhaojun topped four hundred entrants at the Concorso Stradivari, often called the Olympics of violin-making. To be fair, the very top instruments still tend to emerge from Europe. At Music China 2025, Asia's largest instruments expo, Chinese purveyors filled a vast hall, while a solitary corner housed just a handful of European makers. One Cremona luthier sold a handcrafted cello to a Chinese family for €25,000 ($29,000).

Yet for the mainstream market, five centuries of painstaking craftsmanship met thirty years of industrial China—and China closed the distance.

Why does this matter beyond violins? Huangqiao is China in miniature. The same forces that transformed its violin industry shape the broader economy—not only in industrial equipment, smartphones, appliances, and electric vehicles, but also in software platforms, intellectual property, advanced research, and the global brands built on top of them. China's story is not just its vast consumer market but also massive scale, breakneck speed, end-to-end supply chains, and competition so intense it forces constant, rapid innovation across both physical and digital domains.

A Mind-Boggling Scale

Of course, everyone knows the country has scale. Even Marco Polo, supposedly the first European to travel to what we now call China, returned to Venice in the thirteenth century having nicknamed it "Milione." But in China, scale isn't just relative size—it's a size so vast it rewires how companies grow and compete.

In other words, China's scale is not just a static measure of "numerical bigness." It's a dynamic force that consistently over-indexes: relative to its population, income level, and stage of development, China builds more infrastructure, trains more technical talent, and concentrates more industrial capacity than peer economies. That imbalance isn't accidental. It reflects national, societal, and cultural priorities—and it's this compounding scale that continuously generates new economic units, reshapes supply chains, and alters corporate growth trajectories. This is central to understanding China's impact on the global economy.

China has now entered a moderate-growth phase, with most economists expecting 4 to 5 percent annual GDP growth over the next few years. That's slower than its past double-digit era—yet slowing growth doesn't mean shrinking impact. At China's scale, even moderate growth produces staggering absolute numbers. Each year, China still adds economic output comparable to a mid-sized economy such as Switzerland's, and graduates more university students annually than half of Australia's total population.

During its boom years, China poured more concrete in three years than the US had in the entire twentieth century—and it remains a heavyweight today, producing 5.2 billion cubic meters (183.6 billion cubic feet) of pre-mixed concrete in 2023–2024, nearly half of global output. China's 50,000 kilometers (31,000 miles) of high-speed rail network now exceed the rest of the world combined; its 190,700 kilometers (119,000 miles) of expressways exceed that in the US and EU together; and the country saw 263 airports built in two decades. When it comes to consumers, you'll see that China Central Television's (CCTV) Chinese New Year show grabs nearly 680 million viewers, more than five times Super Bowl 2025's viewership.

Any number of mind-boggling stories illustrates China's scale, but one of our favorites involves a homegrown amusement park group that includes the sixth most frequented park in the world with 12.6 million visitors a year. At the original flagship, Chimelong Safari Park in Guangzhou, visitors are immediately swallowed by vastness. Half a dozen roller coasters rise over grounds spanning more than 1,100 soccer fields, and the only surviving giant panda triplets draw millions of visitors a year. At the adjacent water park, a few minutes' drive away, more than twenty thousand visitors crowd in and dance to DJ music in the world's largest wave pool. At peak times it's so packed the water vanishes under a crush of black-haired swimmers.

What makes Chimelong remarkable isn't just its size today but its humble origins. Founder Su Zhigang started his business career by delivering pork to restaurants on his bicycle before opening his own eatery in the early 1990s. He still keeps that bicycle at home beside a life-sized portrait of Deng Xiaoping, whose reforms facilitated his rise. Zhigang was inspired to try entrepreneurship, as he once told Joe, by the line that "some regions and some people may prosper before others."

Growing from frying pork skewers to running six parks that host thirty million visitors required more than ambition—it demanded an ecosystem able to mobilize staff, engineers, capital, and a vast consumer base spread across a cluster of China's mega-cities. Consider Chimelong's customer base. Guangzhou, site of its first park, is home to nineteen million people. Within a three-hour high-speed train ride are Shenzhen, Dongguan, Zhuhai, Foshan, and Hong Kong—aggregating a regional population of more than eighty-seven million in what's commonly called the Guangdong–Hong Kong–Macao Greater Bay Area (GBA); for a park operator, that's massive potential ticket sales. In 2024, Zhigang became the first Asian entrepreneur to receive the Los Angeles–based Themed Entertainment Association's Lifetime Achievement Award.

This kind of scale appears everywhere you look. China already has a vast upper-middle-and-above class—at about 450 million people—and it's still expanding. By the end of the decade, this moneyed tier will swell by another 130 million, reaching a projected 260 million households by 2030—roughly 580 million people. And we haven't even mentioned the 152 million households in middle- and lower-middle income tiers waiting in the wings. "There's no niche market in China. With this scale, any slice of the market is big enough to be worth it," as McKinsey Global Institute partner Jeongmin Seong points out.

China's development is sometimes best seen through the lens of a tiered-city structure. The first-tier cities of Beijing, Shanghai, Guangzhou, and Shenzhen serve as national command centers for finance, government, innovation, and global engagement; some universities in these cities are now cracking the global top tier. Second-tier cities—Chengdu, Hangzhou, Wuhan, to name a few—are rising powerhouses, regional hubs that enjoy rapid growth, strong local industries, and expanding middle classes. Third-tier cities, smaller and less affluent, make up China's vast emerging market and are home to the majority of Chinese consumers.

Of course, "smaller," in China, is always relative: a third-tier city can range from one to nearly ten million people—the population spread from Sanya to Nanyang—and by the way, there are about seventy of these cities. China's modernization is complex, and the country is not a monolith.

Scale extends beyond consumers to talent. China produces more than fourteen million skilled workers annually and five million STEM graduates—the skew toward engineering over law or the liberal arts signaling what the system values. Many countries have skilled workers; few have this many, clustered this tightly. Apple CEO Tim Cook put it plainly in 2017: "China stopped being the low labor cost country many years ago. Companies come . . . because of the quantity of skill in one location, and the type of skill. In the US, you could have a meeting of tooling engineers and I'm not sure we could fill the room. In China, you could fill multiple football fields. It's that vocational expertise—very deep."

Infrastructure gives this scale physical form. In Guizhou's mountainous southwest, crews have erected some of the world's tallest bridges; the Huajiang Gorge Bridge, completed in 2025, rises 625 meters above the river below. China built its high-speed rail network from zero to the world's largest in little more than a decade—accounting for roughly 70 percent of all high-speed rail built globally over the past decade. By 2023, it was scheduling 3.7 billion train trips a year. Railways are connective tissue—binding a vast, geographically dispersed economy into a single operating system.

Scale is also energy, which isn't about keeping the lights on but rather creating a platform for competitive advantage across technology, innovation, and industry, transforming energy from a cost center into an enabling resource. In 2024, China's industrial enterprises generated 10,100 terawatt-hours of electricity, or about 2.3 times that of the US, at 60 percent of the cost. Perhaps even more impressive, in the first half of 2025 alone, China installed new solar power systems with a total capacity of 210 gigawatts—more than the entire installed US solar base and almost double that of Germany.

Despite the already impressive numbers, China's scale is still routinely underestimated. Those trying to gauge the country's potential often fail to take note of purchasing power parity (PPP)—which adjusts for exchange rates and prices—by which China has been the world's largest economy since 2016.

Jim Kralik, an American investor who has lived and worked in China for more than thirty years and now leads Linden Street Capital and Milestone Capital, puts it this way: "If you look at the actual bundles of daily life in aggregate—how much space people live in, how many washing machines, phones, coffees, or services they consume—the scale of what people consume in China now exceeds any other country, even if income per person remains lower."

The reason is simple: unit costs are far lower in China. A Starbucks cappuccino with a breakfast sandwich might run $16 in New York; in China, the same Starbucks set costs about $7.50—or $6 with a monthly card, and with promotions and delivery discounts, consumers can routinely find deals below $5. Moreover, local chains offer options for as little as $3. And there is a no-tipping culture. The pattern holds for TVs, delivery services, burgers, and everyday goods. That means nominal GDP understates China's scale: Chinese incomes buy more units—more "stuff"—than equivalent incomes in the US or Europe. That volume effect is why, in PPP terms, China is already the world's largest consumer economy.

China's scale is part of its strategic advantage. It locks in supply, creates a domestic market large enough to test and refine global products, and concentrates talent at a density no other economy can match. And the scale effect is amplified by Chinese consumers, who are among the world's most discerning.

The World's Most Fickle and Demanding Consumers

The Chinese consumer base isn't just massive—it's complex, aspirational, and restless. China is fully mobile first: discovery, promotion, payment, and delivery happen with a tap, and thirty-minute delivery is routine. Consumers don't just buy—they force companies to evolve.

Shopping in China barely resembles the rest of the world. QR-based mobile wallets collapse discovery and purchase into a single action. Our colleague Xin, for instance, buys everything on his phone—groceries, dinner, even screws for home repair—and his seventy-one-year-old mother does, too, except for the green onions she forgets and buys downstairs. The result is a hyper-engaged, always-on consumer.

Increasingly, this consumption is moving from physical goods to services. Services now account for roughly half of household spending, with growth concentrated in dining, travel, health, education, and on-demand local offerings. Mobile platforms have collapsed discovery, booking, payment, and fulfillment into a single flow, allowing services—from tutoring to home repairs—to scale as efficiently as physical goods.

The short-form video platform Douyin, ByteDance's China-focused equivalent of TikTok, sits at the center of social commerce—though it started as an entertainment platform that later monetized through shopping. Livestreaming isn't fringe; it's prime time. Celebrity hosts, key opinion leaders (KOLs)—influencers—and even key opinion consumers (KOCs) with as little as two hundred followers move millions of units, and people trust them more than they do advertisements. "In China today, consumption is about trust and tribes," says Henry Zhang, the Chinese contemporary novelist and poet best-known by his pen name Feng Tang. "People follow the tribes' shared values, taste, and aesthetics, and with short video and livestreaming, what you see can be bought instantly. A phone, a trusted voice, and a community are enough—and this model works because it fits human nature better than the old model of brands and advertising."

On video platforms such as Bilibili, iQIYI, and Tencent Video, comments fly across the screen, turning passive viewing into a group event. When one of our Shanghai colleagues is searching for advice on topics as varied as which sunscreen is recommended to travel visa requirements, she turns to Xiaohongshu, or RedNote, a mash-up of Instagram aesthetics, TikTok videos, Pinterest taste, and Amazon-style reviews.

This digital machine normalizes what we call hyper-switching: constant comparison across prices and specs, with full transparency—from the composition of skin serums to the chipset inside a refrigerator. As Natixis's chief Asia-Pacific economist Alicia García-Herrero notes, price sensitivity isn't thrift; it's power. "I've never seen anything like the way Chinese consumers compare over pennies," Alicia says.

This ecosystem turns consumers into an active force, giving them a direct line to companies—pushing them to cut prices, raise standards, and speed up launches. "Chinese consumers are more spoiled than anywhere else because of the sheer competition between brands and the volume of interactions they have with companies," says Hai Ye, a McKinsey senior partner leading the growth, marketing, and sales practice. "Companies in the US, Europe, and Japan don't respond to the consumer like this."

Loyalty is fluid. The Chinese keep a short list and rotate through it. "They'll try things," Hai says. "If you're not good enough, they'll drop you. If you get it right, they'll scale you faster than anywhere on the planet." One colleague trusted the Chinese EV brand Li Auto with autonomous driving for his young family only after seventy software updates; he ventures, tentatively, that he's "loyal" now but will still explore rivals. "It's speed dating: mutual exploration," says Michael Hui, a partner at Bain Capital.

Why does the consumer behave this way? We have to understand the velocity of change that most Chinese have experienced. One colleague likes to tell her origin story: in the 1970s, her father borrowed a neighbor's bicycle with an attached flatbed to cart her mother, who was in labor, to a Qingdao hospital; she grew up, studied at Peking University, built a business career, and bought her parents a home and a car—typical for her cohort. Her parents grew up in material scarcity, when meat was an occasional treat, not a daily expectation; their daughter delivered them into affluence in a journey that—from bicycles to SUVs, ration coupons to luxury malls—took other nations nearly a century.

This upward mobility shapes expectations. The average consumer couldn't have imagined such material progress, and our business clients only know breakneck growth. We see a generation experiencing true choice for the first time: Who can blame them for being hardwired for ambition? What they've lived through has seemed an impossible fantasy.

The one-child policy—discontinued in 2016 but still shaping society today—sharpened this psychology further: families concentrate spending on the child's education, health, and experiences. McKinsey finds categories like education, food, health, and travel treated as protected investments in the quality of life, rather than discretionary spending or luxuries. Young adults, despite high youth unemployment, still spend on dining, entertainment, and wellness. Seniors remain disciplined spenders and "invest" in travel, nutrition, and their children. This focus comes with trade-offs: Chinese consumers readily cut back on status goods, home upgrades, big-ticket appliances, and convenience premiums.

What the Chinese consumer wants is shifting from status to meaning. Ownership once signaled success; now consumption signals identity. China is the world's first mega-market where "consumerism itself becomes identity," says Derek Sulger, longtime investor and co-owner of luxury brand Shanghai Tang. "Consumption needs to be understood as a social movement."

The line could be drawn historically: post-WTO consumers chased Western badges—Porsche, Louis Vuitton, Hermès. Post-COVID consumers have inverted the lens and chase quality of experience and technology instead—seamless digital services, health and wellness features, personalized products, and, in autos—infotainment and connectivity.

Generational divides are stark. In the West, luxury habits span generations: the woman who wore Dior at her wedding now buys Dior for her daughter. German families might either be "Mercedes families" or "BMW families." In China, the generations split sharply: the grandmother who lived through the 1960s values thrift, the 1990s mother sees foreign languages and brands as progress, and the post-2010 granddaughter treats luxury as something to experience rather than aspire to. Today's "six-pockets" young people—only children supported by two parents and two sets of grandparents—are digital natives who, as parents themselves, choose robotics over piano and immersive travel over camps. Meanwhile, 77 percent of high-income seniors in top-tier cities say they're confident about the future. Both ends of the demographic hourglass are upgrading into experiences at once.

"Identity through consumption" also explains China's version of tightening belts in a sluggish economy. Consumer confidence has been at historic lows in the past two years. Nevertheless, they're not giving up aspiration—they're reallocating to preserve lifestyle. In search of cheaper hotels after a Hong Kong concert, they'll road-trip back to Shenzhen, even sleep in cars over national holidays—then pour the saved money into food and fun.

Every demographic pocket has its own aspirations and definition of value. As one luxury client puts it, "While Europe has old money and the Middle East has oil money, in China if one pillar falls, you have many others to supplement." But we shouldn't over-generalize.

No single narrative fits 1.4 billion people, and even within one generation, diversity in income, education, and risk appetite is enormous.

Overall, what most Chinese consumers have in common is high expectations, an abundance of information, and many choices—making China one of the world's most demanding retail markets. And the Chinese are sitting on a gross national savings rate around 44 percent—far above the EU's 25 percent and the US's low-by-comparison 17 percent in 2025. As each generation spends more than the last, a massive wave of future demand is building—and waiting for entrepreneurs to tap into it.

"China Speed"

From bicycles to cars, from scarcity to abundance, the Chinese consumer has leapt a distance in twenty-five years that took others a century. Joe's weekly commute since 2002 from Hong Kong to Shenzhen bears witness to that compression of time. Twenty years ago, the drive meant navigating dirt roads and clogged checkpoints into a city that felt like an industrial outpost. "It felt like I was traveling back in time," he recalls. Joe remembers getting out of the car at the Huanggang checkpoint, walking across the short boundary on foot to get his "return-home permit" card checked, and grabbing a meal in a bare-bones cafeteria while Chinese customs processed the driver and car separately—a sensory reminder that he was on the mainland.

The boundary is still crowded, and Joe still gets out of his car to cross—but facial recognition clears him in seconds, long before the car follows. Shenzhen now feels like tomorrow: high-speed rail hubs, eight-lane expressways, glass towers that multiply by the quarter. "Every month I saw a new city," he says. Now he feels like he's stepping into the future.

Nick's "China speed" story centers on a Chinese dairy company that liked to bombard the market with new, exciting yogurt drinks, the only way to stay relevant with incredibly fickle customers. One day he watched the R&D chief approve what felt like a thousand yogurt experiments in one go—whether it was cheese, lychee-infused, green-tea-flavored, or sesame. Sample batches were made on Monday; by Friday, social data and retailer feedback had picked the winners. "The market spoke in a week—and they'd already moved on," Nick recalls. This company went from start-up to Hong Kong-listed within five years to one of China's top dairy companies a few years later—and now sponsors the FIFA World Cup.

"China speed" means that an electronic parts supplier can hire eight hundred engineers to re-design a production line within two months. Clothing retailer SHEIN can reinvent fast fashion to become "on-demand" fashion, designing and producing new clothes in micro-batches of, say, a hundred garments within days, not seasons. Coffee retailers can open thousands of shops in a year, leveraging the resources and enthusiasm of entrepreneurs across the country. We're talking about system-wide speed that also includes the pace of data-feedback loops linking consumers, developers, and manufacturers, as well as decisions around capital allocation and organizational adaptation.

AstraZeneca's executive vice president, international, Iskra Reic, now based in Shanghai, had her "aha moment" watching the company's Qingdao facility come alive. "It was one year from signing the memorandum of understanding to actually opening the first packaging line," Iskra tells us. "The speed, pace, efficiency—all to AstraZeneca standards—were amazing. China's deep expertise in research and clinical development will deliver new medicines at unmatched speed."

Traditional business cycles that once stretched over years have collapsed into months—or even weeks. In Germany, designing and launching a new car model typically took five years or even more. Today, Volkswagen Group CEO Oliver Blume says the company is "using Chinese speed to improve our processes," noting that new platforms are now developed in only two years. In China, local manufacturers routinely complete the same cycle in eighteen to twenty-four months, and Mercedes, Audi, VW, and BMW have now set up R&D centers in China and radically shorten their innovation and development cycles to compete. A sportswear executive tells us that given how quickly fast followers copy, he thinks of China as a "big bucket of speed."

In digital finance, employees of the Italian joint venture partner to 360 DigiTech founder Jun Xu's new start-up work thirty-five hours a week and ask the China side to slow down. "They say it's too much for us. We can't follow your speed," Jun tells us. "My little China start-up works six days a week, twelve hours a day."

"China speed" has a compounding effect. Fast decisions accelerate innovation, which sharpens competition, which then forces even faster execution. Nick calls the speed of failure critical to this cycle. "Chinese companies can stop immediately and move on—they know how to fail fast," says Nick. "Multinationals typically take longer, ironically because of more consensus-driven decision-making and 'face' associated with failure. We joke that in China it's 'fire, fire, aim,' while elsewhere it's 'aim, aim, shoot' or 'aim, aim, opportunity gone.' "

If "China speed" isn't fast enough, try "Shenzhen speed," a phrase that became famous in 1984 after that city's International Trade Center was built at a rate of one floor every three days. Shenzhen itself became a symbol of the speed, boldness, and innovation bubbling up in the surrounding metro area of eighteen million, which is the headquarters location of tech giants Tencent and Huawei and drone maker DJI. "Shenzhen speed" isn't reserved just for that city; consider that Beijing Daxing International Airport, the world's largest single-terminal airport, went from initial design to full commercial operation in just four years before its 2019 opening. Compare that with London Heathrow's runway expansion, which has been in the planning stages for thirteen years and won't be ready until the mid-2030s.

For foreign firms, the lesson is clear: adapt to China's speed, or risk irrelevance. Some have made the shift, while others will likely be headed for the exits. "Anyone can tap into that speed because it's an open ecosystem," says Karel Eloot, a McKinsey senior partner co-leading the global metals and mining practice. "In the West, you do a lot of preparation. In China, you must scale immediately, so you launch 'half perfect' and 'not yet amazing' and then use short cycle times to iterate generations two, three, and four."

Speed, of course, has trade-offs; sometimes what suffers is quality, safety, or compliance. Critics argue that some Chinese companies ship out products before sufficient quality checks at defect or recall rates unacceptable in mature markets. Many multinationals say they can't match the pace—not for lack of ability but because they can't take the same legal or reputational risk. A flawed product in Western markets can trigger recalls, lawsuits, and lasting brand damage; in China, the same risks apply—but Chinese companies have mastered the art of acknowledging faults, apologizing, and iterating in public rather than perfecting in advance. China's speed is real, it drives progress, and standards are rising, but the risk tolerance remains fundamentally different than in the US and Europe.

That difference shapes perception. Some online shoppers might pay close attention to country-of-origin labels and associate "Made in China" with quality or safety concerns, even as they continue to buy large volumes of Chinese-made products through Temu, SHEIN, and other platforms. Roughly two-thirds of safety warnings around consumer products in the US in 2024 involved Chinese companies, reflecting both China's manufacturing dominance and its uneven compliance at the low end.

Yet China now produces both some of the world's most rudimentary goods—for example, textiles, toys, and chargers—and also some of its most sophisticated, as in drones, EVs, and mobile phones. While some companies will meet global standards, their successes will continue to be overshadowed by highly visible failures elsewhere in the ecosystem. China's advantage isn't just speed but a willingness to accept risk early and correct later at scale—the question is whether global trust in Chinese companies can rise as quickly as their capabilities have.

China's Supply Chain Ecosystem

The forces of speed, scale, and demand become most visible in China's supply chain—an ecosystem with no global parallel. It's a complete industrial ecosystem that puts materials, tooling, suppliers, and engineers within immediate reach—enabling unusually efficient cost structures and capital deployment. In extreme but not rare cases, building a plant in China costs roughly 20 percent of what the same facility would cost in the US and can be completed in roughly 20 percent of the time. More typically, companies see 50 percent lower capex and 50 percent faster build times.

This helps explain what happened when Apple's main Zhengzhou plant—at its peak home to hundreds of thousands of workers—was disrupted during the 2022 COVID lockdowns. Apple pushed to diversify iPhone production, with suppliers exploring Vietnam and India, among other sites. Yet within a year, Foxconn, Apple's main final assembly partner, had only shifted about 15 percent of output, according to Kelvin Pan, chief innovation officer of AAC Technologies, one of Apple's primary suppliers of speakers, haptics, and thermal components. "Once COVID ended, the Zhengzhou operation ramped back up again to full speed," Kelvin says.

The reason is simple: China's supply chain advantage isn't just capacity but also muscle memory built over three decades of moving up the value chain. Firms from Hong Kong and Taiwan brought contract manufacturing; Japan brought precision tooling; Europe layered in quality systems; and America pushed scale and automation. "For any other country to come even close, we'd need to invest there for the next ten to fifteen years because that's how long it took China to build this incredibly rich ecosystem of materials, tooling, operations, skilled labor, and know-how," says Cedric Leleu, a McKinsey partner in digital transformation services, who has recently spent time with global manufacturers expanding beyond China.

This supply chain ecosystem—physically clustered across the Greater Bay Area and the Yangtze River Delta and digitally linked through millions of WeChat workgroups, business-to-business (B2B) marketplaces, and factory-to-factory programming interfaces—now produces the world's most sophisticated hardware with precision and speed: hundreds of design tweaks a week, and automation delivered in weeks not quarters. Chinese suppliers feed not only Apple but also Chinese and Western companies such as Volkswagen, Samsung, Lenovo, and Huawei. Tesla has more than four hundred Chinese suppliers clustered around its Shanghai Gigafactory.

In consumer electronics, this ecosystem allows AAC Technologies to move with extraordinary speed. When tasked with supporting a new smartphone model, AAC can ramp up from zero to eight fully operational manufacturing lines in just three months, investing about $100 million to green-light capacity for forty million units a year—at half the cost of comparable overseas production. "We make changes to every sub-station every single day," Kelvin tells us. "You can imagine the volume of changes—hundreds every week—just to keep improving. And the customers are there every day checking the key performance indicators (KPIs) and metrics for each station." Cedric is more direct: "You can ramp ten thousand people in a few days. You can also adjust them in a few days. You can flex labor by the hour. You can't do that outside China."

And it's not just speed; it's also depth. In China, if supplier A can't do it, supplier B, C, D, E, F can, and they're often in the same district. A client's Monterrey, Mexico, plant is so green and technologically advanced as to be declared a World Economic Forum "lighthouse"—but it's not in the Chinese supplier ecosystem. "In China, you can send a request to a thousand suppliers and get twenty bids back within the hour; in Mexico, it's different," says Liang Zhou, a McKinsey associate partner and tech manufacturing expert.

China's edge comes with a cost: the same competitiveness that produces the advantage also squeezes margins thin. A global supplier's COO told us, "China's supply chain is like a vast ocean—but the water is shallow for profits." Work-life balance sometimes feels non-existent, especially compared with what occurs at that client's Mexico plant, where workers enjoy a "Bring Your Pet to Work" day.

Diversification is real and happening—AAC has expanded into Vietnam and Eastern Europe; Foxconn has been deepening and expanding its already global footprint with new investments in Mexico, the US, India, and other locations; and some low-end sectors like textiles and leather have moved out for good, especially the export-oriented factories. But the "small stuff" supply chain—plastics, zippers, buttons, accessories—is still firmly in China. With a domestic market of this size, "Made in China, for China" isn't going anywhere. And as you climb into advanced manufacturing—electronics, EVs, green tech—the high-value work of design, automation, materials, and R&D remains firmly anchored at home.

*   *   *

Massive scale, breakneck speed, demanding consumers, and an irreplaceable supply chain separate China from every other market. And when these dense, information-rich ecosystems meet the ambition of the Chinese entrepreneur, the business landscape can become a "survival of the fittest" brawl. That competitive metabolism is China's final differentiator.

CHAPTER 3

The World's Toughest Gym

The history of progress is littered with casualties. The automobile replaced the horse-drawn carriage, streaming killed the video store, the smartphone swallowed the camera. Each wave of innovation builds on the old, even as it dismantles it.

The influential twentieth-century Austrian economist Joseph Schumpeter popularized a name for this process: creative destruction. His economic theory describes a cycle of innovation, competition, displacement, and renewal—in which the churn of progress demolishes what came before—yet ultimately leaves the system stronger, more efficient, and with economic growth. Chinese business today represents an extreme version of this dynamic, but with a twist—and it's critical to understand this distinguishing feature of China's landscape.

The fuel for this competitive engine is the same cocktail we unpacked in the last chapter: sheer scale, breakneck speed, insatiable consumers, plus a surge of private capital—at times reinforced by state support for strategic sectors from solar panels to satellite towns to electric vehicles. But that intensity has a darker side captured by the term *involution*, derived from the Latin *involutio*, "to fold back upon itself." In Chinese, it's *neijuan*—literally, to "roll inward"—business slang for self-defeating effort and diminishing returns. You're not alone if this term is unfamiliar; it only recently entered English-language business writing, borrowed to describe a phenomenon that's almost exclusively Chinese: competition so extreme it stops being productive, resulting in chronically low returns, inefficient capital allocation, bloated inventories, and eventually deflation.

After decades working with clients in the thick of China's *juan*—shorthand for *neijuan*, terms now often used interchangeably—we've seen a clear paradox: the grind is punishing, but it forces firms to sharpen their capabilities and raises an industry's performance baseline. It's a twist on Schumpeter's creative destruction—progress and damage can, and often occur simultaneously.

Crucially, involution isn't simply hyper-competition. We define it as a market state where output and quality rise while industry-wide returns fall, driven by price wars, overcapacity, and "me-too" entrants. At first glance, it looks like madness: coffee prices falling to bottled water levels, food delivery apps sending noodles to doorsteps for free, sidewalks turned graveyard for abandoned shared bikes, and steelmakers celebrating survival margins.

China may be the only major economy where, for several major industries, annual budgets forecast price declines—and where five hundred million thrifty households enforce a national discipline of low costs and high expectations. Yet China's distinctive pattern is that involution doesn't just erode margins; it often produces stronger supply chains, deeper engineering capabilities, faster iteration cycles, and ultimately a few survivors that break away through genuine innovation.

We often describe China to clients as "The World's Toughest Gym," a mixed-martial-arts "Octagon," or a modern Roman Colosseum—whatever analogy works for you. The contest indeed leaves weaker companies limp on the mat and creates system burnout in ways that no one intends. It also forges resilience and equips the survivors to succeed anywhere in the world.

"Involution is both painful and extreme," says Xin Huang, a McKinsey partner in the consumer practice. "But it's also a core cultural strength, giving Chinese companies a unique way to differentiate themselves both at home and abroad. Firms that harness this involution culture can drive cost efficiency, speed, and resilience—and while multinationals have traditionally lagged in this kind of relentless internal optimization, many are now learning from their Chinese competitors and leveraging this distinctive feature of Chinese business."

The Three Engines: Policy, Capital, Culture

At its core, involution is the result of a uniquely Chinese blend of corporate or entrepreneurial ambition, abundant capital from both public and private sources, a growth mindset, and a culture that celebrates stamina and relentless hustle. Layered onto the defining features of China's market, involution can fuel bursts of innovation while simultaneously compressing margins.

A major strength of the Chinese system is its pro-growth, pro-business government. At every level, often guided by national priorities, local governments have jump-started industries—especially sectors flagged as strategic—with subsidies, low-cost or free financing, and cheap land to achieve aggressive local growth targets. Provinces competed to build the "next Shenzhen," offering loans and industrial parks to clusters of entrepreneurs and suppliers. Consumers got subsidies, too: early EV buyers could receive up to 60,000 RMB (about $8,600) per car—an incentive that shrank as standards rose and ended in 2022, but not before more than a hundred EV brands were born (though only a dozen or so comprise the majority of sales). For years, anything tied to the "new three"—electric vehicles, lithium-ion batteries, and solar panels—was showered with local support. More recently, it's robotics and advanced manufacturing, commercial and industrial drones, semiconductors, aerospace and aviation, and large language models.

Yet it's easy to misread China's system as a state-dominated monolith. "In practice, on measures of competition and private-sector activity, China is often more competitive and more private than most global economies," says Yermolai Solzhenitsyn, a McKinsey senior partner in the metals and mining practice who transferred to

Shanghai after decades with the Firm in Russia. "State-owned enterprises account for only about 30 percent of GDP—far below Russia's 60 to 70 percent, and far lower than much of the Middle East. The reality is a vast system driven by competition—among companies, among local governments, and among regions."

While most sectors have experienced phases of involution, not all have—and involution also isn't limited to government-favored sectors. It appears across many industries, even those without state involvement—from restaurants to tea chains to tour services. In our own field, when we see consulting firms chasing the same work at cutthroat fees, we joke that consulting is involuting, too.

Capital keeps the system moving. Venture funds chase unicorns, state subsidies power strategic sectors, and friends-and-family money supports new ideas. Funding was scarce in the 1990s and early 2000s; after three decades of wealth creation and a maturing investor ecosystem, it's far more accessible today. From 2014 to 2024, China poured $42.1 trillion in capital expenditures into its goods-producing industries—about twelve times the investment of ASEAN, ten times that of India, and five times that of the United States. Between foreign private equity, local and state funds, and wealthy entrepreneurs, promising projects rarely lack financing.

Culture adds its own momentum. Competition isn't just tolerated in China—it's long been part of Chinese life. For 1,400 years, the imperial exam system made upward mobility a winner-takes-all contest, embedding a culture that prizes diligence and *chiku* (eating bitterness). Today's high-pressure ethos is a direct heir to that mindset. The modern national college entrance exam still packs a lifetime of ambition into a two-day ordeal. We've also long struggled with work-life balance in our own offices. We once adopted a global McKinsey initiative that declared "Wednesday Me" nights as time off, but even shutting down air-conditioning to force consultants out of the office simply pushed them into hotel lounges with their laptops to continue working.

The same logic carries into the business culture. Chinese entrepreneurs routinely enter saturated markets—coffee, steel, chemicals, anything—not because they underestimate competition but because they believe they can outwork it—by cutting costs, improving execution, or expanding the market itself. Overcapacity is seen as less a warning sign than a challenge. As one leading synthetic fiber producer explained, making products cheaper and more available can create demand. "We are planning for the long term, and not just for China. Indonesia has three hundred million people," she adds, "and billions more worldwide still need clothing."

There can be a comical predictability to it all, almost as if you could lay bets on the next industry to be involuted. A Chinese friend with a longtime European business partner likes to joke, "A European guy opens a gas station and becomes successful. His friend then opens a supermarket next door. Other friends come and open a school, a medical clinic, a laundromat—soon there's a thriving community and everyone prospers. In China, the first Chinese guy opens a gas station. If he is successful, very soon, a second gas station appears. Then a third, and then a fourth. Before long, you've got ten gas stations on one street—and no one makes any money."

Some friends ask, "Well, why gas stations and not supermarkets?" The answer is yes, of course, the Chinese build supermarkets, too, and pretty soon there are ten others alongside it. It's China. There's more of everything.

Soul Capital founder Herry Han reminds his European investors that China comprises a fifth of the world's population jammed onto land surrounded by mountains—with only a few arable pockets. "When I return to China after a month in Europe, what hits me most is how close people stand to me," says Herry. "Space is not something we've experienced as crucial over our long history. So when a market exists, we Chinese tend to squeeze into any corner of it—even if it's already crowded. Space is an opportunity."

The "9.9 RMB Coffee Wars"—That's a USD $1.4 Latte!

Joe remembers the first time he stumbled upon a Luckin Coffee kiosk. It was a bitter cold Shanghai morning in 2018, and after hours of client meetings, he slipped downstairs in search of caffeine. That first taste turned out to be a preview of extreme competition. The winners didn't just flood the market with cheaper coffee but also built irreplicable strengths in procurement, logistics, operational efficiency, and marketing.

For two decades, Starbucks had defined China's coffee experience: leather armchairs, walnut-colored tables, lattes priced like small luxuries in prime high-rent locations. A Starbucks cup was a status symbol: discerning taste and a white-collar identity. The stores themselves were your "third space" apart from your home and your office. By the time Joe encountered Luckin in 2018, Starbucks had 3,300 outlets across China and plans to open a new one every fifteen hours. From its 1999 Beijing entry, Starbucks had turned a tea-drinking nation into a coffee-loving $20 billion industry.

That day in the lobby of his logistics client on Shanghai's outskirts, Joe found something very different. The Luckin kiosk was built from black sheet metal and barely the size of a street noodle stand. Its footprint was lean and cheap, and so was its staffing: a lone barista pointed to a QR code. A few taps on Joe's phone, and his latte appeared. No line, no cash, no banter. The coffee itself was fine, but the price—barely more than a soda—was extraordinary.

Luckin didn't just enter the coffee market; it detonated it. Its founders, who'd built China's largest car-rental company, applied the internet-venture playbook: raise massive capital, build a model with a vision of profitability, scale fast, and subsidize user acquisition. Phones were flooded with promos. It became the fastest "from zero to Nasdaq IPO" story in Chinese enterprise history—from its October 2017 founding to initial public offering (IPO) in about eighteen months. "Luckin targeted the younger generation," says David Li, Luckin's current chairman and founder of Centurium Capital, an early investor who's now its largest shareholder. "They wanted digital-first, affordable, and more creative drinks. They wanted something new."

Luckin's success—and access to eager capital—drew hundreds of rivals, though the company's rise wasn't linear. In 2020, the company divulged it overstated 2019 revenues by 2.2 billion RMB

($314 million); the chairman, CEO, and COO were ousted, shares suspended and de-listed from the main board. The ousted chairman and CEO soon launched Cotti Coffee, widely seen as Luckin's "second act," and quickly fired the first shot in a nationwide price war with a 9.9 RMB ($1.4) coffee, sometimes as low as 8.8 RMB ($1.3) during marketing campaigns. By comparison, mainstream chains such as Starbucks and Costa were pricing lattes at 25 to 30 RMB ($3.6 to $4.3); suddenly competitors were selling alternatives almost as cheap as a pair of 5 RMB ($0.7) street meat buns.

This competition drove prices to the floor, burned through capital, and made innovation a survival strategy. We regularly see on a single Shanghai block a Cotti next to Manner across from Starbucks, while passersby carry cups emblazoned "Luckin" and the niche chains MStand and % Arabica. Insane—but millions of first-time drinkers embarked on a coffee habit, and ordering on an app was normalized.

"Luckin came in with a totally different way of playing: digital first," says Grace Hu, the former VP of Starbucks China who oversaw strategy and store development during the mid-2010s. "This new generation of competitors lowered the cost of everything—and they had rich consumer data from day one that helped keep the customer engaged." (In many ways, their model is effectively "digital only.")

Luckin had rebuilt its cost stack for exactly this moment. Its scale enabled huge bean volumes and leverage to negotiate with suppliers, while its engineered "coffee basket" flavor—crafted from dynamically shifting blends—allowed the company to arbitrage global commodity swings, cut waste, and extend shelf life. By owning warehousing, transport, roasting facilities, and logistics, it stripped even more volatility out of the system. Hence it was able to price drinks at what David Li calls the "should-be cost"—the industry's theoretical floor—long before it'd achieved it.

Meanwhile, the chain turned coffee into "fast fashion": nearly a hundred new products a year plus thousands in the pipeline: coconut, liquor, seasonal, novelty, orange juice coffee, malt coffee. The innovation seems to be in the drink, but in fact it's in using SKU variety as a weapon. Copying drinks is easy. Replicating Luckin's operational supply chain complexity is not. Cost control plus its optimized supply chain gave Luckin advantages no competitor has been able to match.

To David, the price war was inevitable. Established brands had been living too comfortably on inflated premiums, he says. "That actual profit margin leaves room for other competitors to disrupt the market," David tells us. "If I set my price too high, I give others that kind of room."

Luckin makes money even at 9.9 RMB ($1.4), a price point that sends most rivals scrambling. After turning profitable in 2022, it didn't ease off the gas—it accelerated. In less than a decade, it grew from a few Beijing stores to more than thirty thousand nationwide by the end of 2025 and surpassed Starbucks China in revenue in 2023 at $3.5 billion. In 2025 alone, it launched nine thousand new locations—roughly one every hour—aided by AI-driven designs.

Like many multinationals caught in a price war started by locals, Starbucks refused the 9.9 RMB ($1.4) fight. Starbucks China doubled down on a different philosophy: human connection and experience— the opposite of kiosks, speed, and takeout. Starbucks translated that philosophy into execution: more distinctive store formats, faster delivery, improved digital experiences, and revamped lids, for example. It also trained up baristas to improve those "micro-interactions," the small social touches that make Starbucks "stickier" than a delivery app as mobile ordering and delivery continued to scale. The competition, however, is real. David notes Luckin runs four times Starbucks' volume for twice the revenue—a fundamentally different operating model.

This fierce competition takes a toll on every competitor. After more than a decade as the uncontested growth star of the Starbucks portfolio, Starbucks' China business hit a rough patch: shrinking margins, declining market share, and local upstarts nipping at its heels. The company pivoted. In a move that echoes McDonald's China's shareholder changes a decade ago, Starbucks sold a majority stake in its China venture to the Chinese private equity firm Boyu Capital. Boyu's partner in charge of the deal, Alex Wong, tells us, "We aren't intimidated. There's plenty of value here; this is the world's largest coffee market, still growing, and we have a phenomenal brand." Starbucks expects the partnership will help fuel expansion from eight thousand to more than twenty thousand stores nationwide.

The coffee wars were brutal. While some were successful, many franchisees all over the country, excited about the opportunity to be their own bosses, lost their savings in failed outlets. Yet they together invited more than a thousand competitors, big and small, to try their hand at coffee and expanded the market to about four hundred million coffee drinkers in China. The survivors emerged stronger and more focused. "Hyper-competition has driven innovation. Quality of specialty coffee in Shanghai is on par with that of any leading global city," says Grace, the former Starbucks exec.

Of course, there's no permanent dominance in the world's toughest gym. Delivery wars erupted in 2025 between Alibaba, Meituan, and JD.com, cratering coffee prices to 5.9 RMB ($0.8)—even lower with promos—while milk tea chains and other beverage formats move in on the same consumers. The latest coffee brand? Shanghai's "Taijuan Coffee"—with the Chinese characters literally translating as "too involuted." It offered a 3.9 RMB ($0.6) Americano during morning hours. What will the future hold?

The Electric Vehicle Race

Nowhere has involution burned hotter than in EVs, where prices fell faster than costs even as competition forced eighteen- to twenty-four-month model development cycles and software-first architectures—leaving survivors with a mobility tech stack they can deploy anywhere.

Industrial policy has anointed "green" and "new energy" vehicles—including electric cars, plug-in hybrids, and hydrogen fuel-cell vehicles—as strategic sectors meant to pull the country from low-cost manufacturing into high-value, technologically advanced production. To accelerate the transition, subsidies, grants, tax rebates, and purchase incentives poured in, and early domestic players such as BYD laid the groundwork.

Then in 2019, Elon Musk opened up a Tesla Gigafactory in Shanghai, the first wholly foreign-owned car plant in China. It disrupted a decades-old equilibrium dominated by Volkswagen, Toyota, and the mass-market gasoline cars that had carried China's middle class for years. A generation of Chinese entrepreneurs saw their first Model S, heard Musk speak, and decided the auto playbook could be rewritten. XPENG founder Xiaopeng He switched from a Land Rover to a Tesla and was struck by the acceleration, the quiet, and the unexpected pleasure of listening to music in such silence. But to him, Tesla represented something more than just a great electric vehicle; it reframed who could build great cars. "What left the deepest impression on me was that a company that wasn't originally an automaker could make such a good car," Xiaopeng says. Tesla's history in car-making at the time seemed short, and in fact thinking an outsider could easily make great EVs "was wrong," he says—yet that illusion empowered so many with the courage to try.

One company turned China's intensity into a superpower: BYD. It started as a humble battery shop, then in 2020 launched the Blade Battery, which set new benchmarks for cost and scalability and rendered the lithium-iron phosphate battery as the mainstream default. From there, BYD built a vertically integrated supply chain stack—from mines to materials to batteries to cars—which let it structurally underprice competitors. It then grew rapidly: fewer than four hundred thousand cars in 2015 to more than four million by 2024 to become the world's largest EV maker. Yet BYD's scale cuts both ways: a machine built for massive volume isn't necessarily nimble. Sustaining dominance may require a new phase of innovation as the domestic market inevitably slows.

Other EV makers chose different capabilities. NIO put the customer at the center of everything by working to create a seamless, emotionally resonant relationship with them, while Li Auto simplified product complexity to deliver value-for-money SUVs. Huawei and Aito focused on advanced cockpits and intelligent driving. Geely—a legacy combustion carmaker—pivoted aggressively into platforms and software. Any advantage in China lasts as long as the next new model cycle.

Consumers reaped the windfall. When Tesla first unveiled the Model 3 in 2017, it was pitched globally at about $35,000, though early versions imported into China cost far more. A BYD Dolphin? About a third of that at 80,000 to 100,000 RMB (about $11,000 to $14,000). At the peak of the price wars, entry-level sedans in some smaller cities even dipped below the cost of a scooter in Europe. Famously, the Wuling Hongguang MINI EV launched at 28,800 RMB (about $4,000) in 2020—tiny, basic, and wildly popular, at one point outselling the Model 3 thanks to unbeatable utility for short city commutes.

Competition forced extreme speed: development cycles collapsed from four or five years to under two, powered by agile engineering, continuous iteration and improvement, and clean hardware-software decoupling. The "involutionary" churn of start-ups and legacy original equipment manufacturers (OEMs) fought for survival.

This relentless cost compression forced new forms of organizational creativity. We've visited OEMs that have built lean, digitally-enabled, flat operating models where cost efficiencies have become innovation. Gigacasting, modular production, and AI-assisted design unlocked speed and efficiency, turning survival tactics into repeatable advantages.

But do these advantages last? Usually not, simply because the bar keeps rising. We recently test-drove a Li Auto EV with flawless self-parking, massage seats for every passenger, and a cowboy-hat-donning AI agent executing rapid-fire commands. That's just par for the course in China. Chinese firms have built a deep base in smart-cockpit technology with more than sixty thousand related patents—enough to turn many cars into something closer to rolling living rooms than people movers. Autonomous driving is advancing, too. In summer 2024, Beijing expanded trials to cities including Shanghai and Shenzhen, allowing operators to remove the human "safety" driver and run limited passenger and cargo services. In these pilot areas, riders can watch a movie, relax, or even tutor their children while the car drives itself.

And the leadership title keeps rotating: first NIO captured imaginations with battery swapping. Then Li Auto impressed drivers with extended-range hybrids delivering over 1,300 kilometers. Then Huawei's Aito surged with its Harmony-based cockpit and autonomous driving capabilities. Then Xiaomi stunned the global industry with the fastest start-up development in auto history—just three years from announcing their plans for mass production.

We believe the battle might ultimately be decided by technological capabilities, and many EV players are now full-stack technology companies that can compete across other sectors. XPENG vice chairman and president Brian Gu notes that the same capabilities—AI foundations, chips, sensors, autonomous driving systems, lightweight tech—can scale into flying vehicles and humanoid robots. "We're developing our capabilities toward smart mobility, and there will be multiple solutions. Vehicles will only be a part," Brian tells us.

However, Paul Gao, Mercedes-Benz's global head of strategy and one of the industry's most astute veterans, cautions that it's far from certain technology will decide the winner. "We've seen very rapid commoditization of technology in China such as ADAS, smart cockpit, and electric drivetrain," Paul says. "Today Huawei is supplying a growing number of Chinese and foreign OEMs with its tech stack." When everyone has access to similar technology, Paul argues, the real edge shifts to customer experience, speed of product refresh, and other non-tech differentiators. In short, this race won't be settled quickly.

None of this unfolded by accident. China's leadership engineered the rise of its electric vehicle industry through a full-spectrum industrial strategy: generous consumer subsidies, preferential "green" license plates, production grants for OEMs, and the creation of the world's most concentrated and efficient EV supply chain.

All this played out inside the largest auto market on the planet. Western analysts often focus on subsidies as the source of China's cost advantage. But consumer pull, steadily falling prices, rapid improvements in vehicle quality and technology, and an increasingly compelling value proposition also play a role. In 2024, Chinese carmakers produced nearly three-quarters of the world's electric vehicles, while Chinese consumers accounted for almost two-thirds of global EV sales—by far the largest EV ecosystem in the world.

Serious questions still hang over the sector. A few of the leaders may be profitable, but the supply/demand imbalance remains stark. Without the excess cash flow needed to fund continued investment and R&D, further consolidation appears almost certain. A few players have already collapsed, yet most are still digging in, hoping to emerge among the eventual survivors.

"Digging in" also means competing overseas. Chinese OEMs are exporting this *juan* competition globally onto the streets of Bangkok, London, and Sydney, rapidly capturing market share. Its outward expansion feels relentless. "2025 was a turning point for the auto industry because China became the world's largest auto exporter for the first time," notes Daniel Birke, a McKinsey partner in advanced industries. For Chinese players, overseas markets offer a reprieve from competitive pressures at home—at least at first. Margins abroad are typically higher than at home—at least until the next Chinese entrant arrives and competes margins away. Still, there's cautious optimism that competition overseas will be less purely price-driven. "Given today's competitive landscape, it'll take time before the industry is truly healthy again. In China, these cycles are just really painful," Mercedes-Benz's Paul says.

China's EV story isn't just a story about cars. It's a tale of scale, capital, supply chain, government industrial strategy, speed, involution—and the conversion of brutal competition into innovation.

China's Green Tech Reckoning

In the same way, China's green tech expansion isn't only a climate story. It's an experiment in scale, capital, and involution—what happens when an industry becomes too extraordinarily good at what it does. Chinese solar companies have weathered an environment of steep losses and endured razor-thin margins yet in doing so have helped drive down the global cost of clean energy deployment and reshaped the economics of greening the planet.

The state's push into renewable energy—solar, wind, batteries, power electronics—was rooted in climate goals, energy security concerns, and industrial strategy. As in other priority sectors, support came through subsidies, preferential financing, land access, and guaranteed grid connections. Once the policy framework was in place, the building began.

Solar manufacturing, in particular, became a magnet for capital. Capital poured in, capacity surged, and costs fell—often faster than demand—and in little more than a decade, China became the primary manufacturing base for nearly every major solar component. Today, Chinese companies produce roughly 95 percent of global solar wafers, over 80 percent of cells and modules, and a similar share of key upstream inputs such as polysilicon. Most new installed solar capacity now relies on Chinese-manufactured hardware. China installed nearly 60 percent of new global PV capacity in 2024 and nearly 70 percent in the first half of 2025—more than double the rest of the world combined. Without this industrial surge, the energy transition wouldn't just be slower—it would be more expensive.

For a time, the system was profitable. China's climate goals triggered a rapid post-2020 solar boom, but upstream supply of polysilicon—the critical raw material at the top of the value chain—proved slow to scale. Polysilicon prices surged more than four-fold; the mismatch created a bottleneck which created pricing power upstream, and for many solar manufacturers and developers, 2022 was a banner year.

LONGi Green Energy became emblematic of this boom. An early bet on monocrystalline wafers—backed by subsidies, research breakthroughs, and manufacturing efficiency—helped propel the company to global leadership as it standardized monocrystalline silicon, pushed wafer sizes from 156 to 210 millimeters (from 6.1 to 8.3 inches), and advanced industry-wide cell efficiencies. At its peak, the company generated tens of billions of renminbi in annual revenue.

The boom proved short lived. A flood of new entrants and aggressive capacity expansion collided with cooling demand, sending module prices plunging 70 to 80 percent over the next two years.

Manufacturers responded as they always had—by innovating. Firms accelerated technology iteration with domestic equipment and material suppliers, pushed toward next-generation architectures that convert more sunlight into usable power and reduce use of inputs such as silver, and drove costs lower through automation and deeper vertical integration. From 2010 to 2025, solar cell efficiency rose from 16 percent to north of 25 percent. Even as margins thinned, industry players worked to preserve R&D spending—critical to competing in high-tech spaces.

Still, no company got better at making money, even as the industry got better at making solar panels. Gross margins collapsed from around 20 percent to roughly 5 percent in 2024, pushing the industry into net losses. In some segments, production capacity reached nearly two times global annual demand. The result was widespread financial damage. That year, LONGi reported a $1.1 billion loss, its market capitalization down to roughly a fifth of its peak—and it wasn't alone. The excess has landed even in Shanxi province, home to both a billion tons of coal production a year—about one-seventh of the world's total—as well as the largest single solar panel factory on earth with a target capacity of 56 gigawatts. That's about a tenth of global solar demand. "Most manufacturing industries have become too efficient for their own good," says Haimeng Zhang, LONGi's vice president and chief sustainability officer. "There's oversupply even at a global level," he says.

Geopolitics compounded the pain. Trade barriers rose, and export markets tightened just as domestic demand slowed. By 2024 and into 2025, many solar producers were burning cash, writing down inventory, and idling capacity. "We are building for a world that doesn't exist yet," one executive tells us.

This industrial implosion coincides with China's nearing—or possibly reaching—peak emissions, not because growth has stalled but because clean energy capacity scaled fast enough to decouple economic expansion from carbon output. Wind and solar now account for more than half of new power generation capacity added annually, with China building more than the rest of the world combined. This dominance extends beyond projects built at home: Chinese firms also play a substantial role in solar capacity added abroad through overseas investment; engineering, procurement, and construction (EPC) contracting; and equipment supply.

Though the green transition remains incomplete for the world's largest coal burner, electricity in China is cheaper, cleaner, and more abundant than at any point in modern history. For the planet, the gains are profound; for manufacturers, they've come at a cost. As one client puts it: "It's hard to appreciate the energy transition when you're reporting losses."

That cheap energy is becoming a strategic asset. As AI data centers, robotics, and advanced manufacturing scale, energy costs matter—and Chinese firms now operate at price points few global competitors can match. For now, some of the pressure is being alleviated through exports: Europe, Africa, and Southeast Asia absorb large volumes of low-priced equipment, while Chinese firms operate at thin margins. The question is whether the world pushes back on these renewables as another arena of Chinese "industrial overcapacity," or instead embraces them as a cornerstone of a faster, cheaper global green transition.

Costs and Consequences

As we've described, the process of involution often begins with success—whether it be in coffee, solar, steel, or fashion. Starbucks introduced the Chinese consumer to lattes; Suntech Power led the early charge in photovoltaics; Tesla made EVs aspirational; Zara brought fast fashion to the masses. Success quickly draws new entrants, new money, new factories. This boom eventually devolves into overcapacity, price competition, collapsing profit margins, and the exhaustion of both capital and people.

While China has built world-class industries on this model— "ambition first, profitability later"—the bill does eventually arrive. "Involution and intense competition have been central to China's economic success, but several emerging factors could introduce new uncertainty," says Lambert Bu, a McKinsey senior partner leading digital practice. "Advances in AI may erode traditional advantages in engineering talent and labor, while an aging population and a smaller, more laid-back younger generation could temper the forces that once powered growth."

Those costs arrive as thin or negative returns on invested capital (ROIC), a growing number of "zombie" companies, and misallocated capital propped up by local incentives. Cycles come to an end only when standards tighten, credit dries up, and exports meet resistance.

Oversupply is worsened by the fact that Chinese entrepreneurs rarely stay in their swim lanes. Sure, companies everywhere chase adjacent opportunities, but in China the conviction and speed of these moves are on another level. Consumer appliance makers jump into EVs (Xiaomi), online marketplaces reinvent food delivery and digital finance (Alibaba), and carmakers begin building humanoid robots (XPENG). Luckin's founders came from car rentals; NIO's from internet ventures. When a market heats up, boundaries simply vanish.

At McKinsey, we constantly debate the costs and consequences of involution. Traditional strategy says to stick to your strengths and avoid piling into crowded trends. The Chinese marketplace is full of cautionary examples, and some have been spectacularly costly. Evergrande leapt from real estate into theme parks, EVs, and even bottled water. Suning expanded from electronics into sports and hyper-markets, snapping up Inter Milan and Carrefour China. Vanke, another major developer, even tried pig farming.

But there are also spectacular successes. After a few champions crawl out of the gym, the market might stabilize—or a new cycle might start all over again. In some sectors, the structure eventually settles and profits begin flowing. But more often, the game never ends. The ambition we observe can be intoxicating. "I wanted to be the next Elon Musk," one investor tells us. And so does everyone else.

At the macro-level, the toll is heavy. China's return on invested capital (ROIC) was about 6.5 percent in 2022—well below the EU's 10.3 percent and North America's 11 percent and closer to that of Japan and South Korea—a quiet signal that money no longer works as hard in China. "From an investor's point of view, involution is a nightmare. It's messy and terrible for short-term returns," says Hai Ye, a McKinsey senior partner. "But it rewards deep understanding and long horizons."

As overall market growth slows, deflationary pressures persist. Producer and consumer prices remained unusually weak through August 2025. Together, these trends show how inward-looking competition and supply/demand imbalances are eroding returns, distorting market efficiency, and weighing on economic stability.

These lower returns aren't just a financial curiosity—they're rewriting business strategy. Companies are pulling back on investment, recruiting fewer graduates, and watching both domestic and foreign investors drift toward greener pastures. Provincial rivalries make things worse, with regions undercutting one another in a race to attract capital—often at the expense of their own returns. "Involution basically tells us that Chinese companies work super hard and make amazing things for very little return," says Karel Eloot, a McKinsey senior partner co-leading the global metals and mining practice. "Yet China is a market economy, and if there is not enough return, this will sooner or later limit further development."

This phenomenon has proven difficult to stop. A few entrepreneurs manage to sprint ahead in this corporate "Hunger Games," but many struggle just to survive, while others become zombie firms or simply disappear. "Imagine if prices suddenly shoot up in China in certain sectors. It might really hurt demand because people have become used to lower and lower prices," says Alicia García-Herrero, Natixis's chief economist for Asia-Pacific. "There could be unintended consequences if this race to the bottom ends abruptly."

Behind the numbers lie the human costs: overworked employees, overextended students, and falling birth rates. Typically, we see that consumers cannot stomach price increases, the state stays growth-oriented, and households end up financing this low-margin equilibrium through their own low-return bank deposits.

In a now-famous episode in 2024, then Chairman Qinghong Zeng of state-owned automaker GAC Group openly urged peers at an auto industry forum to stop involution and price wars and focus instead on profits, taxes, and employment. Months later, GAC's Honda joint venture was forced to execute two rounds of layoffs. EV newcomers scoffed: the legacy OEMs, they said, had been sitting on "fat profits for way too long"—and it was time for the challengers to take over.

The Politics of Consolidation

Consolidation is nothing new in business. British textiles, US railroads, Japanese electronics, even Australian beer all saw brutal price wars. What makes China different is the sheer persistence and scale. Industry after industry has run this cycle not once but over and over.

During boom years, this pattern was challenging but manageable. Now, with slower growth, tougher export conditions, and overcapacity everywhere, the same forces have become a societal worry. Even *The People's Daily* has sounded the alarm, warning about the dangers of *juan* and calling for "high-quality development." The central government is trying to temper the excess it once fueled in certain sectors, for example, by raising standards to weed out low-quality players, pressuring provinces to halt new capacity, and pushing for consolidations and exits of money-losing ventures.

Still, consolidation is politically charged. Provinces rarely want to let their own firms die; social stability and jobs come first. In many countries, bankruptcy wipes the slate clean; in China, propping up weak companies delays the kind of shakeout that could lift efficiency across the board. That's how such firms manage to stagger on—kept alive not by strength but by local protection and credit rollovers. What can look like resilience is really capital being misallocated. And with local officials wary of being blamed for failures on their watch, a reckoning for many already doomed enterprises gets pushed down the road.

Still, some sectors are cooling, with clear winners emerging. In chemicals, repeated rounds of involution have already produced "last-man-standing" outcomes. In vitamins, NHU now controls roughly 35 percent of the global market and posted a 12 percent net margin in 2024, even as much of the chemicals industry lost money. Chinese producers collectively supply about 85 percent of global vitamin demand. Similar patterns have played out elsewhere: Lomon in titanium dioxide; Meihua in amino acids. The payoff is capability. Today, US bio-industrial start-ups working on precision fermentation often turn to companies such as Meihua to scale and industrialize their products—not because they're the cheapest option but because it's hard to find others that can execute as well at industrial volumes.

Other sectors, by contrast, remain stuck in open warfare. Coffee chains, EVs, and consumer internet platforms continue to attract waves of entrants, imitation, and price competition. Some industries cool; others simply reset and start the cycle again. In 2025, just when the internet battles seemed settled, Alibaba, JD.com, and Meituan reignited another costly free-for-all in "instant retail," or sub-one-hour delivery.

By the way, this mechanism doesn't always lift capabilities. It works best where scale and speed matter—and less well in fields that depend on long-cycle scientific research and accumulated know-how. Jet engines, high-end machine tools, and parts of the semiconductor supply chain remain notable gaps.

Is it really more competitive today? "China has always been like this," says Yibing Wu, China CEO of Singapore's Temasek Holdings, one of the country's most influential investors. "In the 1990s, PC assemblers fought it out—that was the first generation. Then internet entrepreneurs reshaped the economy, followed by ByteDance and Pinduoduo capturing share. Now we have a fourth generation of entrepreneurs competing in AI. The winners from the PC era are only in their sixties, and they're still hungry. It's the Chinese way—a congestion of entrepreneurs and companies fighting in a very compressed period of time."

When Competition Blurs into Involution

Excess competition? Natural evolution? Involution? Creative destruction? There's no consensus on how to characterize China's hyper-competitive industries, and we see people use these terms interchangeably. In theory, involution has a specific meaning: competition so intense that it destroys profit margins, creates oversupply, pushes prices downward, and keeps zombie firms alive. Lower returns may simply be China's new equilibrium—something investors must accept—but within that landscape, standout firms can still thrive.

On the ground, involution feels both brutal and strangely logical. One client compares it to a movie theater where the first row stands, forcing every row behind them to do the same: "No one sees any better, but no one dares to sit down." Entrepreneurs echo the same mindset, as they consume little and fight year after year to develop cheaper drones, a greener EV, or a skin lotion that promises to reverse aging: "We can go without sleep for two years. We need little to survive. We will outlast the rest."

Playing in this theater is often highly rational for the individual player—a predictable response to an intoxicating mix of tax incentives, abundant capital, government support, national ambition, and the lived memory of personal wealth and glory. Over three decades, China has seen the fastest wealth creation in its commercial history: Alibaba and Tencent in digital, Anta and Li-Ning in sportswear, Xiaomi and Oppo in electronics—and countless regional fortunes in everything from local hotel operators to provincial shoe distributors.

Some business practices practically invite involution—especially in asset-light industries such as software, e-commerce solutions, digital media, and knowledge-based services, where price can become an important lever. Consulting is a case in point. Joe recalls one bid process for a banking project in Beijing: the bank's procurement team invited five consulting firms for a proposal, or what they called a "beauty contest."

Two were immediately eliminated on qualifications, and the remaining three—including McKinsey—were ushered into a conference room and told that we all qualified, but that winning the project would come down to price. The client's procurement leader announced the lowest bid at that point. Sitting across the table from their competitors, *Survivor*-style, firms resubmitted their fees. One more was cut. For the final round, McKinsey and the remaining firm called their investment committees for approval to slash fees further. McKinsey lost. The winning bid? Twenty percent of the initial proposed fee.

Brutal, yes. Nevertheless, the progress is right in front of us across both asset-light and asset-heavy industries: logistics networks that mastered on-demand delivery at near-zero fees; ride-hailing networks that rewired urban mobility through iteration; an EV ecosystem that drove down battery cost and sped up global adoption; a coffee battlefield that converted a nation of tea drinkers into digitally native coffee consumers; and even steel—steel!—that emerged greener through automation and technological renewal.

In some sectors, involution has reset industry baselines and produced an environment in which companies that survive can even thrive. For example, Chinese steel sells at 30 to 50 percent below US prices while industry margins are only a few percentage points lower, according to our colleague Sheng Hong, a McKinsey senior partner leading the global energy and materials practice. In advanced compressors, a high-value segment of industrial machinery, Chinese products are 50 to 80 percent cheaper, yet industry profits trail US peers by only 10 to 15 percent. This mix of extreme cost advantage, modest profit compression, and a complete manufacturing ecosystem positions Chinese firms to compete globally. As Sheng puts it, "I joke that I'd never buy an industry index in China—the sector will always compete itself to death—but the leader makes healthy margins."

China's pressure-driven efficiency doesn't just benefit domestic players. It expands global access to advanced technologies. For example, waste-to-energy plants, once affordable only to high-income countries, are now viable in markets with a per capita income as low as $3,000. In China itself, plant adoption has scaled so quickly that capacity has overshot demand—the country is literally running out of garbage to burn.

Looking Ahead: From Lifting All Boats to Only a Few

We understand the challenge the China market poses. How do foreign entrepreneurs and multinationals build in a place where workaholism is a badge of entry and the primary weapon seems to be cutting prices until rivals starve? Is this a game anyone, much less outsiders, wants to play? And can anyone realistically build durable competitive advantages here?

Of course, for end users downstream of an involuted industry, there's no better place in the world to be. For Chinese consumers: new EVs every few years; 9.9 RMB ($1.4) coffees; a subsidized refrigerator; two-for-one robot vacuums! For professionals: a noodle lunch that costs less delivered than eaten at the restaurant; a collared shirt for the price of four metro rides!

And the great irony is that even companies squeezed by involution in their end markets benefit in procurement upstream; automakers might get steel on the cheap, battery makers scoop up discounted chemical inputs, and appliance firms source components cheaper this year than last. The marketplace shimmers with hungry suppliers.

For industry players, especially the multinationals accustomed to less intense competition and fatter margins in other markets, the choice around whether to stay and how to play can feel agonizing. "Auto companies say it's not an option not to be in China, but at the same time, it's not a great option to be in China," says Ruth Heuss, a McKinsey senior partner in Berlin and co-leader of the Firm's global operations practice. Economist Alicia Garcia-Herrero puts it bluntly: "You decide not to invest, you lose faster. You invest, and then you're in the gym—some people call it a prison. You can't tell everyone 'I'm getting fit,' because the reality is you're getting beaten up."

Our view is straightforward: multinationals can't simply walk away now. China is the only single market that's large enough, with an abundant supply of talent, a comprehensive supply chain, and the infrastructure to enable sustained competition. Other economies might be too small, too fragmented, or lack industrial depth or logistical capacity to offer the same opportunity. To compete here is to get "fit for the fight that's coming to your other markets," as McKinsey's retired senior partner Franck Le Deu puts it. "You can't just say, 'I'm sorry, this race is too difficult and everyone else is too good.' For many global companies—especially in industrial sectors—performing successfully in China is what helps make you globally competitive."

Two final points are worth emphasizing. First, for all the talk of exhaustion and involution, entrepreneurs remain fundamentally optimistic about the market's long-term vitality and potential. They keep piling in because they genuinely believe there's upside, while in stagnant or declining markets, no one bothers to enter. So while it's easy to lament China's intensity, the real warning sign would be if entrepreneurs stopped wanting to invest their capital, reputations, and time.

Second, this is the toughest gym in the world. We've seen companies carve out real success by competing on cycle time, choosing defensible niches, co-developing with customers, or simply resetting their margin expectations for China. Outcomes can be powerful: consumers get higher-quality products at lower prices, companies sharpen their capabilities, and industries move up the value chain. Call it a Joseph Schumpeter–style "creative destruction with Chinese characteristics." Many Chinese companies now carry that confidence and those capabilities abroad.

The Chinese marketplace moves with the restless energy that no middle-aged economy possesses. This ecosystem can be unforgiving, but it's also generative, and those who endure leave stronger than when they entered.

CHAPTER 4

The Price We Paid

When BlackBerry devices came onto the scene a couple of decades ago, one of Nick's financial clients—an influential chairman and CEO—rejoiced. Suddenly he could fire off emails at all hours on tiny devices that could easily travel out to dinner, into the gym, even into the bathroom. He liked to joke, "My BlackBerry can send faster, but I can't make the others reply faster."

But in China, people did reply faster and faster, a reflection of the country's ambition at the time. It was the same ambition that kept the factories of Dongguan and the tech workers in Shanghai and Shenzhen running "996"—9 a.m. to 9 p.m., six days a week. Coupled with tens of millions entering the workforce, massive capital investment, and a government-fueled infrastructure build-out, this relentless work ethic transformed China in just thirty years from an agrarian nation into a global manufacturing and technology superpower.

China's urbanization surged from the mid-teens before late-1970s reforms to about 67 percent by 2024, effectively adding a new Shanghai, of around twenty million people, every year. The country now has 144 cities with over a million residents—compared to Europe's 58 and America's 12—including 18 mega-cities of more than ten million each. This mass migration has fueled both consumption and productivity as China evolved from a manufacturing hub into a comprehensive industrial ecosystem spanning basic goods, advanced manufacturing, and technology innovation.

That progress has come with trade-offs and significant casualties. China's corporate athletes got to the world championship and won gold, but along the way, some players fell, others cramped up, and many more burned out. The medal is real—but so is the shakeout.

We see these pains in a segment of young people who quietly reject the competition they feel is required to succeed. We see it in multinationals contemplating their own version of "wait and see" on further China-related investments as margins and market share erode. We see it in Chinese entrepreneurs who confront a slower economy, lower returns, involution, and sheer exhaustion. And we see it in geopolitical shifts that have slowed the flow of Chinese goods, from electric vehicles to solar panels to AI technologies.

"We haven't seen anything like the rise of China: a capable workforce at least three or four times larger than the US and Europe and working twice as hard. The world isn't prepared for this level of output from such a large economy," says LONGi's vice president and chief sustainability officer Haimeng Zhang. "The decoupling that's underway is destroying a lot of wealth on both sides."

Ironically, the very engines that powered China's rise—investment, savings, ambition, competition—have become drags when pushed to excess. High savings now restrain consumption. Investment fueled infrastructure but left heavy debt burdens. Market-based competition helped industries scale, only to tip them into involution. Educational ambition lifted skills and moved China up the value chain while accelerating burnout. And the demographic dividend—millions moving to cities and joining the urban workforce—has given way to falling birth rates as residents opt out of parenthood.

This chapter is a clear-eyed accounting of the costs of China's rise. Consumption remains too weak to rebalance the economy or offset the property downturn in the short term. Corporate debt has climbed to 1.8 times GDP, twice the global average, and by the end of 2024, nearly a quarter of industrial firms were unprofitable—the highest share in more than two decades.

How long can this burden be sustained? No one knows. But long-term stability depends on faster productivity growth, which in turn depends on stronger domestic demand—and overcoming several key "traps."

Swollen Balance Sheets

In 2010, Nick visited an architect friend whose charming home on Beijing's outskirts had floor-to-ceiling windows overlooking a peaceful lake. At some point, a massive mall appeared across the water, followed by a new metro line. Soon, rows of high-rises began appearing much to the architect's dismay.

For a time, the towers sat empty, prompting talk of "ghost cities." But tenants eventually arrived once the infrastructure was in place as Beijing expanded further into the surrounding countryside. Some other mega-projects were less fortunate, remaining largely unoccupied, and as China's growth slowed, construction in many places continued to outpace population inflows.

For decades, this build-first, fill-later pattern defined an investment-heavy, debt-fueled race to scale. Real estate, infrastructure, steel, autos, solar, even bike sharing—the model was always the same: borrow today, build tomorrow, and assume returns will follow.

It worked well for a long time. Over the past decade, we have had many interesting conversations with our clients—many from emerging markets—who are fascinated by China's model of development. From Southeast Asia to Africa to Latin America, they all want to know: Could it work for them?

Today, this model has reached its structural limits. China once borrowed to build new capacity; it now borrows largely to refinance existing obligations—supporting infrastructure, property, and local governments whose returns no longer cover their costs. We call this China's swollen balance sheet problem: economic growth driven by debt accumulation rather than productivity. China's debt-to-GDP ratio has climbed steadily to a record 293 percent in early

2025—roughly double the level of two decades ago and higher than that of the US, the UK, and Germany.

The roots lie in the urban boom of the 1990s and 2000s, when local governments financed growth by selling land and borrowing heavily. Developers, convinced demand would never falter, built relentlessly. Property values became the backbone of both local government budgets and household wealth. When regulators imposed 2020's "three red lines"—caps on leverage, debt-to-equity, and short-term liquidity—to curb excess, the bubble cracked. The collapse of Evergrande, with $300 billion in liabilities, symbolized the unraveling.

As revenues dried up, local governments rolled forward old debts just to stay afloat. Infrastructure projects stalled; schools delayed construction; government bureaus cut civil servants' salaries. State-owned enterprises kept building projects, some of which made marginal fiscal sense—because stopping would trigger loan defaults, which would then ricochet through local banks and public finances.

Once-flush developers began offering steep discounts. Unfinished towers stood behind locked gates. Banks kept lending simply to avoid recognizing losses. Households, watching property prices soften, tightened their wallets—saving more, spending less, waiting for the rebound that has yet to come. Growth remains, but it is slower, more constrained, and funded by yesterday's money. Each yuan of borrowing now produces less output, while the weight of old debt narrows future choices.

What's the fix? Shifting from a growth model driven by construction and leverage to one powered by productivity and consumption. Other major economies face their own prescriptions—Europe must invest more, and the US must save more—but China's challenge is steeper.

Household, corporate, and public balance sheets are already strained, raising the risk of secular stagnation and slower wealth gains in the decade ahead. The Chinese government is acutely aware of the problem: initiatives such as industrial upgrading and "AI +" aim to lift productivity, with ministries rolling out adoption targets and new

KPIs. McKinsey's analysis suggests that without faster productivity growth, wealth expansion over the next decade could slow sharply, making balance sheet trends a clearer signal of the path ahead than conventional forecasts alone.

The Savings Engine Turned Savings Trap

Consider Jing, a thirty-nine-year-old project manager in Nanjing, who still treats payday like a personal savings ritual. On her commute home, she opens Alipay or WeChat Pay and moves part of her salary as well as her husband's into a three-year deposit or a money market fund. Jing could automate, but she prefers the feeling of being hands-on. She and her husband check the stock market sometimes, but largely out of curiosity—it still feels too unpredictable. For Jing, financial security means guaranteed returns, and where she once carried cash to the bank counter, one tap on her phone now gives her the same sense of control.

For decades, growth has run on an extraordinary engine: household savings. Since the 1990s, China's household savings rate has consistently exceeded 20 percent of GDP. That's the kind of number that makes us rub our eyes and check twice. More than one-fifth of GDP was stashed into savings accounts and low-risk products?

Yes, one-fifth. No country's citizens save like the Chinese. Over the same period, Japan and South Korea saw their household savings rates fall from around 14 percent to just 8 percent, while in the United States and the United Kingdom, it has never exceeded 10 percent. To be clear, that rainy-day money doesn't sit idle. Households trust banks, and banks funnel those deposits into loans for state firms and local governments. Higher-return investment trust products—a form of shadow banking—grew rapidly before high-profile failures reminded investors they weren't guaranteed. For most Chinese households, real estate remained the only serious alternative to bank savings.

This high-savings model powered a once-in-history build-out. Over the past two decades, the country has invested tens of trillions of dollars—often more than 40 percent of GDP each year, into the world's largest high-speed rail network, vast expressways, ports, metro lines, bridges, new cities, and housing for hundreds of millions. Capital spilled into industrial parks and economic zones. For years, this cycle felt like perpetual motion.

But returns have slowed. Economists track this via the incremental capital output ratio (ICOR): in the early 2000s, China's economy needed 3 to 4 RMB ($0.4 to $0.6) of investment to generate 1 RMB ($0.1) of GDP; by the early 2020s, it needed 8 to 9 RMB ($1.1 to $1.3). In other words, it now takes two to three times more capital to produce the same growth. Some new infrastructure—data centers, cloud, digital power—still delivers double-digit returns. But trillions of RMB remain locked in real estate, where clearing existing inventory now takes more than two years, compared to just twelve to fourteen months five years ago.

Weak consumption amplifies this imbalance. Household consumption significantly lags rich-world norms, settling at just 39 percent of GDP in 2024—far below the US at 68 percent, Japan at 55 percent, and the low 50s in Germany, France, Australia, and South Korea.

Why do Chinese households save so much? Part of the answer lies in history. As China shifted from a planned economy to a more market-driven one, the old "iron rice bowl" system of guaranteed jobs and cradle-to-grave benefits receded. Families increasingly assumed the private burden of paying for housing, education, retirement, healthcare, and other long-term needs—prompting them to save more. In effect, households internalized costs that in many advanced economies are socialized through public systems.

China does have a broad social safety net; the nationwide "five insurances and one housing fund" program covers pensions, medical care, unemployment, workplace injury, maternity needs, and long-term housing savings. But payouts are often modest, and demographic shifts mean fewer workers will be supporting a growing retiree population—the classic "inverted pyramid" facing aging societies everywhere.

Uncertainty reinforces this instinct. Youth unemployment hovered just below 20 percent in 2025, and job insecurity runs deeper than the headline. As Chinese families say, "If you can't see the storm forecast, you carry a bigger umbrella."

The savings trap has two sides. On the supply side, cheap funding keeps flowing into lower-return projects, repeating the old formula of steel, concrete, and buildings. On the demand side, anxious households do what anxious households do: they save rather than spend. Overcapacity feeds frugality; frugality worsens overcapacity.

China's economy has navigated shocks before—SOE reforms, the global financial crisis, COVID—but this current adjustment will feel slower. The old playbook of debt-fueled growth no longer delivers, and the next phase of growth must come from innovation, consumption, and productivity.

For now, weak spending reflects two realities. First, deflation makes nominal consumption look flat even when real volumes rise. Second, some consumers are "trading down," shifting from hotels to camping, from Porsche aspirations to BYD practicality.

Expectations also need to be recalibrated. From 2000 to 2020, many assumed property prices, wages, and consumption would rise indefinitely. Property came to be seen as one of the most important investment assets, and the bursting of the housing bubble has been deeply distressing for a generation of savers. Wage growth was likewise expected to have remained in the high single digits, if not double digits; the last few years of slower growth and job cuts have punctured that assumption. Perspective helps. We often remind business leaders that Europe has grown at around 2 percent for decades; Japan closer to 0.5 percent. As expectations normalize, sentiment may recover.

The upside lies in sectors seeded over the past decade: robotics, generative AI, biotech, and green energy. If the 2010s were about building, the 2020s must be about making those assets pay—and turning precautionary savings from a trap back into an engine.

One central question for the next China is simple: How do you unlock 152 trillion RMB ($22 trillion) in household savings and shift some of it from empty apartments and savings accounts into real consumption? The challenge is turning precaution into participation. The potential is obvious. "The desire and the power—and the money—are there. We just need to unlock it," says Kevin Wei Wang, a McKinsey senior partner co-leading the digital practice in Asia. In researching livestream shopping behavior, McKinsey found that even in lower-tier cities, consumers might spend up to two-thirds of their incomes, drawn by community, novelty, and a nudge by influencers and livestream hosts. "You give consumers a chance, and they do consume."

The World's Toughest Gym: The Costs to Society

As we outlined in the previous chapter, involution can result in dazzling success. Whether it's coffee, solar, steel, or the less-reported booms in EV chargers, LED lighting, or home fitness gear, each "next big thing" triggers explosive growth and a stampede of capital. Local governments compete to host factories, and companies sprint to grab market share.

We've already detailed the economic fallout: negative returns, zombie firms sustained by cheap credit, and capital misallocated by local government incentives and investor exuberance. The cycle typically breaks only when standards tighten, credit dries up, and export markets hit their limits—setting off consolidation that's always politically sensitive but economically unavoidable. And even then, involution is hard to extinguish entirely: cycles slow, markets might stabilize, and then—because the opportunity is huge—it roars back to life.

What we haven't yet discussed is the human cost—what this constant over-effort does to sentiment and confidence across Chinese society. Workers feel trapped on the same treadmill that students do: ten years of preparing for the college entrance exam, only to graduate into a job market with another bottleneck and lots of headwinds. "There are too many people running faster and faster, and only a few feel they're getting ahead," says Stanley Wang, a McKinsey partner in the global energy and materials practice. "There's massive fatigue. At some point you ask if it's sustainable."

Can the Chinese economy hold on to the upside of relentless competition without burning itself out? The next two traps emerge from the sheer intensity required just to stay in the game.

The Ambition Treadmill—and Its Generational Bill

Picture Ming, twenty-four years old, sitting in a rented studio on the edge of the mid-sized city of Jinhua in Zhejiang province. The blinds are half drawn. His laptop is open, but he's decided to watch a video rather than work. Ding! His phone glows with yet another message from worried parents, urging him to trade up for a better job, to take the civil service exam, or to get married. He scrolls for a while, then puts the phone face down.

He's not protesting, he's just *tangping*, lying flat, a phrase coined to describe a certain segment of a generation that looks down the road and doesn't like what it sees. Ming is opting out, working an online advertising job that pays enough to get by: no overtime, no pressure. On weekends, he reads or takes a walk. It's an unremarkable life, and that's the point—far from what his parents and grandparents imagined when they poured heart and soul into furthering his education. Ming still hopes to "make it"—whatever that means—just not now.

The one-child era minted a generation of ambition, but now the cost is becoming clear: high expectations layered onto slowing growth have led to generational burnout and in turn declining fertility just as an aging society needs care.

For decades, Chinese families invested heavily in a single child. Households devote a larger share of their budgets to education than any other country—about 17 percent of average annual income, far higher than the 1 to 2 percent typically seen in Japan, Mexico, or the United States. The pattern holds across the rural-urban divide and across income levels: urban families spend more than rural families, and the poorest households devote more than 56 percent of their annual income to education.

By 2024, China had produced 260 million college graduates, forming a large and increasingly skilled workforce. Many have gone on to advanced study at home and abroad, filling out PhD programs around the world, and then returned home to drive the country's emerging industries. The middle class expanded rapidly: households earning 180,000 RMB (about $26,000) grew from a small minority to nearly half of urban households by 2024—and day-to-day purchasing power often stretches further, with a carton of high-quality eggs costing $1.57 in China compared with $4.40 in the United States and $3.82 in Germany.

But the payoff has thinned. The one-child generation was raised to win; now it's asking whether the race is worth it. In one recent interview with a twenty-five-year-old master's graduate on the topic of lying flat, she said, "We used to quote the Chinese proverb—'bitter first, sweetness later'—meaning that you should work hard first for delayed gratification. This is the problem: we don't know whether sweetness will ever come, but you know that it sure is bitter now. I would rather taste some sweetness now, because I know it is definitely sweet."

In other words, a segment of the population has opted out of the race. It is impossible to estimate how large this group is—likely a small minority—but the sentiment is widely felt. At the same time, the "4-2-1" burden—one child supporting two parents and four grandparents—has become a national concern, with the basic pension fund projected to run dry by 2035.

Younger generations are routinely labeled complacent or entitled, a pattern seen in China as well as in mature economies like Japan and Europe. What sets China apart is the speed at which these pressures are arriving. The response, however, is far from passive. Millions are saving more, delaying marriage, or seeking civil service stability—over three million applied in 2025, more than double since 2020—while others turn to gigs, creator platforms, or start-ups, redefining ambition for a slower-growth China.

It's also a gentle warning sign for corporations. Today's young workers didn't grow up in the hardship their parents and grandparents knew. While they're still living modestly by global developed market standards, they've already leapt far beyond the living standards of earlier generations. That shift matters. It means companies can no longer assume that young people will simply put their heads down and accept whatever working conditions or culture they're handed.

A few years ago, we asked young Chinese what they were seeking from their careers, and their answers looked identical to those of young people everywhere in the world: meaningful work, autonomy, flexibility, and the chance to advance quickly. The way forward is purposeful ambition that excites, supports, and endures. That's the dividend China now owes its young people.

China's Demographic Crossroads

Consider Mrs. Zhang, a seventy-eight-year-old widow who lives alone in a small apartment an hour outside Chengdu. Like many women her age, she's outlived her husband, while her son has migrated to Shenzhen and visits only once a year. Most days are quiet. She boils water for tea, watches livestreams on her phone, and chats with neighbors on WeChat—a faint glow of company in an otherwise silent room. A wristband tracks her heart rate and pings her son if she falls. Across the street, the kindergarten has closed—too few children remain and there aren't enough teachers.

China is confronting a demographic reversal: a rapidly aging population, falling fertility, and a shrinking workforce. The country's once youthful age structure—long a growth engine—has run its course. Fertility has fallen to around 1.0, among the lowest globally. Meanwhile, by mid-century the number of citizens over age sixty-five will rise from 15 to 31 percent—that's one in every three Chinese citizens! China is aging faster than Japan ever did, compressing what was essentially a century-long shift in Japan into a single generation. By 2050, the number of seniors in China will double, leaving the country with a demographic profile that looks much like Japan's today.

On the surface, this may look like a caution flag. But the story is more dynamic—and much less dire—than it first appears. From the late twentieth century through the early 2000s, China reaped enormous benefits from a young, mobile labor force as roughly

240 million rural migrants fueled the country's industrial boom. The number of urban Chinese quadrupled to 67 percent by 2024. Yet the population peaked at around 1.41 billion in 2021 and has since begun to contract.

China won't be alone in this shift. Western Europe is expected to have a similar share of older adults by mid-century, and the United States isn't far behind—though both remain slightly younger than China with higher fertility rates and also higher rates of immigration. This demographic wave will shape everything from the labor force to household finances.

Will Mrs. Zhang's son have one child or two? In China's mega-cities, life feels expensive, fast paced, and intensely competitive—and that constant ambition treadmill is eroding the appeal of larger families. Today, roughly five workers support Mrs. Zhang's pension, but by mid-century, that support ratio is expected to drop to just two working-age adults as the share of retirees rises and the working-age cohort declines.

Despite an array of government incentives—tax breaks, subsidies, and the shift from the two-child to the three-child policy—few families are choosing to have more children, especially in major urban centers. The overall fertility rate sits around 1.14, but that number masks a sharp divide: rural areas are closer to 1.35, while large cities are nearer 1.0. Simply put, raising children in urban China feels too expensive, and many young adults hesitate to birth more kids—only to have them start running on that treadmill almost from day one.

Of course, this isn't unique to China; it mirrors a global trend seen in most highly urbanized cities. What sets China apart is the speed and depth of its decline: fertility has fallen into the same ultra-low range as Japan and South Korea, but in far less time. The way out of this trap is adaptation: upgrading labor skills, boosting productivity through technology, and addressing the economic and social barriers facing young households. The alternative is stagnation—an economy that grows old before it grows rich.

What are China's institutions doing to address this? Beijing is rolling out a fertility-boosting program: cheaper childcare, longer parental leave, tax and housing incentives, and a rapid build-out of public nurseries. Local governments are adding work-life balance reforms of their own, from Sichuan's extended marriage and maternity leave to Shanghai's mandate around "family-friendly" positions with more predictable hours. Companies have begun limiting overtime and enforcing clock-off rules to reduce burnout. China's leading online travel agency, Trip.com Group, announced that it will provide 1 billion RMB ($143 million) in subsidies to support employees who choose to have more children; Jane Sun, CEO of Trip.com, tells us she feels "tremendous responsibility" to pave the way for female leaders and has introduced free taxis during pregnancy and company-sponsored egg freezing.

Like many aging societies, China's demographic shift doesn't erase opportunity—it reshapes it. An older population is driving demand for healthcare, services, smart devices, automation, robotics, and productivity-boosting tools, and China still contributes more to annual global GDP growth than any other economy.

In the near term, however, the effects will show up more clearly in classrooms than in offices. Kindergarten enrollment will shrink well before the labor force does. University graduates entering the workforce will still increase over the next decade, reflecting higher university enrollments. The sharp drop in births only began after 2016–2017; its full impact won't be felt until the late 2030s.

In short, the demographic headwinds are real—but so are the markets they create. The questions ahead are not just about population size but also about productivity and innovation. And those are areas where new players, including foreign multinationals, can thrive. Not to be cliché, but boomtowns don't disappear; they evolve.

The Potential Runway to Success

Put the five traps together—high debt, high savings, the costs of "involution," an ambition treadmill, and an aging population—and you get the dinnertime conversation in millions of Chinese homes. The meal looks simple enough—bowls of rice, bok choy with mushrooms, a plate of stir-fried pork—but it probably arrived after a few swipes on an app, steaming hot within thirty minutes and delivered almost for free. The parents sigh, "In our days, things were better." By "our days" they don't mean the 1970s or 1990s but just a decade ago, when wages reliably climbed and apartments seemed destined only to rise in value. Yet they're eating food their own parents could never have afforded so easily. The smart fridge hums beside a countertop full of appliances that once belonged only in glossy magazines. A new EV sits outside. Everyone has one, maybe two phones. Life is materially better, and consumption feels effortless.

What's faded isn't comfort or abundance, but rather the confidence that tomorrow will be better still. Their child—often still an only child—gulps down dinner before returning to hours of homework. Her future looks tighter: slower salary growth, a more competitive employment landscape, high real estate prices, postponed family plans, and the expectation of caring for aging parents and grandparents alone.

Companies feel a similar strain: cautious consumers, workers frustrated by flat wages, and markets warped by constant price cuts. The world's toughest gym built strong muscles; the next phase requires using them more intelligently.

None of this means China is predestined for stagnation. Predictions of collapse often borrow the wrong frame—reading China through Japan's "lost decades" or Western boom-and-bust cycles. China's system per capita income still has room to grow and its policy machinery can redirect credit quickly. And remember: Chinese households are sitting on enormous savings. The energy is there, but the channels to turn savings into spending, scale into productivity, and ambition into purpose need repair.

The positives are real: a measured optimism; a vast domestic market that still allows companies to pivot, test, and scale; and a Chinese workforce that remains among the world's most driven. Chinese entrepreneurs continue to generate world-class competitors in sectors where success once seemed improbable. In AI and robotics, the new class of unicorns are creating wealth faster than ever before, with ever younger whiz kids. In a world of slowing growth, the country's resilience remains singular.

The challenge—and the opportunity—now is to pivot: to move from price wars to productivity, from ghost assets to smarter capital, from forced workaholism to sustainable ambition, and from inward anxiety to outward confidence. Humans tend to fixate on the negative—an evolutionary instinct that's great for avoiding bears and tigers but less great for understanding long-term progress, as Nick and his McKinsey Global Institute colleagues have researched and written about in *A Century of Plenty*. The arc of the past century is unmistakable: global per capita incomes have risen more than seven-fold, life expectancy has extended by three decades, and average years of schooling have increased by more than seven. China has been central to that story, enabling hundreds of millions to lift themselves into the middle class and driving global growth.

A negative outcome is not predestined. "Are we at a precipice?" asks Michael Zang, CEO of Zhejiang Shangbai Group, which operates supermarkets, malls, and department stores across the coastal corridor south of Shanghai. "Whereas periods of 'irrational exuberance' can inflate expectations far beyond underlying economic realities, I like to say that 'irrational pessimism' calls for immediate entry. The more pessimism I hear, the more opportunities there are. We just need to work a little harder to find them."

PART II

WINNING IN THE NEXT CHINA

CHAPTER 5

Waking Up in China's Next Chapter

Over dinner at the legendary Da Dong Roast Duck Restaurant in Beijing, a Chinese retail executive set down his chopsticks, leaned forward, and asked Joe a question we haven't heard in decades: "How do you set a budget when revenues keep going down?"

By 2024, for the first time, revenues in consumer categories such as cosmetics and beauty products were shrinking, and margins were disappearing even faster. Joe's retailer dinner companion genuinely didn't know how to plan for it: Shutter weaker stores? Drop unprofitable channels? Cut product lines? He'd done all these things before, but always in bits and pieces and never at this scale. This felt like a defeat.

We've been having these types of conversations for the first time in our China careers. Sometimes we joke, "Welcome to the rest of the world." In Europe, Japan, and the US, McKinsey has been running cost-efficiency programs for decades; in China we've only been doing so in the last two years.

China has repeatedly reinvented itself, shifting from low-cost to advanced manufacturing, rewiring life around digital super-apps, and urbanizing at a remarkable pace. Growth hasn't always been smooth, but even when we saw hiccups in the infrastructure build-out, a lull in consumer demand, or crashes in stock or real estate prices—any economic consequence typically righted itself before long. "In the past, you could just wait it out, and growth would invariably come back—you could grow your way out of trouble," says Yonglin Xie, co-CEO of Ping An Group, one of the largest financial groups in China.

Yet this moment feels very different. "Consumer confidence has been subdued—the longest slump we've seen—though it's beginning to stabilize after a long period of uncertainty," says Daniel Zipser, a McKinsey senior partner and co-leader of the Asia consumer and retail practice. The post-COVID rebound never came. Property prices have fallen significantly with little sign of a short-term recovery. Digital economy firms, once a surefire landing spot for graduates, have cut staff. White-collar salaries in cities like Shanghai and Shenzhen stagnated and for some declined for the first time.

It's increasingly clear that the next era won't replicate the old pattern of growth. "The playbook is changing," says Bob Sternfels, McKinsey's global managing partner. "But China will continue to export innovation to the rest of the world, and its market is massive and continues to be relevant. From a global point of view, companies will need to have a model that works there."

A Quandary for Global Companies

Multinationals no longer view China as a hyper-growth market. Global boards, especially those in North America, are debating whether China remains "investable"—not because of any single shock but due to concerns about geopolitics and regulatory moves that can be hard to predict. As one Canadian institutional investor told Joe in 2024, "If I put more capital into China today, I have to answer so many questions. If anything goes wrong, I risk my job. If I wait and see, I'm just being conservative like everyone else."

This doesn't mean multinational companies are naive, passive, or standing still. On the contrary, many executives are deeply sophisticated, understand the China market well, and are actively fighting to adapt. For years there was strong alignment and mutual benefit:

multinationals brought capital, technology, brands, and management expertise, and China welcomed them in. Revenue and profits would then flow—often, the country would become their largest growth market overnight. That honeymoon is now over.

Many are meeting this moment head-on. Some clients are doubling down on their footprint and investments in China today, while others are recalibrating more cautiously. What's clear is that the next phase will require a new set of "firsts." McKinsey has spent more than thirty years in China, often pioneering new approaches. Today's environment demands another reinvention of the operating playbook—one designed to thrive in a very different environment.

Exit, Pause, or Pivot

For multinationals, exiting might seem to reduce exposure to risk in the short term, but companies are finding no replacement for the volume that China provides. As one client puts it, "No place in the world has as many people willing to pay tens of thousands for a previously unknown brand of electric vehicle, much less the ecosystem to bring to market an even newer and better car in twenty-four months which people might test-drive or buy. Europe and the US don't have this. Other countries might be too small or lack growth."

More important, step away from China, and you not only lose the Chinese market but also your ability to compete globally, particularly in high-value industrial sectors. As Mingyu Guan, a McKinsey senior partner leading China's automotive practice, says, "China is now offering a spectrum of possibilities that multinationals can benefit from. Rather than just selling into China, it's now a market that will be driving cutting-edge change—millions of engineers and a consumer base that continues to rise. If you can 'get fit' here in China, you'll be fit globally." That logic extends across sectors that depend on complex, high-value products. And no CEO wants to be the first in their sector to give up on China. Therefore, outside of a few cases that make sensational headlines, very few notable multinationals are completely pulling out of China.

Pausing investment or taking a "wait and see" approach may feel safer—and many American, European, Japanese, and Korean companies are doing exactly that. This choice is often frustrating for local China teams, for which needs on the ground feel endless, from re-investing in operations to funding local R&D and technology upgrades. Yet committing new capital to China today is rarely straightforward, leaving many boards divided and hesitant. As Jeongmin Seong, a McKinsey Global Institute partner, puts it, "China is a market where companies feel pressure to keep investing just to stay competitive. If you don't do that, you'll struggle, but if you do, the payoff is harder to predict than before. This creates a feeling of strategic limbo." Yet in a market that moves this fast, standing still means falling behind. Chinese competitors are well funded and moving quickly. Product cycles that once took years now unfold in months. Local firms don't have the option to exit—so they continue investing and innovating.

What we recommend is a pivot. Firms must rethink how to compete in China. Tighten up your cost base, team up with the right local partners, find efficiencies you may not have needed before, and get comfortable with faster, more value-for-money innovation. We're seeing these moves everywhere: chemicals, consumer goods, food and beverage, industrials—you name it. Companies are forming joint ventures, engaging with Chinese private equity to fund the next stage of growth, or shifting to an "in China, for China" model whereby products, processes, and decisions are built for the speed of this market. Dozens of multinationals are also considering the "in China, for global" strategy.

At the same time, we're seeing a new class of investors rapidly increase their exposure to China. Many Middle Eastern clients are expanding their China teams, opening new offices in Hong Kong and Shanghai, and crowding flights to China from Abu Dhabi, Dubai, and Riyadh. With the recent surge of Chinese IPOs in Hong Kong, private family offices are accelerating investment activity—hunting for the next CATL or Pop Mart.

Chinese Entrepreneurs Are Also Feeling Pressure

It's not only multinationals that are facing challenges. Many of our Chinese clients—long accustomed to prioritizing scale and speed—are suddenly considering operating disciplines that German or Japanese firms have practiced for decades. Founders say the past decade rewarded growth, while the next will demand sharper execution and a deeper look at cost structures. The abrupt shift has caught many entrepreneurs off guard.

We often console our clients: "China is still growing at 4 to 5 percent this year. Remember, Europe has been growing at 1 to 2 percent for years, while Japan has endured decades of less than 1 percent growth. If you think that it is difficult now, what will you do when one day China grows at 3 percent?"

The pressure is real. Companies across China are freezing salaries, cutting pay, and shutting business lines. Layoffs are hitting both internet platforms and traditional industries, and even some state-owned enterprises are trimming compensation. "Cut costs and boost productivity" has become the new mandate.

Where will growth come from? For the first time in their business careers, Chinese entrepreneurs must actively search for it. In the past, opportunity seemed to be everywhere; the challenge was focus. Now, with domestic markets slowing and the competition intensifying, global expansion is becoming a serious consideration—just as geopolitical complexity reaches generational highs.

A more nuanced picture of the "next China" is taking shape.

Navigating the Next China

The China market is no longer a tide that lifts all boats—the era of breakneck growth is behind us. Competition has shifted from how fast companies can grow to how well they can endure; from growth papering over inefficiencies to an environment demanding productivity, discipline, and profitability.

Michael Hui of Bain Capital puts it bluntly: "Ten years ago, all you needed was access and the courage to invest, and the market carried you. Now you need real techniques and investing discipline. If you look at the top line, there's much less to celebrate these days—but look 'bottom-up,' and there's a lot of very interesting things happening."

Exiting or pausing is not an option for Jebsen Group, distributor of Porsche, Dyson, and Blue Girl Beer in China. "If you surrender now, the problems you have in China will come to your home markets in five years," says its CEO, Alfons Mensdorff-Pouilly. "It's investment time right now, and then by 2029 or 2030, it will be harvesting time again. If you tap some entrepreneurial guts and think outside the box, the market can still be as rewarding as it was ten or fifteen years ago."

China's business landscape is too big, too fast, and too varied for any single strategy to be exhaustive or for prescriptions to apply uniformly across sectors, competitive positions, and company sizes. What we offer instead are signposts to help leaders chart their own path.

Unleashing the Entrepreneur's Advantage

Over the past decade, multinationals have been steadily losing market share to local competitors in China. There are plenty of reasons for this; Chinese firms will have built-in advantages around localization, cost structures, and deeper insight into the consumer. But we maintain that the biggest problem is around governance, incentives, and organization.

At the core, China subsidiaries of global multinationals tend to be led by executives operating within large, complex organizations, while competitors are typically entrepreneurs fighting as though everything is on the line. One side is navigating global structures; the other feels like they're locked in a battle for survival. The trick is to unleash the same entrepreneurial energy inside multinational teams and equip executives to compete with speed, agility, and hunger.

McDonald's and other corporations have adopted private equity–style ownership models to sharpen incentives and enable more local decision-making. Yet not every multinational has to give up control or majority ownership to make itself sturdier. For example, the Swiss dental technologies company Straumann Group localized its product portfolio.

Ultimately, multinationals must treat China not just as a market to be served but as a business to be built to sustain over cycles—with local autonomy, accountability, and entrepreneurial drive. Without this, the advantages that once helped them succeed will continue to erode as the market matures. The competition in China's "gym" is relentless, and multinationals must learn to match the hunger, resilience, and adaptability of the rest of the market.

The Land Grab: Converting Scale into Staying Power

China has long been defined by scale—bigger factories, larger markets, faster growth. But the old "land grab" mentality, which once rewarded speed and size at any cost, now no longer ensures strength. As growth becomes costlier, scale must be paired with strategic focus, operations excellence, structural advantage, and a clear path to profitability. Companies that build regional or technical moats are far more likely to achieve durable, sustainable returns. Alibaba used its broad user base and data assets to double down on its core e-commerce and "cloud + AI" businesses. Luckin Coffee turned its massive store network and tightly integrated bean-to-cup system into cost discipline, which enabled innovation and pricing power that competitors struggled to match.

Crucially, sufficient scale isn't about being the largest overall, but about dominating a specific segment. Concentrated market power can help create pricing power, supply chain leverage, and defensible margins; Shuanghui, for example, may be smaller than Muyuan and other players overall, but it has created a "black hole" in the sausage category, where it is three times the size of its nearest rival, with more than 50 percent share. That level of concentration yields high, stable margins. Companies that dominate a single segment often achieve better profitability and resilience than larger players spread across multiple businesses.

In the next China, rapid scaling must be matched with focus, quality, and a line of sight to profitability. Scale still matters, and remains a core reason for multinationals to compete in China, but its value now lies in supporting cost efficiency, brand strength, access to talent, supply chain leverage, and operational synergies.

Seeking Granularity for Growth

Top-line numbers won't dazzle the way they once did, so winning in the next China requires looking past the averages to uncover real opportunities. McKinsey colleagues published the book *The Granularity of Growth: How to Identify the Sources of Growth and Drive Enduring Company Performance* in 2008 for Western audiences, and China's market has now matured to the point that those concepts apply here as well. And there are plenty of ways. China isn't a monolith; it's a mosaic of regions, income bands, demographics, and tastes, and growth will come from identifying and quickly capturing these micro-pockets of opportunity.

We see openings everywhere we look: resilient consumers in lower-tier cities, Gen Z leaning into experiences, even outdoor enthusiasts lifting a flat apparel market. PepsiCo, for instance, approaches snacks with a 3D "Rubik's Cube" strategy, segmenting by city tier, occasion, consumer cohort, and channel, to name just a few. China's *baijiu* liquor producers—including the world's largest, Moutai—are toying with alcohol content and repackaging for new occasions. Remember that in China, even a "niche" is enormous. For example, China's express delivery sector in 2024 generated 1.4 trillion RMB ($200 billion).

Going from Factory to Innovation Lab

China's innovation engine has shifted decisively—from imitation to iteration and increasingly toward originality in select fields. In other words, Chinese companies are evolving from copycat to innovator, from fast follower to global originator. Breakthroughs in EVs, batteries, AI, biotech, and new models of online retail and social commerce are no longer merely adapted in China—many are now conceived, tested, and scaled there. Innovation is no longer a one-way flow from West to East—it's circulating through dense ecosystems of engineers, suppliers, researchers, and demanding consumers at speed.

Global companies are already plugging into this system. Merck and AstraZeneca are licensing and co-developing innovative new therapies with Chinese biopharma companies. Mercedes-Benz is rebuilding the Smart brand by tapping into Geely's massive EV supply chain, engineering ecosystem, and rapid iteration speed. L'Oréal uses its China R&D center to design skincare and makeup formulations with local partners, with some products heading for global markets.

In the next China, innovation is not just about invention but about who can learn, optimize, and scale fastest—and who can harness China's ecosystem without being outpaced by it.

*   *   *

The real question for companies goes beyond whether China is rising or stalling but where and how companies can still compete. "It's foolish to get too positive or too negative—instead, companies must build a business model that's resilient to all kinds of outcomes," notes Bob Sternfels, McKinsey's global managing partner. After three decades of working alongside companies navigating a variety of challenges in China, we know that success will be possible only for those willing to adapt, learn, and relearn. And do it all over again.

CHAPTER 6

Unleashing the Entrepreneur's Advantage

When McDonald's golden arches first arrived in China more than three decades ago, they soon became a ubiquitous symbol of modern urban life. By the 2010s, China had become McDonald's second-largest market in terms of restaurant count and also one of the most competitive consumer arenas on earth. Yet scale brought new challenges. The China leadership team sat at what we call "CEO minus three"—a few layers removed from the decision-makers in Oak Brook, Illinois. Organizational distance isn't just geographic—it often shapes how quickly, and whether, China leaders can act.

Competing at "China speed" can be structurally tough for multinational corporations. Typically, China CEOs have latitude over local matters, particularly on marketing and sales, but the biggest decisions still climb from China to Asia-Pacific to global headquarters. The multinational governance ladder is world-class at control and consistency but not necessarily built to match hungry and agile local competitors. In quick-service restaurants, for example, while China teams of multinationals might be polishing Power-Points for distribution and approvals, local rivals can open new stores rapidly and roll out innovative products at a frenetic pace without navigating decision chains of command: Pineapple and pork rib burgers! Cheesy potato ball afternoon snacks! Sandwich-and-milk-tea sets!

The contrast highlights a broader challenge: How can even the most nimble multinationals compete with founder-led Chinese rivals in a market where quick service means not only KFC and Burger King but homegrown chains Tastien and Wallace, small-format look-alikes, and thousands of casual independents?

Multinationals have long succeeded in China, but relentless competition from local rivals has exposed the structural limits that keep many from matching the market's pace. Chinese firms benefit from ownership-style incentives, real decision autonomy, and a culture built for speed and local experimentation—while multinational governance, incentives, and culture are increasingly misaligned with this environment. The heart of the question: How do corporate executives compete against entrepreneurs?

Consider the journey of McDonald's in China. A Big Mac felt expensive when McDonald's first opened in Beijing in 1992. It wasn't a luxury item, but it was definitely a premium foreign import: 6.4 RMB ($0.9) for a hamburger was more than half a day's wage for the average Chinese worker. A Big Mac purchased in the US costs three times as much in absolute terms, but the average worker could pay for it with less than fifteen minutes' worth of work.

A Big Mac in China today, at a cost of roughly 28 RMB (about $4.07), eats up only a fraction of the average monthly wage—making it broadly affordable and a mid-market product. That flip didn't happen because McDonald's got cheaper—it happened because the average Chinese got richer. Chinese wages have surged more than forty-fold since 1992.

It didn't take long before McDonald's became a sensation with young urban families eager for new lifestyle and consumption experiences. Western brands weren't merely offering alternatives; they were often introducing entirely new categories. There was no life insurance before AIG, no hyper-markets before Walmart and Carrefour, no personal care industry before Unilever and P&G, and no coffee industry before Starbucks. Of course, there was no quick-service restaurant industry before KFC and McDonald's.

By 2015, McDonald's had more than 2,200 restaurants in mainland China (the US had 14,259). But as consumers matured, competition intensified; rivals flooded the market with bubble tea, fried chicken, and new quick-service formats. While US headquarters was rolling out drive-throughs, China's food-and-beverage space had moved onto app-based delivery, and consumers expected burgers at their doors in minutes. Though China remained one of the company's fastest-growing international markets; sustaining momentum required significant investment. Yet corporate headquarters—balancing global priorities—didn't always see China as a top priority, even as access to capital was critical locally. For many global quick-service chains, China had become a paradox: a hyper-competitive, low-priced brawl where new stores didn't offer returns superior to other markets.

Against this backdrop, a strategic opportunity emerged in 2017 for McDonald's to strengthen its operating model. The company sold 80 percent of its mainland China and Hong Kong operations to a consortium including state-backed CITIC; its private equity arm CITIC Capital (now called Trustar Capital), and US private equity firm the Carlyle Group. "The structure was deliberately designed to unlock the next phase of growth," says Alwin Poon, a former managing director at the Carlyle Group who was in charge of the deal. "CITIC brought local knowledge and government connections, while Carlyle contributed financial discipline, corporate best practices, and the ability to help bridge cultural gaps among the parties."

Governance shifted materially: profit-and-loss (P&L) ownership and capital allocation moved to a China-based board, and the leadership team adopted private equity incentives tied to growth and profitability. "We instilled an owner mentality into management and empowered them to re-evaluate all aspects of the business to more effectively compete—from menu innovation to supply chain localization," Alwin tells us.

Phyllis Cheung, CEO of McDonald's China, and her team began building China-first systems, such as a proprietary digital backbone for two hundred thousand employees, supplier co-design to develop new chicken products that excite customers, and idea-to-launch cycles as short as three months. The ownership change further enabled faster investment decisions and shortened innovation cycles, aligning the organization more closely with the pace of local competitors.

McDonald's China entered a phase of rapid expansion, opening 1,000 stores per year since 2023 to arrive at around 7,700 stores today, and is targeting 10,000 by 2028. "Now we report to a board that sits in China. It's essentially one layer, and critical decisions can be executed faster than before," Phyllis says.

Success and confidence in China's upside set up the next phase. In 2023, McDonald's agreed to buy out Carlyle's minority stake while Trustar Capital retained 52 percent; the move reinforced the strategic value of the partnership model with a local Chinese institution.

This being China, the battles never stop. A snacking price war that erupted online has driven the price of milk tea down to 1 RMB ($0.1), wiping the advantage of premium locations. And in mid-2025, delivery battles between Alibaba and Meituan pushed prices even lower. It's always a tough battle out there, but with greater local autonomy, multinational leadership can decide more deliberately when and how to engage.

This chapter is aimed primarily at multinationals, and the lesson is straightforward. In China, you have to find ways to unleash corporate entrepreneurship and sustain it despite governance challenges. In practice, that means treating the China unit as a full-fledged business, not a sales outpost. McDonald's illustrates that when ownership sits in China, autonomy becomes real, "China speed" becomes instinctive, and entrepreneurial energy moves to the front line.

"Localization is the key to success," Phyllis tells us. "Being truly customer-centric to adapt to fast-changing Chinese consumer needs can be achieved if headquarters is willing to delegate authority while maintaining good governance structures." What every global company should recognize is that China is filled with founders and competitors backed by local capital, driven by a cultural instinct to fight every day, and operating with little to lose. Not every fast-moving, hungry Chinese competitor succeeds—in fact, most don't—and among the downsides of extreme speed can be wasteful expenditures and spectacular failures. Yet from an incumbent multinational's perspective, when corporate processes meet a freewheeling entrepreneur, hunger usually has the advantage. "Competing in China is very different from competing in Japan, Southeast Asia, in France and Germany, where you can reliably forecast six or twelve months out," says Hai Ye, a McKinsey senior partner leading the growth, marketing, and sales practice. "To manage China, you need a high tolerance for ambiguity and uncertainty, and you must break down silos so that decisions move quickly—something difficult for global headquarters that want to stay in control."

Every company will shape the solution differently, but the principles remain constant. To optimize your China business to best compete, leaders should examine the following elements:

- *Decision Autonomy:* Define who can give the green light.
- *"China Speed":* Move fast with conviction in the face of ambiguity.
- *Localization:* Consider an "In China, for China" model.
- *Entrepreneurial Spirit:* Build an organization with smart risk-taking and "can-do" drive.

Enabling Local Decision-Making Governance

How can you grant the China team the authority and autonomy they need to make quick decisions?

In the weeks after COVID first hit, a curious thing happened inside one of China's quiet industrial champions. Demand for mask-making equipment soared—and operating them required programmable industrial controllers. As supply chains tightened, factories rushed to expand capacity; many plant managers, fearing shortages, were hoarding controllers in their apartments.

Most automation suppliers saw the opportunity—few could act on it. Entering a new sector meant diverting production and R&D from existing lines, a short-term profit hit many multinationals struggled to absorb. Their organizations were segmented by region and industry; moving into mask making first required deciding who "owned" the business, a bureaucratic process that could take months. Reassigning engineers also put managers' performance metrics at risk. While teams debated responsibility, the window closed.

Inovance—a rising Chinese industrial automation company with more than thirty thousand employees—had never operated in public-health equipment. But chairman and co-founder Xingming Zhu made a different call. Watching mask demand explode from Shenzhen, he made mask making a company priority the same day a sales director flagged the opportunity. Speed, he knew, would decide the outcome.

Engineers were shifted from long-cycle industrial projects. Together with customers, Inovance studied imported Japanese machines, which went quickly out of stock, and helped customers replicate them at scale—but with Inovance controllers. Engineers realized that mask-making machines didn't require micron-level precision; tolerances of a few millimeters were acceptable. Customers needed speed, not perfection. Teams reviewed drawings, made substitutions, tested configurations on the fly, and fixed issues directly on the factory floor.

The most decisive advantage lay in Inovance's supply chain. Years before COVID, Inovance had pushed aggressively into servo products—feedback-controlled motion components—and stockpiled significant volumes of chipsets. When the semiconductor shortage hit, Inovance had inventory; its competitors did not. And while multinational rivals often needed a year to qualify a new supplier for any parts, Inovance could do so in two to three months, in part by using other large manufacturers' approved supplier lists, accepting calculated risk to be able to move faster. Within weeks, Inovance's systems were shipping nationwide. Above all, leadership made the difference.

Other Chinese firms moved just as decisively. The EV maker BYD assigned three thousand engineers to build mask-making equipment as COVID began to spread. Masks rolled off the line within seven days; eventually BYD was producing five million a day plus three hundred thousand bottles of disinfectant.

Mask making was short lived, but this story illustrates how Chinese companies move when the market shifts—fast, even instantly. Western and Japanese incumbents had the technology to capture this market, but pushing a new initiative through headquarters on another continent took too long. Approvals would come after the moment had passed.

Structural autonomy isn't cosmetic. It means giving China leaders real control over funding, staffing, marketing, and R&D—the full stack of decisions—and requires headquarters to become comfortable shifting control. This is where the tension lies: trust, compliance, and risk. Headquarters worries that full autonomy may lead to brand dilution, regulatory missteps, or misalignment with global priorities. Yet without autonomy, local teams can't move fast enough to compete. "That's where corporate governance comes in," says Dai Feng, founder of CareCapital Group. "If multinationals build truly indigenous organizations with localized products and services, and still maintain control, they can perform as well as Chinese companies."

McDonald's sold a majority stake to a local investor to grant greater autonomy to its China operations; but not every multinational will—or should—take that path. The real challenge is designing mechanisms that simulate ownership without changing shareholding structure. How do you rethink culture, re-design incentives, and create an environment where China executives think like owners, not employees?

Giving China leaders real "skin in the game"—for example, letting them invest in the China entity with private equity–style upside—could shift behavior quickly. But true upside requires real authority. That's the dilemma: how to give owner-level incentives while still maintaining essential reporting lines and governance. "I know some multinational CEOs operating in China with plenty of entrepreneurial spirit. These leaders are global CEO 'minus-one' who are able to directly influence and deploy real authority around investment resource allocation," says Phyllis of McDonald's.

At McKinsey we debate this issue for our China practice. We run China locally but operate within a global firm with strict risk controls, quality standards, and a shared reputation. We're also a partnership—our leaders have partnership shares and long-standing relationships—which helps build trust. Even so, the trade-off between local autonomy and global control is a constant balancing act, and most multinationals lack this structural advantage when it comes to China. When China leaders are hired externally or global CEOs have limited China exposure, trust isn't a given. It must be built.

Trust also comes from familiarity. Many European company board members fly into Shanghai for a day and fly out the next, says Alfons Mensdorff-Pouilly, CEO of Jebsen Group, which has been operating in China for over a century. "They don't visit Wuxi, Wuhan, or Chongqing—and without seeing 95 percent of China, it's hard for them to really understand the country."

By contrast, China-savvy leaders such as Hank Greenberg, AIG's former CEO, and Steve Schwarzman, Blackstone's founder, are legendary for their frequent visits and deep ties to China. Apple CEO Tim Cook's trips are always given top-level attention from officials and media alike. A smaller group of committed executives also serve on the International Business Leaders' Advisory Councils for the mayors of Shanghai and Beijing, maintaining direct lines into local decision-making.

Another approach is to strengthen China expertise at the board level. This can mean appointing Chinese directors or expatriates with long operating experience in China. Gordon Orr, McKinsey's former China chairman, for example, now sits on the board of European private equity firm EQT.

It's not feasible for most CEOs to be often on the ground, but, as Alfons notes, "Your No. 2 probably should be there, with the resources to truly understand the market. And bring Chinese talent into global headquarters so the Chinese consumer stays close to the center of gravity."

Operating at "China Speed"

How do you move fast amid uncertainty—without falling into "analysis paralysis"?

If autonomy is the foundation for survival in China, speed is the weapon. China's business environment runs on a mix of ambition, improvisation, and ruthless competition that forces companies to move faster than anywhere else—that's "China speed." Survival depends less on being perfect than on being first.

Take instant noodles. Japanese and Taiwanese brands introduced the category to China in the 1980s and 1990s and dominated for decades, becoming household names. By the 2010s, the market was stagnating as consumers turned away from "fried junk food," and local players such as Master Kong, Uni-president, and Jinmailang were moving into the lead. Baixiang, a regional brand from top wheat-producing Henan province, was closely trailing but still concentrated in smaller inland cities.

Baixiang chose speed as its strategy, rapidly adopting advanced technology to outpace rivals. In 2018, Chairman Yao Zhongliang crushed a rival's pack of instant noodles in the workshop before his engineers and told them, "What we lack isn't capacity—it's a reason to make young people proud." The company pivoted its R&D toward healthier, non-fried noodles and began experimenting with freeze-drying technology.

Its speed was tested in 2021 when catastrophic floods hit ninety-eight-million-strong Henan province. Within three hours of the first SOS call, trucks rolled out of Baixiang's warehouses, delivering noodles to a children's welfare home in Zhengzhou. In the following days, the company donated thirty thousand boxes of food and 5 million RMB (about $0.7 million) to the relief effort. A viral livestream showed one worker using sign language while packing boxes—"Ship slowly, because we package with care."

Baixiang didn't let the goodwill fade. While competitors were negotiating supermarket displays, Baixiang pushed into new channels, placing hot-and-sour noodles in thousands of milk-tea shops and snack cafés frequented by Gen Z consumers. This was start-up speed for a thirty-year-old company, creating new demand in a category many thought was stagnating.

In 2023, Baixiang's instincts struck again. On Douyin—the original ByteDance video app known globally as TikTok—the hashtag #cilantro surged past 10.5 billion views. Within three months, Baixiang's engineers launched "Super-Fragrant Cilantro Noodles." Co-created with Douyin's Super Brand Day and promoted through influencers, the product sold out in twenty-four hours and became one of the platform's most shared foods that year.

By 2025, Baixiang had evolved from a regional underdog to a symbol of national pride. Its premium Tang Hao He line—featuring six-hour slow-simmer bone broth and freeze-dried toppings—recorded 3 billion RMB (about $430 million) in annual sales with an ROIC seven times the industry average. At a Forbidden City press conference, Chairman Yao lifted a bowl: "Some said domestic products are low end. Now, in this bowl, there's the confidence of six hundred years of imperial kitchens."

Speed, for Baixiang, isn't just about moving quickly. It's about sensing shifts early, mobilizing instantly, and turning every burst of momentum—from a viral clip to a national crisis—into competitive advantage.

Many Chinese companies are wired for speed because decision-making hierarchy is flat, engineers talk directly to clients, and managers are rewarded for growth, not caution. "Many local companies rigorously require their sales teams to have at least a product management background, often having an engineering or technical background, which cuts out a decision-making layer," says Jan Milark, a McKinsey associate partner who works with industrial clients.

And as Nick notes, the secret isn't perfect aim—it's firing often—the business equivalent of taking more shots on goal. The more you fire, the more likely one will hit. In practice, that means shipping version 1.0, seeing what breaks, fixing it, and launching versions 2.0, 3.0, 4.0 in quick succession. It's a culture built on iteration.

The electric vehicle industry, for instance, is defined by speed. Market leaders have learned to move quickly in a hyper-competitive environment. BYD uses an extreme 24/7 R&D model—engineering shifts covering all hours on seven days of a week. This helped compress development and mass production of its Blade Battery into eighteen months, while EV development cycles were whittled from five years down to two. Toyota engineers working on its joint venture sedan bZ3 were stunned by BYD's practice of revising designs late in the process—almost unthinkable for traditional automakers, which are accustomed to locking prototypes much earlier.

"You need to be set up for speed in this environment; you can't expect three committees to approve headcounts, to lock every investment in advance, or to have an absolutely perfect platform," says Jan. A former colleague visiting a Shanghai robotics firm found executives in their twenties and thirties who'd just decided—at 9 p.m. on a Wednesday—to triple production. When asked about their annual plan, they were puzzled. "Annual plan? We can do it, so we did it."

Let's be clear: "China speed" has its downsides and trade-offs. Some companies move too fast—slashing prices, cutting corners, or releasing products that aren't ready. These aren't learning cycles; they erode trust. Multinationals can wield a contrasting advantage, displaying strong quality, safety, and risk controls that can allow premium pricing; the goal isn't to discard those systems—but to prevent them from becoming bottlenecks.

That's the harder question: How to preserve quality while increasing firing frequency? Speed doesn't mean recklessness. It means building a China business that learns faster, empowering engineers to engage customers directly, shortening feedback loops, measuring progress by iteration instead of annual plans, and acting even without perfect data. The ambition isn't for multinationals to mimic the excess—it's to selectively import the speed.

Investing in Localization

How do you develop the conviction to localize—despite the cost and the divergence from global standards?

Rooted in the Latin *locus*, meaning "place," the word *localization* literally means "making something belong." For Straumann Group, this wasn't a slogan—it was their China business model.

A dental implant pioneer founded after World War II as a family-owned materials science lab in Basel, Switzerland, Straumann entered China about twenty years ago. Crucially, it didn't try to "export Switzerland" but instead plugged into China's local ecosystem. Straumann built relationships with clinicians and distributors, invested in local R&D and manufacturing, and adapted its portfolio and economics to Chinese conditions.

Dentistry varies widely from country to country—insurance, certification, costs of schooling, and rules about which clinicians can perform what procedures all differ—and dental technology companies are more accustomed than most medical technology firms to adjusting their management models accordingly. That flexibility helped European and Korean family-origin multinationals thrive in China.

Straumann entered China in the early 2000s through a local dealer. A strong dealer can help navigate hundreds of decisions: where to expand, how to price, which dentists to target, what training to offer, and more. Only after Straumann gained real familiarity with China through these accumulated decisions did the company begin acquiring select dealers, integrating them, and turning them into the operational backbone of its China business. That humility—local first, global second—became a cornerstone of Straumann's success in one of the few healthcare categories where a multinational still dominates.

Then came volume-based procurement (VBP), a government initiative targeted at reducing drug prices and increasing accessibility. For most multinationals, this means lower margins and a big damper on their China business. Straumann instead saw opportunity.

It engineered a lower-cost implant line and opened a Shanghai manufacturing site in 2025 to train local dentists and meet rising demand. The result: an expanded portfolio, solid margins from a new customer base, and implants affordable for millions more patients.

Today, China is a major business for Straumann. Shanghai is part of its global manufacturing footprint and an R&D base for key product lines. China accounts for more than 15 percent of global sales and is the company's biggest driver in the Asia-Pacific region, which is already 24 percent of revenue.

Everyone knows localization matters, but a full "in China, for China" model requires commitment and capital—and often requires stepping away from global frameworks. The real question in the next China is how far you're willing to go and what you're willing to trade-off. For years, multinationals succeeded with partial localization because global technology and standards were true differentiators. That advantage is eroding. Chinese competitors now engineer and manufacture at global quality—and in some categories define the benchmark—while moving faster and at lower cost. Volkswagen is the latest example of an "in China, for China" strategy; by shifting R&D, design, and production to its Hefei hub, the company says it can cut EV development costs by half and cycles by 30 percent.

We also find "de-costing" to be a critical factor. Chinese customers are unwilling to pay for marginal features they don't need, pushing companies to "de-engineer" cost out of the product or tailor quality or performance to match what the market wants. Clinging to global architectures risks "under-localizing" and being priced out.

Localization also means adopting a China cost base. Input costs, from supply chains and utilities to labor, land, and capital, are far lower than in most Western markets, forcing hard trade-offs. One client struggled over whether to re-design its China organization and salary structures to match local competitors, which would create tension when it came to global standards and operating models. Another quick-service restaurant client debated local store fit-out standards; adopting Chinese local structures would halve the cost but dilute global methodology and branding. All these are real decisions that come with non-trivial trade-offs.

Moreover, deep localization comes at a cost. It requires new domestic capabilities, fresh investments, and a different governance model. More fundamentally, it requires acknowledging that legacy global standards and technologies are no longer decisive—or, in some cases, have become the burden. It's a hard pill to swallow, and it sits at the heart of the strategic tension many multinationals now face.

"Localize more" is easy to say; placing capital to stay relevant in China's next cycle is much harder.

Building a Culture of Entrepreneurialism

How do you build a culture that rewards a can-do mindset, smart risk-taking, and strong ownership?

French economist Jean-Baptiste Say defined entrepreneurs as people who move resources from lower to higher productivity. Europe built its version through mercantile trade and craft; America's grew from a frontier belief that anyone could make something from nothing. From industrialist Henry Ford's "Whether you think you can or you think you can't, you're right," to Jeff Bezos's "it's generally human nature to overestimate risk and underestimate opportunity . . . thinking small is a self-fulfilling prophecy," US business culture has celebrated boldness and possibility. Silicon Valley turned that spirit into a system powered by venture capital and speed.

China has now entered that arena. In just over three decades, the country has layered one of the world's most dynamic entrepreneurial ecosystems on top of a substantial state-owned foundation, resulting in a system where market-driven competition and state influence coexist—sometimes uneasily and often differently across sectors. Much of this intensity is often described through the idea of "wolf spirit," a business metaphor that Huawei founder Ren Zhengfei helped popularize, capturing perseverance, acute sensitivity to opportunity, a relentless drive to survive, and a collective dimension. Wolves hunt in packs, after all.

Many clients ask, "Does my company have enough wolf spirit?" We tend to prefer "animal spirit," borrowed from economist John Maynard Keynes, who defined it as the "spontaneous urge to action rather than inaction." Whether you channel wolves, horses, or Keynesian economics, the point is the same: in China, incentives drive ownership, and autonomy fuels speed, but culture unlocks the final gear. Thriving in an ultra-competitive environment requires more than strategy or structure: it means building organizations that enable hustle, tolerate small failures, and empower even junior team members to make real decisions.

Take WeBank, China's first digital-only bank. Founded in 2014, it faced a paradox: How could a sector known for hierarchy and risk aversion cultivate entrepreneurship? Chairman and CEO David Ku's answer was to push decisions to the front line. "The person closest to the problem should have the power to solve it," David says. When a junior employee, fresh out of university, spotted two clunky steps in the lending journey, he quietly reversed their order, tested the change, and delivered a fix that produced a nine-fold jump in click-through rate overnight.

David reflects, "As CEO, I might make this business nine times better in ten years. But there's no way I can make something better in twenty-four hours. That's the power of letting the little guy make the call." David tells us he spends hours each week thinking about how to create the right culture, allowing the people who know the customer shape the experience, enabling model-builders the space to make mistakes, and ensuring innovative ideas reach decision-makers—all while containing risks so errors don't "dig a hole and bury you."

That philosophy extends to WeBank's deployment of AI; while major strategic initiatives are driven top-down, David promotes a "horse-racing," bottom-up approach that encourages many teams to race and test similar ideas, around, say, AI-generated advertising content. The winning formula will be adopted. "If you ask smart young people, they'll always come up with something impactful," he says.

This mindset is rare in banking but critical for a new digital institution. "Our internal culture and how we encourage staff matter as much as the business model," David explains. By 2024, WeBank had served nearly four hundred million customers, making it China's largest digital bank.

The lesson applies irrespective of the industry. China's market economy is only forty years old; many industries are still led by first-generation entrepreneurs in their prime, and the competitive landscape reflects their energy and urgency. As one apparel executive puts it: "It's not about size—it's about agility. If you're not nimble, you're already behind."

But the spirit we're describing isn't uniquely Chinese—it appears in markets where the entrepreneurial environment is intense. This isn't a Chinese versus multinational story; it's everyone versus everyone. State-owned enterprises (SOEs) are losing share to hungrier private firms. More established companies are getting challenged by nimbler start-ups. As Andreas Tschiesner, a Munich-based McKinsey senior partner, notes, "In EVs, the West has the same capabilities and similar talented engineers; they're simply lacking the culture. At 11 p.m. in China's R&D centers, the lights are still on. People would rather build something that could change the future than sit in a hotel room watching TV."

Of course, wolf culture has a dark side. In Chinese business circles, "wolf" is a controversial term. It can mean hungry and relentless—but also reckless, corner cutting, and willing to bend rules. We've seen the consequences: substandard buildings, manipulated financials, regulatory blowups. These aren't entrepreneurial bets: they cause real damage to society.

And the lifestyle itself can be punishing. Does anyone enjoy being a wolf? Many leaders prefer the professionalism and humanity of more structured environments—one reason our colleagues choose McKinsey. At the same time, some Chinese entrepreneurs thrive on the intensity, especially when financial rewards are substantial. But what feels exhilarating in one's twenties and thirties can become exhausting over time—and for a younger generation raised in greater comfort, the appeal is fading even faster.

Having Conviction About the Future

We'd like to impart a lesson about conviction. For multinationals, China is one market among many; that optionality is both a strength and a weakness. When every incremental dollar could go anywhere, the China business must compete for attention. "They can hedge China," says Leon Meng, founder of Ascendant Capital Partners. "Local companies can't. China is their only game—and that single-market conviction fuels speed, resilience, and a higher tolerance for risk."

The mindset gap creates an uneven fight. The entrepreneur wakes up with no exit or fallback plan. For a corporate CEO—who may rotate out in a few years—conviction on China is conditional, shaped as much by career risk as by market belief, and can sometimes be fleeting. The China CEO sits in the middle, constantly reading headquarters' mood, gauging how far they can push, and sometimes hedging for their own next role.

Conviction, in the end, isn't declared. It's engineered. McDonald's China didn't succeed by pushing harder; it re-designed itself to unlock corporate entrepreneurship—shifting ownership, collapsing decision layers, empowering local innovation, and rebuilding supply chains for speed—while adhering to the discipline of a global firm. As Phyllis tells us, "It's not sustainable that home delivery should cost less than eating in the restaurant—but while food delivery wars are ongoing, we need autonomy and speed in deciding when to dance with the wolves, so to speak, in business terms."

McDonald's is a clear example, but it's part of a broader pattern. At BASF, China-based leadership teams control major investment and R&D decisions at local Verbund sites—highly integrated production complexes—treating the China business as a full operating platform rather than a downstream market. At Nike and adidas, local product, digital, and supply chain teams are empowered to design for Chinese consumers and run faster test-and-learn cycles. Schneider Electric has given China management teams P&L ownership and engineering authority, enabling them to re-design products and cost structures to compete head-to-head with domestic players while operating within global governance.

Phyllis created a culture of entrepreneurship and innovation inside one of the world's most recognized brands. You don't necessarily need to be a wolf in China—but you need a system built to dance with them.

CHAPTER 7

The Chinese Land Grab: How Scale Becomes Power

The Chinese have always loved steel. Leaders see the country's "industrial backbone" as a symbol of progress and rebirth—a marker of national strength. The sector's transformation has been remarkable: a nation once short of rebar for basic construction now produces more than half the world's steel output.

Yet the story of Chinese steel also exposes the fragility of a capacity-driven growth model—especially in a downturn. To understand the constraints of a "scale at all costs" model, it helps to examine how the industry rose. After the Mao-era backyard furnaces gave way to reform, the sector drifted until the 1980s and 1990s as private ownership and competition took hold. During the 2000s and 2010s, demand from autos, machinery, and construction surged. Mills scaled relentlessly, fueled by cheap land, easy credit, and local governments chasing growth. As China urbanized, its steel output would eventually exceed the rest of the world combined.

Yet the reckoning came when demand slowed. In the winter of 2015, benchmark steel prices collapsed to what traders called "cabbage-like lows," plunging from over 5,000 RMB ($714) per ton to barely 1,800 RMB ($257). At its peak in 2016, China's steel sector was producing around 800 million tons a year—enough to build the Burj Khalifa or Golden Gate Bridge more than ten thousand times over—yet capacity had surged past 1.1 billion tons nationwide. More than five hundred producers were operating over a thousand mills.

"When the market was expanding, everyone felt there were more pies to go around," says Antonio Sun, a McKinsey senior partner in the global energy and materials practice. "When capacity pressure becomes severe, survival increasingly depends on cost competitiveness, R&D, quality, and how the business operates—not just how cheaply it produces."

A few early movers had already begun shifting focus. One was Jiangsu Yonggang, a private steelmaker founded in the early 2000s. This regional player raced to scale like everyone else, with its founder, Wu Dongcai, betting that bigger output meant survival. In 2002, the company famously completed a one-million-ton blast furnace in just 341 days. Yet Yonggang's leadership also began to see that an expansion-at-all-costs model might become a trap, especially in the face of declining demand. Instead of pushing more tons into an oversupplied market, it began upgrading its facilities, pouring around 3 percent of revenues back into R&D, and pivoting toward high-value specialty steels used in wind turbines, autos, and heavy equipment. It also doubled down on its home-region advantages: coastal access, scrap supply chains, and relationships with local customers—and even away from steel to invest in a digital AI company.

The strategy eventually paid off. As the number of mills nationwide consolidated from more than a thousand to fewer than six hundred by the late 2010s, dozens of competitors vanished. The sector stratified into national champions such as Baowu and Ansteel; regional private players leveraging local strengths; and specialty producers competing on technology or environmental performance. Yonggang emerged not as the biggest—but as one of the best—known for quality and premium pricing, and profitability improved sharply within just a few years.

The company's arc mirrors China's broader business story. For decades, scale was the organizing principle. Entrepreneurs chased national dominance, and every multinational entered for one reason—growth. From autos to insurance to consumer goods, the key was to expand fast and let volume create advantage. In the old China, scaling fast was cheap and effective, as hundreds of millions of consumers bought their very first mobile phones, insurance policies, apartments, and cars.

The internet era pushed this logic to its extreme. Delivery, ride hailing, e-commerce, and bike-sharing companies sprinted for users. Companies such as Alibaba, Tencent, Meituan, and Didi became national champions. Scale was power. Speed was survival.

But China's market is maturing. Incumbents crowd every space. GDP growth has slowed from double digits to around 4 to 5 percent. Customer acquisition costs online have risen ten- to twenty-fold. Foreign markets, once eager for low-cost Chinese goods, are more protectionist, while capital once addicted to "China growth" is now cautious.

As Leon Meng, founder of Ascendant Capital Partners, puts it, "Scale is still very important, but investors are getting pickier now and going five levels deeper: What's the company's point of differentiation? Is there a path to sustainability? What's the underlying engine that creates long-term value?" When investors posed similar questions before, they didn't seem as urgent at a time that growth could mask fundamental weaknesses.

In the next China, scale still matters, but it must be matched with strategic focus, operations excellence, structural advantage, and profitability. Winners will build regional or technical moats—competitive advantages—invest in quality, and deliver sustainable returns. "Having a hundred customers who try your product once because of big discounts is nothing like having a hundred loyal customers who come back every month," says Alex Wong of Boyu Capital, who remains bullish on China's consumer market.

The real shift is from "any growth" to "quality growth"—a repeat customer, a profitable product, a defensible niche. Put another way, the obsession with getting big is giving way to the discipline of getting big *and* better. That's the lesson of Yonggang—and of the next China:

- Don't expect to grow your way out of trouble.
- Capital is increasingly expensive and expects discipline.
- Build that line of sight to sustainable economics—as soon as possible.

The Era of the Land Grab

From the 1990s through the 2010s, China was an open field—no dominant brands, no entrenched incumbents. For entrepreneurs, it was a once-in-a-lifetime opportunity. Whoever reached scale first was more likely to win, and China was teeming with venture capital, optimistic and ready to power the competitors.

Companies borrowed heavily, spent future profits early, and used rising valuations to borrow even more. Easy credit made it feel rational to build ahead of demand. Many founders even pledged their own shares to keep growing, tying their personal fortunes to growth. The reasoning was simple: when markets rise, leverage amplifies returns. The result was massive debt buildup. China's total debt now exceeds three times GDP and corporate debt nearly twice its GDP—roughly double their 2000 levels and far above global norms.

Insurance led the first scale wave. When AIG introduced Western-style life insurance to China in the 1990s, it brought the agent model—legions of commission-hungry door-to-door salespeople. The more agents you had, the more you grew. Domestic firms such as China Life, Ping An, China Pacific Insurance Company (CPIC), and Taikang copied the approach, building the world's largest sales forces. The scramble reflected that moment in China's economic story. For the first time, millions had money in their pockets and were looking for ways to protect—or multiply—it. A local agent could sign up half the village within weeks. Every new policy might bring a new agent recruit, who'd then pull several more into the fold. "At that time there were a lot of part-timers making side income," recalls John Cai, Prudential's China CEO.

The barrier to entry was low: sit for training and licensing exams, tick a few boxes on required paperwork, and you were ready to start.

Anyone could join—friends, neighbors, your kid's teacher, new college graduates—and selling to family and friends made every new agent productive for the first few months. "We called those 'bloodline policies,' because every customer was related," recalls Yonglin Xie, the co-CEO of Ping An Insurance Group. "The test would be whether the agent could move beyond this and become a real salesperson."

By 2015, China Life had six hundred thousand agents, Ping An nearly nine hundred thousand, and CPIC four hundred thousand. This pyramid of ambition stretched across the country from Tier 1 cities to remote townships. "We let the least sophisticated distributors sell a complicated, sophisticated product," John says. "It was a mismatch of management capabilities."

Still, the land grab worked. By 2017, China Life's market cap hit $123 billion, Ping An's $150 billion, and CPIC's $54 billion—proof that for a time, in insurance as in China's broader economy, sheer scale was the preferred strategy. (Over time, professionalization followed: training improved, products grew more complex, compliance tightened, and the industry learned to educate consumers.)

Manufacturing and consumer goods also joined the race for scale. Midea built bigger factories and expanded into nearly every household appliance category, using its size to improve efficiency, gain share, and strengthen supplier leverage—ultimately enabling global expansion. In athletic wear, Anta, Li-Ning, Nike, and adidas opened thousands of franchise stores. Channel growth was the key metric: *How many new outlets this quarter?*

SF Express poured money into infrastructure, including its own cargo airline, becoming China's premium logistics player, surpassing FedEx and DHL in the market while simultaneously fighting off multiple lower-tiered local competitors also gunning for scale.

Real estate developers Evergrande, Country Garden, Vanke, and Sunac pursued the same strategy from the late 2000s: build fast, sell faster. Joe once met with a developer who dreamed of 100 billion RMB ($14 billion) in annual sales—a moonshot at the time, since in 2009, most large real estate companies were doing a tenth to a third of that. Within a few years, to the developer's surprise, his company reached the target; but he wasn't alone. Before long, doing 100 billion RMB ($14.5 billion) wouldn't even put a company in the top twenty. The now-infamous Evergrande would sprint past that number; by the late 2010s, it was selling more than 600 billion RMB ($86 billion) a year, making it the world's largest developer.

The internet era supercharged everything. Scale shifted from factories to users and clicks as Alibaba, Tencent, Meituan, JD.com, and Didi waged an all-out customer acquisition race. The strategy was simple: subsidize early users, seize market share, and worry about profits later. China's digital infrastructure—mobile payments, super-apps, real-time data, and digitized supply chains—made it possible to iterate, expand, and optimize at extraordinary speed.

At the peak of this race for scale, tens of billions of renminbi poured into coupons, discounts, and cashbacks. What began as Alibaba's playful 11/11 anti–Valentine's Day "Singles Day" marketing scheme in 2009 became a national shopping phenomenon generating tens of billions of dollars in twenty-four hours; the one-day sale still dwarfs Black Friday in the US—with Chinese e-commerce platforms recording 845 billion RMB (roughly $120 billion) in 2024 sales, far exceeding Black Friday's $10.8 billion.

A now-legendary JD.com story captures the mood of the era. In 2006, investor Kathy Xu, founder of the venture firm Capital Today, met JD.com founder Richard (Qiangdong) Liu late at night at Beijing's Shangri-La Hotel. When Richard asked for $2 million US, Kathy waved off the request: "That's nothing, you need to run. Take ten million." Later, Richard approached Hillhouse's founder, Lei Zhang, for a $75 million loan. Lei concluded that Richard would need multiples, telling him, "Seventy-five million isn't even enough to test and validate your model. Either you take the $300 million [in financing] I'm offering, or I won't invest at all." When JD.com was listed on Nasdaq in 2014, Kathy's early stake had grown more than 150-fold and Hillhouse's $300 million investment had soared 13-fold to $3.9 billion.

Fintech also became a hotspot as financial and non-financial firms and start-ups jumped in and jostled for users. "We spent billions of renminbi a year acquiring customers and funneled everyone into our ecosystem; profitability came later," says Jun Xu, former CEO of 360 Finance. At the peak, over a thousand online lenders from Ant Group and Du Xiaoman to WeBank and countless start-ups vied for millions of borrowers. Capital poured into payments, digital wealth, insurance, and the financing of small and medium-size enterprises (SMEs).

Offline, the "sharing economy" boom launched by companies such as Airbnb and Didi materialized in the "rainbow" wars, as red, canary-yellow, cobalt-blue, lime-green, and other brightly-colored bicycles blanketed city sidewalks. Start-ups Ofo, Mobike, and competitors burned through subsidies, populating streets with more than twenty million shared bicycles and raising billions in capital to subsidize growth. Similarly, in what was dubbed the "Hundred-Power Bank War," Street Power, Diandian, and other players tried to blanket every mall, restaurant, and transit hub with shared power banks to chase growth in an industry expected to expand 20 percent a year, exceeding 40 billion RMB (about $6 billion) by 2029.

The logic was familiar, but the scale was unprecedented. Chinese companies embraced the Silicon Valley playbook—grow first, monetize later—and applied it to a 1.3-billion-person market. Private capital poured in. Local governments offered tax breaks, land, and deployment subsidies. Venture capitalists openly acknowledged a large portion of the capital they deployed was devoted simply to "buying" users. Metrics like gross merchandise value (GMV), market share, and growth became the scorecard. With these incentives, China's consumer base exploded to more than nine hundred million fintech users—nearly double the number five years earlier. By the late 2010s, more than 350 million Gen Z Chinese had become digitally native smartphone users who'd never known a world without apps, forming a base five times the size of the US. Alipay and WeChat Pay processed over $80 trillion in annual digital transactions, with mobile payments hitting 332 trillion RMB ($47 trillion). Fintech had become the financial bloodstream of everyday life.

The first firms to scale often became national champions and sometimes global leaders. For these winners, and for their founders and backers, extraordinary financial success followed. Success was so intoxicating that everyone expanded onto neighbors' lawns: property firms launched insurance companies, and internet players ventured offline into finance and medical services. If scale built dominance once, maybe it could again.

For a generation, the land-grab approach defined success, and it worked in a China that was young, growing quickly, and flush with capital. As the market matured, the sprint to dominate began to collide with a new reality.

The Land Grab Worked—Until the Music Stopped

When growth slowed and capital tightened, investors began looking under the hood. The "grow first, fix later" model that had powered China's boom was no longer sustainable. Sector after sector, firms were forced to confront what that scale was built on: borrowed capital, inflated valuations, and a model that only worked in an ever-rising bull market.

Expansion had come cheaply in the early years. Mobile users jumped from zero to a billion in five years, and digital lenders could acquire customers for less than 100 RMB ($14.3). "Traffic cost much less back then," recalls Jun, the 360 Finance entrepreneur. "You just paid Tencent or Baidu, and customers flooded in." By the mid-2010s, every new user was already someone else's customer, and acquisition costs had risen ten-fold, Jun says. "Today you have to work with eighty different small apps, cutting deals one by one just to get visibility. And there's still no guarantee that you can control the spiraling marketing spend."

Rising wages and tougher regulations raised operating costs, and subsidies began drying up. Many companies had stacked their balance sheets with debt or pledged future equity to keep growing, only to find themselves squeezed when revenues flattened and repayments came due. What looked like competitive pressure was, for many firms, the sudden exposure of structural fragilities that years of easy growth had masked. Many global players still envy high single-digit growth rates, but for firms—and investors—built for double- or triple-digit expansion rates, resetting expectations has been painful.

The numbers tell the story. Between 2010 and 2024, industrial revenues rose a steady 5.1 percent annually—yet profits grew only 2.5 percent per year. The gap isn't a mystery: debt costs surged, with the commonly cited BIS debt-to-service ratio climbing from 13 percent in 2009 to 19 percent in 2024, directly eroding margins. Nearly one in eight firms were losing money in 2010; by 2024 it was about one in four.

In insurance, companies' legions of agents had become unmanageable. The model deteriorated under the weight of increasingly expensive recruiting, unproductive agents, tightening regulation, and digital disruption. Ping An has cut its ranks from its peak of about 900,000 agents to roughly 350,000 today. The new mantra: smaller, more professional sales forces with better productivity. "Insurance is a long-term business—you can never skip generations or take shortcuts as you can in technology," says John Cai, the former CEO of China Pacific Insurance Company, the country's third largest life insurer. "We're now back to the fundamentals: building trust and professionalism, which is in knowledge and experience. That takes time." (That said, a "smaller" agent force of 350,000 still equates to the population of Florence, Italy, or Bilbao, Spain.)

In real estate, the bigger the developer, the harder the fall. Evergrande, once China's most aggressive, had built at a breakneck pace on borrowed money. At its peak, it owed 2.44 trillion RMB ($344 billion)—roughly 2 percent of China's GDP. When demand collapsed, the empire imploded under its own weight. Projects were abandoned, suppliers went unpaid, and millions of homebuyers were left stranded. A company once valued in the tens of billions at its peak, owned by a founder who was momentarily China's richest person, has since become Chinese corporate history's largest bankruptcy.

Cautionary tales exist in every sub-segment. In fintech, many players exited, merged, or sharply reversed course. Bubble tea chains such as Nayuki and quick-service restaurants such as Taier Sauerkraut Fish had scaled quickly and dazzled the market with IPOs—only to soon see their stock prices drop precipitously. In cosmetics and fast fashion, dozens of once-hyped brands burned through capital to chase visibility, only to fade into relative irrelevance. Perfect Diary, the first Chinese beauty brand on the NYSE, raced to a 2020 IPO on Gen Z buzz and digital marketing, only to produce five years of losses amid soaring costs and slowing growth. Its stock price has dropped more than 90 percent from its high.

At times of exuberance, it all made sense to grab share first in the largest developing market in the world. Everyone believed it. The stock market rewarded it. Each IPO confirmed scale as the number one, two, and three priority. We wondered whether this growth could be sustained. But how could you sit it out?

The New Playbook: Build Strength at the Core

The rules of the game have changed. In the old era, chasing scale meant racing outward: more users, more platforms, more regions, more everything. You could grow your way out of legacy problems, so why look back? Just keep pushing. Now the priority has flipped: companies must look inward and strengthen the engines that sustain the business.

Across industries, the land-grab logic has given way to a push for sustainability. Steelmakers are shifting toward higher-value products; insurers are professionalizing leaner sales forces; retailers are rationalizing stores; developers are de-leveraging; internet platforms are optimizing for monetization; fintechs are prioritizing profits and cash flow; and consumer brands are focusing on repeat customers and healthier margins.

All the while, they're defending scale advantages that keep costs low, drive productivity, and offer financing and procurement power. While sectors sit at different points in their cycles—and many remain vulnerable to "involution"—the broad direction is toward more sustainable economics.

It almost sounds like "back to basics." China's new reality demands solid, high-quality businesses that generate quality growth—returns that exceed the cost of capital—if not immediately, then soon. This sounds simplistic, but it hasn't been easy in practice. For our first twenty years in China, McKinsey never ran a real operations excellence project—we saw executives skip over those recommendations in favor of revenue growth. Few companies had a chief operating officer or professionalized procurement and finance functions; most were organized around business units focused on growing market share. For that era, it mostly worked.

In the next China, winners will bake sustainability and quality into their business plans—not bolt them on later. That doesn't mean every company must be profitable from day one. In capital-intensive, long-horizon sectors—robotics, biopharma, semiconductors, rockets and satellites, and the emerging "low-altitude economy" spanning drones, air taxis, and aerial logistics—early losses are often inevitable. Rapid expansion can still make sense when paired with a laser focus on decreasing costs and a credible path to returns. What has changed isn't the tolerance for investment, but the tolerance for undisciplined growth.

The Midea Group, one of the world's largest home appliance and technology conglomerates, illustrates this shift. After achieving scale, it moved aggressively into smart manufacturing and digitalization to raise efficiency and establish advantages over competitors. As Xiyuan Fang, a McKinsey partner and leader of the private equity practice, puts it, "The market economy and investment situation have changed. Investors are still willing to back growth, but they want clear economics, repeatable models, and a path to profitability so that if you don't eventually go IPO, the business can be sold."

Yet executing remains difficult in practice. Many sectors still exhibit irrational pricing and destructive competition that undermine long-term economic sustainability, as we've mentioned. For firms caught in fierce crossfires, theoretical paths to profitability offer little comfort. Still, there are signs of change: local government funding is drying up, while the central government is stepping in—regulating below-cost pricing, lowering targets for production output, and encouraging more industry self-regulation. The difference between "big" and "defensible" will separate the last era's casualties and the next era's winners.

Dominate a Well-Defined Segment

Companies that define their segment precisely—by product, price point, region, or customer—can build dominance that's both defensible and profitable. China's coffee market has no overall leader, but zoom in and patterns appear: Luckin rules the mass market, while Starbucks has the biggest brand presence in the premium tier. The same logic applies across industries: Shuanghui leads sausages, Meiyijia rules mass convenience stores, and Wallace wins in affordable fried chicken. These "hidden champions" aren't flashy, but their margins are strong. Shuanghui, for instance, is smaller overall than the integrated agricultural giant Muyuan, yet in sausages it's a "black hole"—so dominant it pulls in demand and slowly crowds out competitors—at three times the size of its nearest rival, with more than 50 percent share. Insta360 is the leading company in the global 360-degree camera segment. Such dominance isn't confined to new sectors; even mature industries have niches waiting to be captured.

Given the extreme degree of competition in China, it's perhaps impossible to expect permanent leadership in any segment. As soon as margins feel comfortable, the next price war will come and the next competitor will appear. Nevertheless, it pays to focus, build quality, and pick your battles. "Another way to think about the segment is geographic," observes Xin Huang, a McKinsey partner in its consumer practice. "One example is Chongqing Brewery. It's significantly smaller than its national rivals, but it has built up a dominant market share in the Western China region with a strong distribution network that makes it difficult for others to compete."

Achieve Structural Advantages Through Scale

Companies should turn scale into structural advantage—reshaping cost architectures or operations in ways competitors can't easily copy.

Segment leaders can command disproportionate resources from suppliers, channels, media, and even regulators. Capital markets, in turn, reward these leaders with significantly higher valuations. These advantages must be intentionally built.

"Hard" advantages—supply chain efficiency, technology, and capital-intensive investments—create far more value than "soft" advantages like brand equity or membership programs, which are more vulnerable to market shifts. Shuanghui, Luckin Coffee, MiXue, and Wallace succeed because their scale allows high degrees of cost efficiency within well-defined segments. Scale in China turns into a highly-effective weapon when used properly.

One long-term investor reminds us, "Scale matters—this is China, after all. If you don't build it, others will. It all depends on how much you can use it to your advantage. The question is: Are you building something distinctive and defensible through scale, or are you just adding bulk?"

Build Functional Excellence and Professionalism

The next competitive edge will come from how companies operate: sharper procurement, smarter supply chains, stronger execution, and tighter cost control. For years, many Chinese firms functioned as loose federations of business units—fast, entrepreneurial, and driven by general managers accountable primarily for market share and growth. Japanese and German firms, by contrast, operating in more mature markets, built success on operational discipline. The next China will require companies to blend both, adding structure and discipline without killing speed.

Given the widespread digital adoption across Chinese businesses, there is plenty of potential upside. "Once you digitize, you put every process under a microscope and it becomes easier to find efficiencies," says Phyllis Cheung, McDonald's China CEO. "Multinationals always set high quality standards—but you need to flex your muscle on both quality and cost efficiency, because your competitors can survive beautifully on slim margins."

Kelvin Pan, chief strategy officer of major consumer electronics components maker AAC Technologies, says, "We are now looking into procurement best practices, and we're finding many areas of improvement. It's like discovering a muscle that we've never trained up."

Track Quality Metrics

In the next China, we push clients to measure not just how fast they grow but what kind of growth they're generating.

The earlier era's fixation on top-line metrics such as market share, customer counts, and gross merchandise value (GMV) has often obscured weak fundamentals and even encouraged unhealthy behavior—from banks buying short-term deposits to companies stretching the definition of "customers" or "revenue" to hit unrealistic targets. We now ask clients, "What percentage of your business is low-quality and unprofitable? Which customers are money-losing? Do you even know?" And as important: "How are your executives measured and compensated? Are they incentivized to build quality businesses or just to hit revenue targets by any means?"

We often find companies with large portfolios of marginal businesses: money-losing customers, channels that require prohibitively high commissions and remain hyper-price sensitive, or revenue that's effectively "borrowed" or "bought" to allow executives to meet their targets. These situations raise tough questions: Do you cut off these segments immediately or transition over time? How do you explain a shrinking top line to investors? Do you create a new baseline for growth?

Companies will need to understand customer lifetime value, focus on loyalty and profitability, and build durable, high-quality business models. That starts with tracking the right metrics and aligning incentives around quality growth.

In the following pages, we illustrate these concepts with examples: how Alibaba restored its momentum through clarity of focus, and how Luckin's coffee executives developed pricing power by leveraging its massive size.

Alibaba: From Empire to Core

After years of sprawling into entertainment, logistics, healthcare, and physical retail, Alibaba hit a turning point in September 2023. Under Chairman Joe Tsai and CEO Eddie Wu, the group didn't just cut unprofitable ventures—it proceeded to dismantle its fragmented business portfolio to refocus on two engines: e-commerce and "cloud + AI."

This was not a retreat but a reboot: a shift toward an AI-powered ecosystem in which Alibaba's scale becomes a true competitive moat. By shedding non-core assets and pouring resources into high-return, defensible areas, Alibaba transformed its once unwieldy size into an edge. Cost discipline tightened, data started to work harder, and investment now concentrates in places where Alibaba's user base, data depth, and infrastructure create value that competitors can't replicate.

The shift is nonetheless visible in its core businesses. In commerce, Ele.me's food delivery and Taobao Flash Sale were folded into a unified ecosystem—replacing siloed operations with shared data, logistics, and supply chains. The payoff has been sizable, even at Alibaba's scale: by July 2025, combined daily orders for Taobao Flash Sale and Ele.me had topped ninety million, unlocking new value from existing users without the cost of building new platforms. In cloud, the strategy is even clearer: Alibaba Cloud is leaning on its data-center footprint with more than nine hundred global nodes to serve enterprise clients, with AI emerging as its fastest-growing revenue engine.

A clear leadership mandate drives the transformation. "We will focus on two core strategic directions: e-commerce and cloud + AI," Joe Tsai declared at Alibaba's 2025 Family Day. "Within three to five years, every business must be AI-driven to break through new internet entry points."

Luckin Coffee: Discipline at Speed

Luckin Coffee is a parable of the new playbook, proof that speed can coexist with structure. Founded in 2017, the company expanded at record pace, surpassing Starbucks in China revenues by 2023. Luckin understood that to sell high-quality arabica coffee and latte-style beverages at roughly half the price of premium chains, they needed to turn scale into cost discipline. Yet the company's efficiency doesn't come just from scale—it's built on a fully integrated "bean-to-cup" operating model linking store operations, product innovation, and supply chain.

Luckin launches more than a hundred new products each year to keep customers hooked. This pace of innovation would overwhelm most supply chains, but the company manages its complexity through precise coordination. Menu switchovers—normally costly and wasteful in food services—generate minimal loss across more than thirty thousand stores thanks to careful orchestration across marketing, procurement, and R&D.

Its layered system is designed for streamlined execution at the front lines. Recipes are standardized from the start: simplified raw materials, consistent base liquids, and fixed ratios. Baristas don't learn complex steps—they just need to know where ingredients are stored. Training modules reinforce this formula, and equipment is streamlined to a single machine with one-button operation. Even with weekly menu updates, Luckin's operating model keeps stores efficient and consistent.

When global arabica prices doubled between 2021 and 2023, most competitors saw margins evaporate. Luckin instead adjusted its sourcing mix, blending beans from different origins to keep both taste and input costs stable. "The strategy of product innovation, cost stability, and the ability to manage extreme operational complexity has created Luckin's economic moat," says Fox Chu, a McKinsey partner leading the logistics practice. "Running a business governed by a two-hundred-page supply chain manual is a fundamentally different challenge. Most competitors can't handle it. If they chase innovation, costs and complexity spiral; if they clamp down on costs, they miss product opportunities that grab the attention of the consumer."

Luckin's strategy allows it to keep latte prices far lower than premium brands—levels that are incredibly difficult to match. Investor and chairman David Li calls this pricing "healthy" and "strategic": "If competitors match my price, consumers win. If they undercut me, they lose money." Scale, he argues, delivers not just efficiency but pricing power.

Operationally, Luckin runs with digital precision. Every app order becomes a data point feeding its AI-driven demand forecasting system, which optimizes roasting schedules, inventory replenishment, and labor planning. Competitors can copy Luckin's drinks, but not its system. Stores average eighty-two-second service times. And customer ordering is becoming increasingly driven by AI. "Our AI agent is named Lucky," David tells us. "You can instruct it to buy your coffee, and it'll let you know when it's ready."

The Land Grab Continues—with More Discipline

Scale will always matter in China. It delivers cost advantages, brand strength, talent access, supply chain leverage, marketing synergies, and resilience. It's the platform from which world-class companies have emerged—Alibaba in e-commerce, Tencent in social media, Xiaomi in electronics, Huawei in telecommunications, Anta in sportswear, just to name a few—and companies with scale consistently outperform those without. Yet in a slower-growth economy, companies now need a clearer line of sight to profitability.

"Investors want higher returns, more secure returns," says Hai Ye, a McKinsey senior partner leading the growth, marketing, and sales practice. "They're still long-term thinkers, but they also want to minimize risk. That raises the bar for management: sharper analytics, better talent, and more disciplined execution."

The lesson of the land-grab era is not that participating in the race for scale was misguided, but that scale without sustainability might eventually collapse under its own weight. Of course, that land-grab instinct persists—it's embedded in China's entrepreneurial DNA.

New battles keep emerging, from instant commerce with Meituan, JD.com, and Alibaba to Xiaomi's Lei Jun diving into electric vehicles. As one race ends, another begins.

The required shift is not away from boldness but rather toward sharper execution. The winners will be those who pair ambition with discipline. Scale only becomes an advantage when it can be made durable—strong enough to fend off the competitors waiting at the door of the gym.

CHAPTER 8

Seeking Granularity for Growth

For two decades, the Finnish elevator and escalator maker KONE climbed China's urbanization boom to the top of the sector. China became KONE's single largest market, at one point contributing over a third of its global revenues of $9.9 billion. Its logic was simple: China was building, and KONE—like many other companies—simply rode the surge.

It's no surprise "granularity of growth" never caught on with our clients back in 2008. That year, our US and European colleagues published a book by that title, arguing that in flat markets, companies must "de-average"—drill down into the smallest meaningful "cells," or micro-markets, micro-segments, and precise plays—to cobble together a growth strategy. The book was a global business hit.

Clearly, *The Granularity of Growth: How to Identify the Sources of Growth and Drive Enduring Company Performance* was written for mature markets, and China in that era was anything but. Its economy grew nearly 10 percent the year after the book launched and spent the next decade cruising in the high single digits. No company needed a microscope to find opportunity—and we sometimes say you barely needed a map. Low baseline penetration rates made broad categories like "snacks," "fresh coffee," and "EVs" sufficient, and a single Unilever soap could serve consumers from Tiers 1 to 4 simply because it was considered a famous brand. When segmentation appeared at all, it meant sorting cities by tiers—crude but effective when everything was rising.

That was then, this is now. As China's economy slows, market share will no longer be won on wide, growing plains, but in pockets containing specific behaviors, micro-tribes, and still-rising hyper-local curves. For example, it's important to know that China's most optimistic consumers today live in smaller cities, not in Tier 1—yet even "tiers" are too blunt. Growth now depends on matrices gridded by tastes, occasions, experiences, brands, and behaviors, to name just a few.

We see young single women in city cores, pet owners, health enthusiasts, "silver" consumers seeking travel experiences, China-chic fans, anime-manga communities, and other micro-groups, each fueling distinct categories of spending. Even in seemingly commoditized sectors—elevators, noodles, package delivery, industrial chemicals— growth is now district by district, flavor by flavor, segment by segment. "Granular growth isn't just about finding a new sub-segment and shifting your portfolio," says Antonio Sun, a McKinsey senior partner in the global energy and materials practice. "It's also about extracting value—whether upstream, downstream, or into adjacent capabilities like digital—and how you participate in that."

Whereas the old game was "show up and scale big," the new game is "compete surgically." KONE's new reality reflects this shift. Its earlier model was built around mega-developers during the greatest real estate run in human history; the country's top builder casually booked more than $50 billion in sales—many times the $1.8 billion that Blackstone's US development arm made in 2015.

In China, a single fifteen-tower complex could mean dozens of elevators—a gold rush so strong that Beijing sometimes felt like a Finnish "satellite" in China, as a McKinsey Helsinki partner would joke. At Nick's daughters' primary school in 2010s Beijing, entire classrooms of Finnish children gathered on Saturdays for Finnish lessons so they wouldn't lose their mother tongue. The names on their parents' business cards: Nokia, KONE, Stora Enso, Suunto.

China's property cycle eventually turned. Housing starts fell more than 60 percent in 2024 from their 2019 peak, elevator and escalator installations dropped by a tenth, and KONE's China story seemed to fall straight to the bottom of an elevator shaft. In 2022, Joe Bao, former head of Microsoft China, was brought in to reset the trajectory, and his approach was "in the granular," so to speak. "Our way out would be to learn and grow and innovate," he told us in Shanghai recently. "Figuratively speaking, there are no high-rises in Finland."

There would be no grand transformation. Instead, KONE made a sharp pivot to services. China's eleven million installed elevators—40 percent of the global total—each require maintenance every fifteen days, creating a huge service economy dominated by thousands of small operators. KONE set out to consolidate that market through selective acquisitions, raise the productivity of its twenty thousand technicians, and deliver tangible savings through digitizing operations and maintenance. Next came modernization and green retrofits, and a targeting of niches: "Think about freight, data centers, villas, and rural buildings," Joe Bao says, ticking them off. KONE has had to go deep—district by district, county by county, community by community—to find pockets of potential growth.

We see the same logic across consumer goods, healthcare, education, food services. For one coffee client, we found that Beijing and Shanghai had plateaued, while Tier 3 cities accounted for 38 percent of all outlets in China and were expanding twice as fast. Going a level deeper, we found real growth came not from daily loyalists but from "occasional drinkers" who indulge once or twice a week—a micro-behavior with potential.

"In the past we didn't focus as much on smaller segments because the overall economy was growing so fast," says Frank Tang, chairman, CEO, and co-founder of Chinese private equity player FountainVest. "Today, those pockets define where the opportunities are because the segments are already at scale. If the whole market is only growing at 3 to 5 percent, then the right geography and consumer segment become everything. It's bottom-up now."

China executives see it, too. Phyllis Cheung, CEO of McDonald's China, has recently re-read McKinsey's *The Granularity of Growth*: "I appreciate that book. It's very relevant to us right now." Anne Tse, CEO of PepsiCo's Asia Pacific Foods, says, "No China chart has a single dimension; everything is something by something. Step one is the 'average need,' and then it's about city tier, cohort, occasion, price tier, then channels, and then competition in these slices. The whole Rubik's Cube is super-complex."

There's no universal playbook for finding granularity—opportunities differ widely, and each pocket is uniquely shaped. By the way, identifying growth pockets is only half the job. The real test is execution: empowering employees who directly interact with customers, moving at the pace of local dynamics, and adapting as micro-markets shift in real time.

In the pages ahead, we'll look at how several companies dug deep, adapted, and built growth opportunities cell by cell.

First, What Is Granularity?

We sometimes describe the "granularity" shift in asset management terms as moving from "beta" to "alpha." In the 2000s, buying almost any property in Beijing or Shanghai could earn a ten- to twenty-fold return—townhouses, apartments, business districts—it barely mattered as long as you were willing to invest. Today, real estate growth is still there, but the game has changed from riding the market ("beta") to earning returns through precision ("alpha"): the right street, the right building type, the right floor, the right price, the right leverage.

Geography offers the simplest form of granularity. Coastal hubs remain huge but have lost post-COVID momentum, while lower-tier cities have become growth engines. Yet even there, companies must slice thinner. Try demographics: nearly 75 percent of millennials in lower-tier cities are confident about China's economic outlook, compared with 65 percent in top-tier hubs. And companies that focus by income will see that confidence among mid- and high-earning millennials climbs above 80 percent. Lower living costs, cheaper housing, and more stable jobs—often in government or large enterprises—translate into higher purchasing power than that experienced by mega-city peers, even if absolute wages are lower.

But picking the right city is only the beginning. Within each city, you still need the right district, street, and channel. Some value comes from pricing and distribution; other pockets emerge through sub-brands, in-store experiences, or digital ecosystems. And the "tiers" categorizations themselves need macroeconomic context. Northern provinces remain tied to steel and other legacy industries, and young workers have moved south.

As McKinsey's Asia consumer and retail co-leader Daniel Zipser puts it, "China has more than nine hundred cities and thousands of counties. Where do you put your marketing money? Where do you actually distribute? It's a critical strategic question—this ability to pinpoint what is promising." For example, in targeting the consumers considered "very important"—the power shoppers spending north of €15,000 ($17,400) annually on a single luxury brand—it's critical to have a deep understanding of each local market, explains Michael Straub, the China commercial director of Loewe, the Madrid-based luxury house owned by LVMH. "For instance, Shenyang remains a top destination for silver generation 'older money' luxury shoppers," Michael says. After two decades of expansion, growth in China's beauty industry has stalled, and one skincare executive tells us he's thinking about the hundreds of cities in China as distinct markets, some growing, and many requiring precise targets and hyper-local execution.

How to tap granularity depends on your category, customers, and model—whether you sell infrastructure, snacks, or medical devices. Our playbook isn't a marketing checklist but rather a strategic shift: if the floodlight worked before, now you need a spotlight.

ANE Global Logistic: From One Hub to Forty-Four Spokes

For fifteen years, ANE Global Logistic grew by blanketing China: thirty-three thousand franchise partners—mostly mom-and-pop couriers handling the first and last mile. The company specialized in less-than-truckload (LTL) cargo—too big for a courier yet too small for a full truck—connecting the noodle maker to the neighborhood stores, the appliance factory to the township warehouse, the auto parts plant to the repair shop three towns over.

ANE's scale enabled a cost structure and speed that few could match. But e-commerce growth was slowing, average delivery prices were flattening, and a price war was inevitable. That realization prompted ANE to pivot early—well before a roughly 15 percent industry price collapse in 2025. ANE's story shows that granularity is not only about spotting micro-pockets of growth but also about rewiring its organization so those pockets can be captured.

Under founder and CEO Xinghua Qin the question shifted from "How large can we grow?" to "Where exactly is growth hiding?" Xinghua eliminated the "regions" layer and split the national profit and loss (P&L) into forty-four district-level units, each with its own balance sheet, profit targets, and mini-CEO. "Let the headquarters feel the battlefield. We put our back offices onto the front lines," Xinghua says.

The new structure unlocked route-level visibility. ANE could analyze profitability by lane, weight band, and service type—pinpointing which corridors and customer clusters created value and which quietly eroded margin. Their analysis was so granular that it distinguished between a washing machine delivered to a home versus a construction-site dormitory—different occasions, different price points. Some corridors outperformed, especially those serving large enterprise clients in the east, while others in remote western provinces required subsidies. "This opened our eyes to what sub-segments we were betting the future on, and which were dragging us down," Xinghua tells us. "It was time we migrated into a more granular, more scientific approach to our operations."

With automation and real-time dashboards, ANE improved operational visibility and could shift resources quickly. Decision-making became data-driven, and pricing became tailored: premium, guaranteed-time services for electronics shippers in major cities, with slower, consolidated routes in smaller, price-sensitive markets. Each micro-market became its own experiment.

Incentives were rewired. District mini-CEOs earned unlimited profit sharing above targets, which re-energized the network. Prospective franchisees received income models comparing ANE with rivals, often showing higher earnings within a year by switching.

ANE's franchise system kept costs low, enabling a near-zero profit policy on trunk hauling and last-mile delivery. It could offer next-day for some routes at roughly a third of air-freight costs, setting the bar for delivery speeds and real-time tracking. Profit came not from shipping fees but rather from volume efficiency, network effects, and adjacent services such as dispatch surcharges and documentation fees, which ANE reduced by 95 percent through digitization. With county-level coverage across 99 percent of China and AI-guided routing and sorting, ANE offered value while rivals raced to the bottom.

This two-step strategy—drive costs down, then optimize by segment—powered ANE's recovery. In two years, the bottom line swung from roughly 200 million RMB ($29 million) in losses to nearly 960 million RMB ($137 million) in profit. Depot productivity rose 20 percent, trucks were going out more than 85 percent full, and route-level profitability strengthened.

Most importantly, ANE shifted its mindset. Managers stopped measuring success by gross volume and instead focused on micro-markets, order density, on-time delivery, customer satisfaction, and lifetime value—creating advantages that its competitors couldn't capture.

Baijiu: Softening China's Oldest Spirit

It took Nick a few years to master the strategy of surviving a Chinese business banquet. The negotiations might be complete, but there's still work to do in handling a blur of tiny shot glasses. "Ganbei! Ganbei!"—"Empty glass! Empty glass!"—and down it goes. You must imbibe without appearing ungracious—but also avoid ending the night face down. Korean colleagues, seasoned in ritual drinking, had taught Nick the craft: the hand towel beside your glass could discreetly absorb a portion; plain water could be swapped in at key moments; and toasts could be made early—to fulfill that social obligation and reduce the likelihood of being targeted for later, more punishing rounds.

What's normally in those glasses is Moutai, China's national spirit, 52 percent alcohol by volume, distilled from sorghum, aged and fermented to create different aromas. Also called baijiu, it's more than a drink; it's a social lubricant and currency of relationships in Chinese business. The market for baijiu rode the country's economic rise, and it's huge: roughly 700 billion RMB ($100 billion), dominated by a small number of national giants and hundreds of regional houses.

For decades, growth was straightforward. Baijiu's core consumers were established men in government, banking, and real estate—and rising incomes and banquet culture helped fuel margins of 30 to 40 percent. State-owned Kweichow Moutai sat at the apex—around a quarter of industry revenue, nearly half its profit, and a market cap of about $250 billion. At its peak, a bottle sold for 3,000 RMB ($429), the sort of price that signals prestige rather than pleasure. But the market has shifted, and per capita consumption is declining. Producers must adapt.

In short, younger consumers drink differently: small groups, late at night, and always online, and they're a latent growth engine. Distillers are halving alcohol content to 19 to 20 proof, launching 200 ml mini-bottles, and re-designing packaging for emotional appeal. Wuliangye, the No. 2 producer, has launched a low-alcohol "Love at First Sight" bottle at 300 RMB ($43). Others target mid-tier price bands to expand its market reach and even to create new occasions for consumption.

Though per capita volume may be flat, drinking moments are rising. "Because the industry is innovating—beverage lines, packaging, online channels—the younger segment is picking up even as consumption slows," says Michael Chi Chen, a McKinsey consumer partner who leads the Firm's work in beverages.

Even category leader Moutai is adjusting. In 2025, it launched an invite-only released on WeChat, tested smaller 200 ml packs at a third the usual price, and pushed expansion into ten key markets across the US and Europe.

Regional champions are strengthening their home turf. Kouzijiao—a 6 billion RMB ($857 million) brand in 63 million-strong Anhui province—is mapping growth by county and point of sale, using AI to optimize planning. Its producer, Anhui Kouzi Distillery, is tailoring products to local tastes and building "liquor-tourism" parks and immersive brewery experiences to deepen home ties. With 80 percent of its revenue still in Anhui, Kouzijiao is prioritizing consolidating local turf over national expansion.

Distribution is being rewritten. Bottles historically moved through five to six intermediaries; online platforms now allow producers to bypass them. "Older consumers go to mom-and-pop stores; younger people buy online," Michael says. E-commerce has grown at double-digit rates for three consecutive years, driven by Douyin and RedNote livestreams that can sell thousands of bottles in minutes. Influencers frame baijiu as a part of life's milestones—weddings, births, big family dinners.

Global expansion is the next frontier, though baijiu's bold flavor and tight link to Chinese dining make adaptation harder than for Japanese sake. Producers are testing lighter blends, Western pairings, cultural sponsorships, and heritage-led branding. Baijiu's next wave of growth will come from re-engineering its occasions, formats, and markets.

PepsiCo: Fine-Tuning a Rubik's Cube of Growth

PepsiCo was the first Fortune 500 company to invest in Shenzhen—a landmark in China's economic opening. Its debut product was Pepsi-Cola, launched in 1982 out of the Shenzhen Yinle Soda Factory at just 0.55 RMB ($0.1) a can—five times the cost of a Beijing movie ticket or subway ride at the time. Foreign yet affordable, the red, white, and blue cans captured Chinese interest and ushered in modern soft drink culture. The company's food business entered China a decade later; Lay's and Cheetos were two of the first packaged snack brands introduced, and later, Quaker Oats helped create demand for these products, building the supply chain needed to make and distribute them across the country.

Over the decades, PepsiCo expanded from market education to market leadership—broadening its beverage lineup, localizing production, and introducing brands like 7UP, Mirinda, and Gatorade—constantly fine-tuning to local tastes and lifestyles. Snacks show this granular strategy clearly. Agility is far higher than in beverages, and consumer tastes are more nuanced, says Anne Tse of PepsiCo's Asia-Pacific Foods.

And there's plenty of potential: in savory snacks, per capita consumption in China is just two kilograms (4.4 pounds) a year, compared with seven kilograms (15.4 pounds) in Australia and fifteen kilograms (33.1 pounds) in the US. To capture market opportunities, PepsiCo's China strategy operates as that Rubik's Cube, as we've mentioned, solving for multiple dimensions at once.

First, the snack market is not "just snacks." Its complexity requires examining the market via different cells: city tiers, age groups, lifestyle "states," social media ecosystems—each with different growth dynamics. When geography is overlaid, the story gets even more detailed. Consider township- and county-level markets, which have grown faster than those in top-tier cities as more people return to lower-cost hometowns. And within any single tier, consumer needs vary widely. Tier 4 cities, for example, aren't just one cell: younger consumers often enjoy more relaxed lives than their mortgage-burdened Tier 1 peers, while older "silver" (over age sixty) consumers are wealthier, healthier, and increasingly drawn to wellness and more personalized experiences.

Granularity, or occasions for consumption, also plays out in moments: in Quaker, PepsiCo is designing products for specific needs: quick breakfasts, wellness options for white-collar workers, grain snacks for teens, and porridge-based meal replacements for families, to name a few.

Further segmentation centers on emotional meaning; Lay's is developing province-level flavors that turn regional tastes into identity markers, tapping rising demand for belonging and "China-chic" aesthetics. Anne points to Gen Z youth who cut back on food to spend 600 to 800 RMB ($86 to $114) on video game "skins"—cosmetic digital items—or professional cosplay makeup. "Brands that tap into emotional value are thriving," says Anne. "When you look at the aggregate, things seem tight. But once you de-average, opportunities emerge."

Media varies not just by geography but by consumer mindset, or "state." In Shanghai, discovery happens through RedNote. In Tier 4 cities, consumers may still be in category education—what are chickpea crisps?—and in-store promotions can do the job. Same brand, same packaging—different attention architecture. The "when" matters, too: inspiring the right occasions. "It's all a question of different intentionalities," Anne tells us.

This is granularity—not just finding the segments but also building an operating system capable of dozens of small, local, fast, autonomous moves. PepsiCo's snacks division is just one example of a native granularity model inside a multinational: a five-to-six-dimensional "cube" of growth that never sits still: "It's very dynamic. The rate of change is very high," says Anne, "and powering decision-making at that level is very difficult to do."

Louis Vuitton's Ship—Seeding Desire

Louis Vuitton's newest Shanghai activation isn't a boutique. It's a hundred-foot-tall stainless-steel-and-glass vessel called The Louis, docked on West Nanjing Road and engineered to create feelings and emotions.

For years, LVMH, the world's largest luxury house, could move handbags by the thousands to China's rising urban elite. In peak years, LVMH drew a third of its fashion and leather goods revenue from China, while Chinese consumers at home and abroad spent $115 billion on luxury—a third of global spend. But as consumers grow more sophisticated, brands now face sharper, more selective, and value-conscious audiences after a softer 2024 and a steadier 2025. The new granularity is around creating experiences and seeding desire, which invites consumers to "come *feel* something, even if you buy later or elsewhere."

Hence the surge of cultural activations, bars, pop-ups, film sets. Nearly every major house now runs a cinematic experience. Luxury in China has become a stage, not a shelf, because "Chinese consumers decide inside China what they'll buy in Tokyo or Paris, and that's why brands are working so hard to create aspiration there," says Daniel Zipser, head of McKinsey's Asia consumer practice.

Experiences are central to this strategy. Nodding to Shanghai's maritime heritage, The Louis is the most ambitious of these moves, declaring, "We create culture—come and experience it." When we visited in fall 2025, the vessel had a waiting list. Visitors drift through floating monogram trunks, a stairwell lined with pastel perfume bottles, Shanghai-inspired cuisine, and film screenings curated by Jia Zhangke—and take pictures to share.

Conversion rates—the share of visitors who actually buy—are low, below 5 percent, says Natalie Liu, a retail senior manager at Louis Vuitton Shanghai—but that isn't the point. The ship is an experiment built for the social media era, and engagement has exploded; by the year's end in 2025, #TheLouis had clocked more than twenty-seven million hits on RedNote and over two hundred million on short-form video platform Douyin. "We're seeding our future customers," Natalie says.

The ship also widens the funnel of the market. Half its visitors are still in college and might leave with nothing but a charm attachment and photos. Middle-class tourists from smaller cities may buy a classic logo purse or simply file away the aspiration. VIPs—more than thirty monogrammed trunks at 400,000 RMB (about $57,000) were sold in the first two months—receive access to a private café. "Consumption habits across cities and classes are distinct," says Natalie. "We have to adjust."

But even theater has its limits. "China has matured. Values are changing. Perhaps people just don't want to spend that much on a handbag," says Alicia García-Herrero, chief Asia-Pacific economist at Natixis. Max Mara's China CEO, Asina de Branche, agrees: "The new generation is shifting their engagement with luxury. Resale value is important. They're asking 'Are the prices worth it?' How do you create the experience and the value they are looking for?"

The Louis is a major marketing win and part of a fast-growing list of experiential bets by luxury brands. Hermès has turned its Beijing flagship into a multisensory showcase; Chanel's Shanghai atelier takes clients behind the scenes; Dior is staging immersive fashion-and-art exhibitions; Moncler's 2024 "City of Genius" in Shanghai spanned thirty thousand square meters (322,917 square feet) and drew eight thousand guests with fifty-seven million livestream views. Tiffany & Co. built an entire showcase inside a historic Shanghai shikumen (stone gate)–style neighborhood in 2025.

Taken together, these efforts capture China luxury's paradox: slightly softer product demand paired with a powerful hunger for experiences—a category in which spending is still rising 7 to 9 percent a year. The question is whether these spectacles are the blueprint for luxury's next phase—or a sign of searching for growth after the boom.

The Real Question: How Do You Rewire a Company to Execute Granular Growth Strategies?

Everyone talks about targeting micro-segments, but few companies know how to do it. Rewiring an organization to act on micro-pockets is a completely different game; it requires shifting decision rights, incentives, and capabilities so that teams can make sharper, speedier, and more local choices in pricing, channels, product design, and activation. When we look at KONE under Joe Bao, what has mattered isn't just the strategic pivot toward servicing and modernization but also how the company reorganized to train entirely new muscles.

The first move was talent. KONE retrained thousands of staff and recruited aggressively from automotive, consumer electronics, and tech—industries with exactly the skills the company needed for its plans: digital field service, predictive maintenance, consumer-grade experience design. "They brought insights that didn't exist in our industry," Joe Bao tells us. KONE then rebuilt its operating model around these skills, pivoting from a master-apprentice service model to Internet of Things (IoT)–based operations—wiring elevators so technicians could seen problems before they occurred. It allowed servicing of *this* elevator in *that* building under *these* conditions— each a data-rich micro-system with different service levels, pricing, and customer conversations.

Sales had to be rewired, too, with teams pivoting from developer boardrooms toward residents' committees, local property managers, and homeowners' associations—an entirely different customer base with a diversity of needs. Incentives shifted accordingly: less celebration of one giant developer win, more reward for accumulating dozens of smaller ones.

KONE's acquisition strategy also turned granular, buying locality instead of scale by stitching together the most promising "orphans" in a market dominated by thousands of small operators. It expanded the portfolio into niche micro-markets and also re-branded itself accordingly: industrial gray color schemes were out and warm blues and greens were in, signaling digitization and sustainability. "I never thought I'd be thinking about colors," Joe Bao tells us. "But modernization is a consumer play; we have to win hearts and minds." The company is now engaging with key influencers.

The company continues to evolve. KONE's most profitable pockets come from the most difficult part of its strategy: shifting from B2B to B-2-small-B or B2C, which include building and individual owners. Profitability overall has declined, yet KONE has steadily flipped its China mix from 80/20 new equipment versus services to a more durable 50/50.

ANE also re-designed its operating model to capture granularity. As we discussed, the company broke its market into forty-four micro-P&Ls based not only on geography but also shipment purpose and weight class. Once they saw the pockets, they rewired to tap them: each mini-CEO was incentivized with uncapped commissions and the authority to move pricing, channels, and product offerings.

Downstream execution shifted, too. ANE didn't wait for franchisees to discover the company. Operators walked into non-network last-mile delivery stations and showed—using that franchisee's own volume—how profitability could change if they joined. Delivering on such a micro-level required an architectural overhaul: new resource allocation logic, a re-designed incentive stack, and decision rights placed closer to the market.

The lesson is straightforward: granularity creates value when organizations have the information, the structure, and the teams to act on it.

Weak Demand? Or Lower Prices Masking Real Consumption?

While we've just discussed finding opportunities amid slower growth, it's worth noting that China's consumption may not be as weak as it seems. "People say China has a demand problem. But does it really? The numbers are distorted by pricing and scale especially in hyper-competitive categories," says Jeongmin Seong, an economist and McKinsey Global Institute partner. "Consumers are still spending, often more than ever, but at lower prices. When we look at volumes, the picture is far more dynamic than headline data suggest."

Here's what we mean. China's household consumption share of GDP—about 38 to 40 percent—is low by global standards, and this metric is cited often as evidence of weak domestic demand, especially compared to the US's 70 percent and European economies' 55 to 60 percent. But that share sits atop an economy that's about ten times larger than it was in 2000. In absolute terms, Chinese consumers now account for an enormous portion of global spending, contributing roughly 10 to 15 percent of worldwide consumption growth over the past decade. In other words, Chinese households generate a massive amount of demand.

At the same time, nominal indicators understate the momentum of real consumption. Volumes continue to climb even as prices fall under deflationary pressure and involution. In fact, volumes have been rising across many categories. Auto sales reached about 31.4 million units in 2024, up from 30.1 million, with new-energy vehicles nearing 40 percent of total sales. Per capita coffee consumption rose from nine cups in 2016 to nearly seventeen cups in 2023, amid fierce competition from low-cost local chains. Similar patterns appear in smartphones, appliances, and food services: rising unit volumes alongside declining average prices.

For middle-class households this means drinking more coffee, streaming more content, and purchasing more home goods than they did a year ago—while spending the same or even less. In short, consumers aren't necessarily retreating. They're optimizing: trading down, discovering cheaper substitutes, and extracting more value from each renminbi. With inflation near zero in 2024, nominal spending naturally looks soft even when real consumption remains resilient.

*   *   *

China was never a monolithic market, and today the differences are sharper than ever. Think of the country as many markets moving at different speeds in hundreds of directions. The question is no longer "Is China growing?" but "Where exactly is the growth and how can we capture it?"

Yibing Wu, one of McKinsey's earliest Beijing senior partners now leading investment company Temasek's China division, frames the economy as two systems operating at once: an "old" economy that is contracting and a "new" one that keeps re-forming. "GDP is an outdated measure," he argues. "You wouldn't index-invest across all of China, because there's a whole bunch of things that don't grow. Every seven years, the country generates a new set of emerging industries. The job is to find them—and execute."

We're spotting pockets of opportunity everywhere. In China, niches are not small; such markets will add billions of RMB in the next cycle. This shift also presents a capability test. Can companies see the market at finer resolution, act on weak signals fast enough, and build systems that make precision repeatable? Doing so will require sharper customer insight, test-and-learn marketing, real-time data loops, and organizational models that empower customer-facing personnel without losing strategic oversight.

CHAPTER 9

From Factory to Innovation Lab

Innovation rarely begins in a vacuum. In China's long artistic tradition, it often starts with learning by imitation—mastering the craft before creating something new.

One of China's most celebrated painters began by learning through copying. Qi Baishi—born in 1864 to a peasant family—spent years tracing the brushstrokes of master calligraphers, patiently absorbing the logic of every line. Only later did he start iterating on form and proportion, sketching from life, and gradually simplifying his subjects. In his fifties, he finally broke away with a signature style that transformed simple subjects—shrimps, crabs, flowers, mountains—into living poetry. His *Twelve Landscape Screens* sold for over $140 million in 2017, cementing Qi's reputation as "the Picasso of Chinese ink art."

Like Qi Baishi's path from student to master, Chinese firms' innovation journeys have moved from imitation to iterative excellence—and increasingly toward creation in fields where they hold distinct structural advantages. We argue that while Chinese companies and institutions are making progress in certain inventions and frontier technologies, their sweet spot continues to lie in iterative innovation—and this focus is likely to sustain China's technological and industrial momentum for the near term.

For much of the past half century, Chinese companies copied fast and implemented faster. Entrepreneurs adopted—and adapted—useful foreign ideas, echoing writer Lu Xun's 1934 call for "Take-ism." The Chinese were hardly the first to imitate, but their business world elevated the practice. Borrowed concepts became raw materials: reworked, improved, and commercialized. Executives still recall early-2000s pirated CD-ROMs. Baidu learned from Google, Alibaba's Taobao mirrored eBay, HiPhone riffed on Apple's iPhone—and McKinsey once shut down a fake Chengdu "branch" whose "managing partner" had been distributing a pirated *McKinsey Quarterly* and collecting fees.

But imitation was never the end of the story. Amazon and Facebook pioneered e-commerce and social media; Tencent, Alibaba, and ByteDance stretched those ideas into full digital ecosystems. Chinese firms iterated within sectors—Alibaba's Taobao refining early digital marketplaces—and across them, as with Alibaba's leap into finance through Ant Group. Tesla ignited the electric vehicle revolution; BYD and XPENG brought cars to market faster and cheaper with better features.

What began as adaptation evolved into capability. Foreign automakers now partner for local supply chains and software. Multinationals such as P&G, Roche, L'Oréal, Bosch, and Apple are expanding their China-based R&D. China has narrowly become the world's top R&D spender at $786 billion—about 27 percent of the world's total—just more than the US's $782 billion and roughly four times Japan's total. China's ecosystem also now generates nearly half of all patents worldwide, or more than three and a half times the US output.

Copying and actual IP theft remain real concerns, though protections have strengthened as Chinese companies build their own IPs. The bigger shift is this: guard ideas too tightly and you may keep them safe—while falling behind. In China's speed-driven ecosystem, the greater risk is being "out-innovated."

The Chinese are "at parity or pulling ahead of the United States in a variety of technologies, notably at the A.I. frontier," former Google

CEO Eric Schmidt wrote in a 2025 op-ed. He urged US companies to share more AI technology and research, innovate faster, and spread the technology across the economy—learning "from what China has done well." Elon Musk said in 2022 that Twitter should become more like WeChat and long stated a desire to develop an "everything app."

In tech circles, "zero to one" refers to inventing something truly new; the term "one to one hundred" has come to describe the furious process of improvement and commercialization once an idea exists. China's scale—millions of engineers, vast consumer markets, and low-cost iteration—often allows firms to move products "from one to one hundred" faster and cheaper than global peers in "the world's toughest gym," in which competition forces constant refinement. Yet we're also increasingly seeing some companies start moving upstream from "one to one hundred" toward the "zero to one"—China's own "Qi Baishi" moment.

Patent Cooperation Treaty filings—international patent applications that signal intent to seek intellectual property (IP) protection across multiple countries—illustrate this story. By 2024, China led the world with just over seventy thousand—ahead of the US's fifty-four thousand and Japan's forty-eight thousand. It's a steep, sustained rise. Quantity doesn't settle the debate about quality; in fact, China leads in total granted AI patents but ranks only fifth in average citations; and other countries hold an enduring edge in fundamental science. Yet sheer volume signals intention and momentum.

Copy: The Origins of China's Upstream Shift

Chinese companies' move up the value chain started long ago with foundational advantages we've described in earlier chapters: the country's scale created dense learning environments in which clusters of firms, labs, and engineers gained capabilities simply because they were doing so much, so often. "These ecosystems were intense, highly competitive, and innovative, and altogether lifted the baseline across a number of industries, including pharma," says Fangning Zhang, a McKinsey partner in the life sciences practice.

China's biopharma industry illustrates this transformation from scale to capability. Nearly half a billion Chinese live with chronic diseases, and more than eight million die each year. China's population base creates one of the world's largest pools of patients that can be tapped for clinical trials—and the country's biotech ecosystem continues to mature. "Altogether, that scale and growing capability enable foreign and local pharma companies alike to identify new disease targets, enroll trials, and develop life-saving drugs far faster than elsewhere—to the benefit of all," says Fangning.

As in most industries, China's rise in pharma didn't begin with breakthroughs—but with imitation. For decades, Chinese pharma grew by reverse engineering Western drugs and expanding through generics—a familiar path for late-industrializing countries. As capabilities improved, firms climbed the drug development ladder, first producing active pharmaceutical ingredients and then becoming a destination for outsourced biopharma manufacturing.

At every step of this progression, a vast ecosystem of contract research organizations (CROs) and contract development and manufacturing organizations (CDMOs) accumulated expertise in ever more complex scientific and engineering processes—often at the behest of foreign pharma companies. CROs took on the lab work and clinical trials; CDMOs helped develop the manufacturing processes and made the drugs. Over time, alongside domestic pharmaceutical companies, these firms became part of the backbone of China's pharma sector.

A decade ago, this ecosystem was in its infancy. In 2015, Chinese pharmaceutical firms contributed just 4 percent of the global innovative drug pipeline; the country's top five pharmaceutical companies were worth only $15 billion and generated under $100 million from "innovative drugs"—new molecular entities rather than generics and biosimilars. Investors were wary of them, citing long development cycles, heavy capital needs, and limited IPO pathways for pre-revenue biotechs.

Clinical infrastructure lagged as well. Fewer than six hundred hospitals could run trials, and patient data quality and consistency varied widely. Yet these early capabilities became the foundation for China's biopharma innovation stage.

Iterate: China's "One to One Hundred" Innovation Engine

Understanding China's innovation surge starts by separating fundamental from applied science. The US and Europe still dominate in "zero to one" scientific discovery, supported by large public funding pools—the National Institutes of Health, Horizon Europe, national science agencies and councils, world-class universities, and an open research culture (which in the US is increasingly debated amid shifting political priorities). What changed, and quickly, was Chinese companies' mastery of applied innovation, turning ideas into competitive products and ecosystems through engineering, design, cost innovation, manufacturing scale, and business model recombination.

Innovation in the biopharma industry, again, provides a clear example. "Chinese pharma companies are flipping drug discovery from a slow, hypothesis-driven science into something closer to fast, engineering-led iteration," says Jin Wang, a McKinsey senior partner and leader of the Firm's China life sciences practice.

From its base as generics-makers and contract manufacturers, Chinese biopharma companies moved up the value chain. For example, in antibody-drug conjugates, those precision "bombs" that target cancer, these companies became master iterative engineers. The components aren't new—antibodies, linkers, payloads. What's novel is Chinese firms' ability to "test different combinations—A with C, B with D—thousands of experiments through trial and error until they find what works best," says McKinsey life sciences partner Tina Hou. "And they can do it really, really fast, at a fraction of the US cost."

Healthcare investor Wei Fu describes China's advantage in drug development with a poker story: "It's like playing Texas Hold'em—in China, you can play ten hands for the cost of one in America, and even with a lower success rate, you win more often. It's probability. You simply get to see more hands," Wei tells us. He's describing an ecosystem-level advantage: China's large talent pool, founder-friendly capital, and a cost-effective supply chain help move a molecule from idea to preclinical testing two to three times faster and at a third to half the cost of global peers.

China's pharma sector has scaled at remarkable speed. The top five firms, which we noted were worth $15 billion a decade ago, had grown into a $160 billion cluster by 2025, with more than seventy biotechs listed across Hong Kong, STAR, and Nasdaq. Chinese companies now contribute nearly a third of the global pipeline of drugs in development. In the first quarter of 2025, about 32 percent of worldwide biopharma out-licensing deal value came from China, up from around 21 percent in 2023–2024. Global pharma players, including AstraZeneca, GSK, Pfizer, and Roche, are partnering with Chinese innovators such as Harbour BioMed, Hengrui, 3SBio, and MediLink Therapeutics. Clinical capacity has expanded, too, and roughly 1,700 hospitals can now run clinical trials, nearly triple the number eight years ago.

As Pfizer CEO Albert Bourla puts it, "In biopharma, China's dramatic speed, cost, and scale have triggered a shift in the global competitive landscape. I've never seen a country advancing in science as quickly, as fast, as powerfully as I'm witnessing China doing today." Chinese biopharma companies should continue to move up the value chain. "If you look at how much China's already leapfrogged in building its innovation ecosystem, the obvious conclusion is that we'll see a lot more breakthrough innovations in the decade ahead," says Jin. "Though individual companies have suffered setbacks, the industry is resilient, bolstered by the large number of entrepreneurs who keep trying and advancing."

This iterative innovation model doesn't belong only to biopharma—it now spans a number of industries: autos, aerospace, chemicals, batteries, AI, robotics, and mobility, to name a few. Shanghai alone hosts roughly six hundred foreign-funded R&D centers. Global firms have embedded in China's landscape: Bosch employs over ten thousand engineers, physicists, mathematicians, and other researchers; BASF has opened a €280 million ($325 million) innovation campus in Shanghai; Airbus designs next-generation components in Shenzhen.

Autos provide a dramatic example of this acceleration. When the Shanghai Auto Show reopened to the world in 2023, foreign executives were "overwhelmed and shocked," recalls Mingyu Guan, leader of McKinsey's China automotive practice. Visitors rode in autonomous cars, examined battery breakthroughs, and tested in-car AI assistants.

Tesla's decision to manufacture in China in 2019 had catalyzed a new generation of entrepreneurs and also helped create a core supply chain, and in time "the innovation capital shifted—from Stuttgart and Detroit to Shanghai, Beijing, and other Chinese cities," says Andreas Tschiesner, a Munich-based McKinsey senior partner and global co-leader of advanced industries. "COVID was like a twenty-year catch-up period for China's auto industry." One German luxury-brand CEO called headquarters from the show floor: "We're far too slow. We must move faster." Chinese vehicle development cycles now run eighteen to twenty-four months versus three to four years in Europe—and are still compressing.

Consumer electronics is another area where Chinese companies have leapt forward in applied innovation. In mobile phones, the camera specifications on Oppo and Vivo phones are often one to two generations ahead of the flagship models from Samsung and Apple. Huawei went further, launching Mate XT—the world's first commercially available tri-fold smartphone—before anyone else in 2024.

Haier, the leading home appliance and consumer electronics company, illustrates how this iterative model extends beyond products into organizational design. Over the past decade, Haier has dismantled much of its traditional hierarchy, reorganizing itself into thousands of self-governing "micro-enterprises" that interact directly with consumers. The goal, which Haier describes as "zero distance" to the customer, isn't centralized control but faster feedback, experimentation, and recombination. In practice, this structure has supported the company's evolution from a manufacturer into a broader smart home and industrial IoT ecosystem where appliances—from smart refrigerators to AI-driven laundry systems—are co-created with the people who use them.

The pattern has been consistent; once an idea emerges, a wave of Chinese companies is ready to plug it into the ecosystem and iterate quickly. And with more than five million STEM graduates each year—many educated abroad—and a demanding "996" (9 a.m. to 9 p.m., six days a week) work culture, this ecosystem has been dubbed by one European executive "a continuous-motion machine" activated at salaries that are typically meaningfully less than those of their US and European peers.

Create: Moving Toward "Zero to One" Scientific Breakthroughs

What was once the world's factory, in select areas, is becoming a laboratory, with a few emerging sparks of the "zero to one" variety— the rare breakthroughs that reshape entire categories on the scale of CRISPR, the smartphone, and the first practical lithium-ion battery.

Creativity takes two forms: the iterative kind that advances through a thousand small refinements, and the conceptual kind that breaks with precedent altogether, like Picasso's first Cubist canvas or a biotech team assembling a molecule no one's seen before. This shift is uneven across industries, but the direction is clear: Chinese companies—after mastering the engineering-driven incremental cycle—are now starting to make the conceptual leaps that signal emerging capability of creation.

Some of these sparks show up in consumer models before they show up in laboratories. European retailers are now looking to China's quick-commerce models, where shopping is fast, finely tuned, and intensely personal. In the practice of "digital clienteling," store associates build ongoing, personalized relationships with customers through WeChat or the business-focused WeCom. Chinese platforms are also using behavioral signals, rather than personal data, to segment consumers and tailor micro-strategies around discount seekers, new-product chasers, and annual occasion shoppers—potentially allowing companies to double or even triple sales, says Kevin Wei Wang, a McKinsey senior partner and co-leader of the Asia digital practice. "This is the model you can copy to France, even though there's no WeChat." These aren't optimizations—they're new ways of organizing data and marketing.

At the tech frontier, a similar pattern is starting to emerge. In AI, DeepSeek is introducing architectural innovations like "sparse attention" schemes which prompt models to focus on more relevant parts of an input. In batteries, Chinese companies are pairing incremental improvements with true breakthroughs in materials science and manufacturing; for example, CATL's condensed battery technology has demonstrated energy densities around 500 watt-hours per kilogram, which could push into aviation territory—a departure from conventional lithium-ion battery chemistry. In quantum science, physicist Jianwei Pan's teams have delivered world firsts from satellite-based quantum teleportation to next-generation orbital communication networks. These are breakthroughs in the truest sense: new architectures, new science, new possibilities.

These advances didn't emerge in a vacuum. They arose in fields where Chinese firms enjoy structural advantages—whether a deep bench of scientific talent or mastery of the "one to one hundred" cycle. Battery breakthroughs grew out of dense engineering clusters and supply chains; AI from massive digital adoption and data-rich platforms; biotech from a well-honed clinical and manufacturing ecosystem; and quantum computing from decades of state-supported physics research. Once the factories, platforms, hospitals, and laboratories existed, Chinese scientists, engineers, and entrepreneurs operating inside them worked to expand scientific and conceptual frontiers.

Still, the trajectory will continue to be uneven. Fundamental breakthroughs often require state sponsorship or university lab infrastructure—deep science, frontier technologies rather than the fast-cycle incentives of the markets. "China is not particularly strong at zero to one," says Henry Zhang, the contemporary Chinese novelist and poet also known as Feng Tang. "The system is cautious about failure, and the cost of being wrong is high. China's strength lies in what it does after the first step."

The most cited foundational AI work still comes from US and European institutions. In global pharmaceuticals, no Chinese firm ranks among the top twenty in 2025; long-established American and European firms such as Johnson & Johnson, Merck, and Novartis still lead. Only about 7 percent of China's R&D spend goes to basic research each year, compared with 12 to 15 percent in advanced economies. "IP imports are still 4.5 times larger than exports, and reliance on foreign inputs persists in several core technologies," says Jeongmin Seong, a McKinsey Global Institute partner. "These contradictions are exactly what make China's innovation trajectory one of the most consequential variables in global competition."

China's space sector illustrates this mixed picture. It hasn't yet matched SpaceX on the efficiency and scalability of putting payloads into orbit or Tesla's Starlink system on global satellite networks. But Chinese programs have achieved milestones that distinguish them in the global arena, such as the first soft landing on the far side of the moon, advanced lunar and sample return missions, and sustained robotic exploration underpinning long-term lunar and Mars ambitions.

This debate feels largely beside the point to the Chinese entrepreneurs we know. They're not pondering the divide between "zero to one" and "one to one hundred"; they're too busy creating and competing, building and testing, launching and iterating again.

Reframing Intellectual Property Risk: Being Outlearned, Not Just Copied

Whenever the topic of China and innovation emerges in conversations with multinational clients, one question reliably surfaces: What about intellectual property protection? It's a fair concern, and we should be clear up front: IP theft remains a real issue, and despite improved enforcement, there is work to be done to address and eliminate it. But the debate often conflates two different issues: outright

IP theft and capability building through engagement, in other words, how joint ventures, outsourcing, and partnerships help Chinese firms move up the value chain. The latter is far less discussed, yet often more consequential.

Apple didn't just outsource iPhone production for lower costs; it outsourced process engineering, tooling precision, and supply chain orchestration at scale. That ecosystem didn't steal Apple's IP—it learned to build at global standards and then kept going. In autos, Volkswagen and General Motors built joint ventures that secured decades of dominance while also training the engineers behind today's competitors like BYD and NIO. In each case, collaboration helped accelerate Chinese capability building.

The old fear of copying as the dominant risk doesn't reflect the reality. China today is simply not the China of twenty years ago. IP theft still occurs, but this pilfering nests inside a dense system of IP ownership, enforcement, and domestic rivalry. China now accounts for roughly half of global patent filings and the majority of AI patent owners worldwide, backed by a national-level IP tribunal under the Supreme People's Court. Rising IP enforcement, especially in high-value and high-tech cases, often reflects more IP ownership rather than greater infringement: Chinese firms now hold so much IP that weak protection would hurt their own interests. European and American business surveys likewise report improving protection.

Crucially, most IP battles in China today are Chinese versus Chinese. In the top court, only about one in ten IP cases involves foreign parties. In other words, the real action is a domestic cage fight where firms wield IP lawsuits as strategic weapons: Tencent versus ByteDance, DJI chasing rival drone makers, Huawei enforcing patents against smaller telecoms, and Baidu versus Sogou or Oppo versus Xiaomi in patent and unfair competition disputes. This is no longer a system organized primarily around copying; ownership and enforcement now matter internally (even as major international IP disputes involving Chinese firms continue).

For global companies, that shifts the center of gravity. The key concern isn't IP protection alone but also the speed and agility at which they can operate. In markets that move at China's pace, protecting IP may offer comfort but erecting "keep out" fortresses can often make an underlying technology obsolete.

Pharmaceuticals present additional complexity. Drug R&D takes a decade and billions of dollars, with low success rates of 10 percent. Those barriers create a degree of natural protection even as progress depends on collaboration. As Merck's Hong Chow puts it, "No single company or country can be self-sufficient in innovative medicines. The business is high-risk, and no one can develop treatments for all diseases alone. Collaboration is essential—at the same time, competition makes us better."

And when those lines between collaboration and competition get blurred, IP conflict increasingly transcends China altogether. Foreign multinationals don't just litigate against Chinese firms; they also pursue IP claims against other global rivals. In 2025, for example, Disney, Universal, and Warner Bros. sued Chinese AI start-up MiniMax in US federal court for copyright infringement and unauthorized use of its characters—and filed parallel suits against US-based AI companies. It's a reminder that IP tensions haven't vanished; they've shifted from factories and hardware to algorithms and data. In lidar and other frontier technologies, joint development and supply chain partnerships have sparked new disputes over who owns and monetizes shared capabilities.

Protecting IP remains essential, but capability building, speed, and strategic learning matter more. The real question is whether firms can engage China's innovation machine without being overtaken by it—using collaboration not as a risk but as a way to evolve faster. As innovation cycles accelerate, the greatest vulnerability for Western firms may simply be falling behind.

Three Strategic Paths

As we discussed, in the next China, local companies are creating and innovating at speed and scale. The next wave of breakthroughs may not just be tested in China—they may be *born* there.

We advise multinationals to plug into China's innovation networks, co-create with local talent, and use China's fast-moving market as a proving ground for ideas that can scale worldwide. "These are the decisive years," says Ken Wong, executive vice president and president of Lenovo's fast-growing unit, Solutions & Services Group. "If companies don't accelerate now, they risk becoming historic brands with no future."

We outline three strategic paths for engaging with China's rapidly evolving landscape.

1. *Source innovations or partner locally.* Find innovations from Chinese firms, or license or co-develop products for China or for global markets.
2. *Build and develop in China.* Use the local ecosystem as a high-speed laboratory to develop products for China and the world.
3. *Adapt Chinese innovations.* Take inspiration from China-origin products, techniques, and business models for potential application in your home market.

Strategy: Sourcing Innovation from Chinese Firms

Jiangsu Hengrui Medicine embodies China's push toward best- and first-in-class innovation. Founded in 1970 as a maker of generic drugs, the company spent decades in the industry's back rows. Then it reinvented itself—investing nearly 20 percent of revenue into R&D and moving from "me-better" drugs to true "me-first" breakthroughs. Among them: potentially the world's first oral lipoprotein inhibitor and a therapy targeting the once "undruggable" KRAS G12D mutation.

Hengrui's rise caught the attention of Merck, the 358-year-old German science and technology company with more than a century of history in China. Today, China accounts for €3 billion ($3.5 billion)—about 14 percent—of Merck's global revenue, and the firm employs 4,500 employees across major Chinese hubs, but this partnership didn't begin in a boardroom. It started at a 2023 oncology conference when Merck's business development team spotted

Hengrui's drug development pipeline. Hong, who is leading the commercial organization for Merck in China and the international region, messaged Hengrui's chairman, Piaoyang Sun, on WeChat for a meeting. "I was surprised when he immediately replied, 'Sure, let's organize something,'" Hong says.

That exchange led to one of the year's landmark deals. When Chairman Sun met Merck's former Healthcare CEO Peter Guenter in Shanghai, "there was immediate chemistry," Hong says. "It was a conversation between entrepreneurs with passions for science." Within months, the two sides finalized a $2 billion licensing partnership—"genuine co-development, not just a multinational taking over a local asset," she adds, fueled by speed and trust.

AstraZeneca's relationship with China reflects a similar shift from market access to innovation engine. Since opening its first office in 1993, the company has built hubs across Beijing, Shanghai, and Wuxi. At its Shanghai R&D center, quiet hallways and glass-walled labs for bioanalysis, proteomics, and mass spectrometry reflect a shift toward earlier-stage, more innovative research. "We're aiming for a qualitative leap in R&D," a scientist explains. "Not just taking projects from global."

That ambition is expanding: a new $2.5 billion Beijing R&D campus will host AstraZeneca's second global AI and data science lab and connect directly to local biotech clusters and hospitals. China now plays a central role in the company's development pipeline, with local teams leading nearly twenty global clinical trials and contributing to approximately 15 to 20 percent of all patient enrollments in AstraZeneca-sponsored studies.

Partnerships span China's biotech ecosystem, from multi-specific antibodies with Harbour BioMed to macrocyclic peptides with Syneron Bio. "From signing the memorandum to opening phase one on the first line took one year," Iskra Reic, AstraZeneca's executive vice president, international, notes. "That's how fast we're moving—pace, speed, and efficiency, and at AstraZeneca standards."

The company has also launched a healthcare investment fund supporting more than two dozen early-stage Chinese biotechs, aiming to bring China-origin innovations to global markets. Early engagement is a necessity, says Tina, McKinsey's life sciences partner, as multinationals increasingly "shop in China's very crowded supermarket" for new drug candidates and platforms. "If you look at a collaboration when an asset is already on the table being shopped for licensing, it's too late," she adds. "If you've promised eight blockbusters by 2030 and only have three in the pipeline, where will the other five come from—quickly and at lower cost? China."

Strategy: Building Inside China's Ecosystem

At dawn in Hangzhou Bay, the glass facades of Smart Automobile's new complex catch the pink light rising over the port city of Ningbo—one of China's busiest shipping hubs. Inside, mixed teams from Mercedes-Benz's Smart unit and Geely review full-vehicle simulations.

This setting—two hundred kilometers south of Shanghai—is where Mercedes-Benz has anchored the future of its small-car brand. Smart's gasoline micro-cars, born in 1990s Europe, never cracked electrification. Its reboot as an electric vehicle is now unfolding not in Stuttgart but in the world's largest EV market. Mercedes-Benz still leads design, but engineering, software, and industrialization have moved into China's ecosystem.

"We're in China for global," says Mandy Zhang, global CMO of Smart Automobile. "Sixty to sixty-five percent of the world's new-energy vehicles come from China, and our headquarters is close to Geely's. We benefit from its scale and speed."

That scale has been transformative. Geely's three million-vehicle supply chain gives Smart purchasing leverage it couldn't achieve alone. "We share many components and benefit from their negotiating power," Mandy says. The effect is clear in iteration speed. She recalls a planned facelift: a 14.8-inch screen was approved; two weeks later, Geely's procurement team sourced a 15.4-inch version at the same cost; the change forced an instrument panel re-design and rapid human-machine interface safety and ergonomics validation.

"The spec changed immediately—that's the speed of China's supply chain," Mandy recalls.

Smart is asset light with no manufacturing plants, and it taps Geely's EV architectures—the same platforms used by Geely's Zeekr, Volvo, and Polestar models along with the fast-evolving advanced driver-assistance systems (ADAS), the driver-assistance systems developed by shared engineering teams. These capabilities come at "almost commodity cost," says Mandy. Smart #1 moved from design to launch in two years—about half a European development cycle.

Smart's success in the crowded EV market remains to be seen, but global automakers are following suit. Volkswagen, BMW, and Tesla use China's ecosystem not simply for manufacturing but also for iteration and innovation. The logic has flipped: global firms once formed joint ventures to sell into a booming Chinese market; today, they turn to China for software systems, platforms, engineering talent, supplier speed, scale manufacturing, co-development with tech partners, and rapid commercialization—to sell both into China and globally.

As McKinsey senior partner Ruth Heuss puts it, "Europe doesn't yet have its own fully formed digital-innovation ecosystem. The next generation of Europeans will choose cheaper, more digital cars—and if automakers cannot rapidly build up their own capabilities or selectively import technology from China or the US, they'll face a period of decline."

Legacy carmakers use strategies that range from full localization to selective partnership. Volkswagen Group has poured at least €2.5 billion ($2.9 billion) into a new R&D center in Hefei, giving the company faster, cheaper, end-to-end development capability in China, and has also invested in or partnered with XPENG, Horizon Robotics, and other local players. Others use China as a manufacturing and export base; Tesla shipped roughly 260,000 vehicles in 2024 to global markets. Still others rely on joint ventures, localized platforms, or China-designed models aimed at Southeast Asia and other growth regions.

Whether automakers shift their thinking around China will determine which survive the next decade, argues Mingyu Guan, a McKinsey senior partner and China automotive practice leader. "Those like Mercedes, Volkswagen, BMW—who see the trend and commit to the future—will remain," Mingyu says. "The ones who stay in their comfort zone, who refuse to partner or explore beyond what they've done for decades, will struggle. Some players haven't moved an inch toward next-generation products."

The global market is big enough for European, American, and Chinese players, Mingyu adds, but only if they evolve. Daniel Birke, a McKinsey partner in advanced industries, sees progress: "Many multinational car companies are now making serious efforts to fundamentally change their operating models; it's not only about catching up with the status quo in China but also about defending their home markets as the industry baseline continues to rise." Competing globally now requires plugging into China's ecosystem through joint platforms, shared architectures, co-development with tech partners, and leadership teams that spend meaningful time on the ground. As Soul Capital's Herry Han, who is also an early investor in EV maker XPENG, says, "China is where the music of innovation is being played."

Strategy: Copying and Adapting Chinese Innovations

The global pilgrimage for innovation has long had as its destination Silicon Valley's garages and glass campuses. Lately, executives, investors, and entrepreneurs are heading east—to Shenzhen, Hangzhou, and Beijing—in search of the next big thing.

At first glance, this seems counterintuitive. Foreign direct investment into China has slowed, and the economy faces headwinds. Geopolitics look increasingly complicated. Yet the flow of people and ideas remains vigorous. Leaders across consumer goods, pharmaceuticals, AI, and industrials are visiting China to understand how its vast, digital-first market operates. At recent industry forums, the attendee list resembled a mini-Davos: the heads of Siemens, BMW, Qualcomm, AstraZeneca, Nestlé, and FedEx all made the trip. Joe recently visited RoboSense's Shenzhen headquarters and was among two dozen visitor groups that day; all were asked to place a metallic red sticker over phone cameras for confidentiality purposes before entering its lidar-sensing factories.

There's good reason for the interest. China's digital ecosystem is among the world's most sophisticated. E-commerce platforms have evolved far beyond online shops into hybrids of entertainment, community, and retail. Millions tune in daily to livestreams on RedNote, where farmers sell peaches straight from their orchards, fashion influencers push the latest streetwear, and wineries pour samples for viewers thousands of kilometers away. Every sale syncs instantly to payments, logistics, and data feedback loops that direct producers where to focus—as soon as the next hour.

These innovations are already shaping global commerce. TikTok Shop—born from Douyin—has reset expectations for social commerce worldwide, making most other e-commerce platforms seem "like a collection of analog items on a scrolling website that feels like the Stone Age," says Herry, our investor friend. In fintech, super-apps WeChat and Alipay have long merged messaging, payments, transport, entertainment, and retail into a single seamless customer journey; consumers outside China still juggle half a dozen apps to accomplish the same tasks.

Multinationals are finding their China operations often outpace headquarters, especially in digital innovation. McDonald's China has built a customer engagement and CRM engine more advanced than its US parent. Starbucks' China app integrates delivery, digital loyalty, and social features that make other global versions look dated. AstraZeneca sends global R&D leaders on multi-month rotations to its China research hubs, and Bosch Mobility's Suzhou factory—designated a green, technologically advanced World Economic Forum "Global Lighthouse"—includes among its best practices AI-driven predictive maintenance and automated optical inspection.

Such lessons are increasingly exportable. McKinsey recently worked with e-commerce players across Latin America and Southeast Asia to accelerate digital transformation using ideas inspired by Alibaba, Temu, and SHEIN. These foreign executives made repeated trips to China to observe supply chain operations, swap stories with sellers, and study business model innovations on the ground.

These are big shifts. For example, many Western and Southeast Asian platforms still rely on e-commerce home pages with "fixed columns organized by category or campaign—not conducive to customers' in-depth browsing and discovery," says Peng Xia, a McKinsey partner in China's digital practice. China's platforms, by contrast, feel like infinite feeds—digital street markets tailored for you: endless scroll, hyper-personalized recommendations, and content that constantly refreshes. One e-commerce company saw both click-through and conversion rates jump after adopting this model. An increasing number of non-China platforms have begun locating their technology R&D centers in China to leverage its vast tech talent pool. One Asian leading e-commerce company has scaled to more than a thousand engineers in Shanghai and Shenzhen to power on-site search, seller support tooling, real-time video creation, and recommendation AI. Yet another European e-commerce company has opened a China office with a 150-person team to recruit and support local sellers, curate product lines, and run logistics—linking Chinese sellers with international consumers.

Meanwhile, many platforms are eyeing Meituan and Taobao's instant-delivery model—the kind where you can get mie goreng in Jakarta, Indonesia, in nineteen minutes or a new umbrella in San José, Costa Rica, just as storm clouds start to gather. But adoption isn't plug and play—it requires rebuilding both the online interface and the offline network of couriers, micro-warehouses, and routing algorithms. Other platforms are adding influencer-led live e-commerce, which blurs the line between entertainment and shopping, leveraging influencers' credibility and charisma to drive impulse purchases. Examples include a beauty vlogger testing skincare products, a chef demonstrating instant noodles, or a tech reviewer unboxing gadgets. However, scaling this model globally requires adapting to local influencer ecosystems, building content production and personalization-of-product capability, and integrating with e-commerce transaction infrastructure to maintain the seamless user experience that defines success in China.

By drawing on practices honed in China's brutally competitive e-commerce arena, companies can reinvent both customer experience and fulfillment operations. The ideal payoff: faster user growth, deeper engagement, stronger unit economics, and a new blueprint for digital commerce.

"This is China's fundamental sauce. With its massive consumer market, abundant STEM talent, and policy support for tech infrastructure and education, you'll see continuous Chinese innovation over the next ten to twenty years," Peng says. "We could be heading toward a global innovation duopoly: Silicon Valley and China's Yangtze Delta–Greater Bay Area."

A Tale of Divergence on the Ground

When we talk about innovation in China, we're referring to the frontier edge of a nation of 1.4 billion people that now produces nearly 20 percent of global GDP. This slice doesn't represent all of China—just as a visit to Meta or Google wouldn't explain the United States. Large parts of the economy remain far from the cutting edge. In capital markets, for example, the depth and sophistication of local institutions still lag the global financial centers of New York and London. And within China itself, the contrast is stark: alongside the gleaming first-tier cities are hundreds of third- and fourth-tier cities where many enterprises continue to operate with older technologies and management practices. Yet it's precisely this frontier slice—small relative to China as a whole but vast in what it signals—that previews where the next wave of global innovation is likely to emerge.

Yet global understanding of this frontier is narrowing just as its importance grows. As one former Google executive who spent a decade in China told us, "Westerners have about 10 percent of the knowledge of China that Chinese people have about the West." That's why immersion matters. Time spent in China has a way of resetting assumptions, and upon their return home, we've seen many executives realize that ideas they'd once dismissed as "too Chinese" might hold the seeds of their next big move.

China's innovation story is also one of divergence. In areas such as robotics, electric vehicles, and advanced manufacturing, the country's scale, speed, and engineering depth are already resetting global benchmarks. In others—biopharma, aerospace, semiconductors—the gap with Western research ecosystems remains meaningful, though its durability is increasingly uncertain amid ongoing debates in the US, in particular, over public funding for university research and government science programs. "It took the US a century to build the university and research foundation that drives fundamental scientific discovery," says Tina, McKinsey's life sciences partner. "In areas like biology and basic science, that foundation still gives American research an edge. Chinese institutions haven't yet mastered that."

Overall, though, the direction of travel is unmistakable. "Multinationals still have a five-to-ten-year advantage in branding, design, and heritage," says Alfons Mensdorff-Pouilly, CEO of Jebsen Group, which has been operating in China for more than a century. "But ultimately, you have to be in China to develop products for the future. Surround yourself with the right partners, the right engineers, and the right work ethic—and access the ecosystem."

We recently brought a group of Scandinavian executives inside China's most dynamic technology clusters for a weeklong immersion we call "Innovation Execution." Leaders from some of Scandinavia's largest commercial vehicle and industrial engineering companies moved through factories, robotics labs, and automation start-ups—to understand the operating processes behind them. What struck them was a pattern of execution that repeated itself: development cycles that would take weeks in Europe were compressed into hours; targets were ambitious; authority was delegated to frontline decision-makers; and supplier changes could be executed in hours. Key calls were made in one room. Communication ran through integrated platforms such as Lark, with response times measured in minutes—rather than days lost in email chains. Our clients observed flat organizations with wide spans and minimal matrix structures. "The week revealed just how powerful Chinese innovation practices can be," one executive tells us. "These are all approaches that can help multinationals stay competitive globally."

Every company must make its own choices about how to engage with China's innovation ecosystem. Some will keep core R&D at home and use the China ecosystem for scale; others will co-develop or compete inside Chinese markets. The US, Europe, and China bring world-class capabilities—different strengths, distinct systems, increasingly intertwined. As AstraZeneca's Iskra puts it, "The real question is how the balance between them will reshape global innovation over the next decade."

While no country has a monopoly on fostering or scaling innovation, China's ecosystem is showing increasing sparks of creative momentum—and a formidable ability in turning ideas, wherever they originate, into products and business models quickly and at scale.

WHAT'S NEXT, CHINA?

From Hard Goods to Soft Power

No one saw Labubu coming. With bulging eyes, furry ears, and stubby legs, this toy doll is a mischievous gremlin—ugly enough to feel comforting in an Instagram- and TikTok-perfect world. Its colorful vinyl and plushy figurines hit a cultural nerve, drawing fans from the tennis star Naomi Osaka and Blackpink's Lisa to teenagers in Tokyo and collectors in Copenhagen.

At the Pop Mart, Labubu's distributor, near McKinsey's Shanghai office, we see adults and children shaking "blind boxes" for clues—a gram of weight, the tap of the box lid, the rustle of an accessory—to divine whether they hold a common one in twelve designs or the ultra-rare prize. Shaking boxes nights and weekends, one father said his nine-year-old amassed a hundred different figurines in a few months. That kind of obsession has pushed Pop Mart global, with flagship stores from London to Los Angeles and nearly $2 billion in revenue in the first half of 2025. Pop Mart has turned its toys into a new form of consumer expression—rooted in a hyper-digital youth culture that collapses the line between online and offline identity.

For decades, China's most recognizable form of soft power was the panda, carefully loaned to foreign zoos as a gesture of goodwill—diplomacy embodied in black and white fur. We're now talking about something very different. China may still be the world's $3.6 trillion factory floor, but a handful of companies are beginning to export something new: culture, characters, and aspiration, helped along by what we call a "cultural supply chain" ecosystem that connects creators, social media platforms, e-commerce entrepreneurs, and consumers in a giant digital loop.

This is the early flicker of China's emerging "soft power"—the late Harvard professor Joseph S. Nye's term for influence achieved through "attraction rather than coercion or payments." Soft power isn't just a geopolitical concept; it shows up in many arenas, including the commercial realm, where culture, values, music, movies, fashion, and brands travel across borders and shape how people perceive a country. Hollywood and the NBA are pillars of America's soft power; K-pop has the same role for Korea.

Chinese companies are now beginning to cross into this world after decades of being better at making stuff than creating intellectual property (IP) for a global audience. This move feels late in their evolution; they've been so dominant in global manufacturing that this gap between their "hard" capabilities and "soft" appeal feels that much wider. In the next China, we are beginning to see the rebalancing of this discrepancy.

Whether it be TikTok's global reach, the video game *Black Myth: Wukong*'s breakout success, or the on-demand fashion machine SHEIN's popularity, several Chinese consumer-facing companies are learning to build loyalty, aspiration, and cultural relevance. We expect that Chinese firms will increasingly attempt to project themselves globally not just through technology and manufacturing strength but also through culture and aesthetics. "Ten years ago, no one would wear a Chinese brand to show off. That's changing," says Michael Chi Chen, a McKinsey partner in the consumer practice. "Companies like Huawei in phones or Laopu Gold in jewelry or Zeekr in electric cars are beginning to be seen as aspirational in some parts of the world. These companies are investing in design, storytelling, and global ambassadors, and they're starting to appeal in new ways."

The Shift: From Building to Branding

It took Chinese companies around a decade to master manufacturing, starting from the late '80s and early '90s. But once they did, the next step was inevitable: they wanted their names on the box. By the mid-1990s, factory champions who'd built fortunes producing generic goods for foreign brands began creating identities of their own. Apparel moved first. Hong Kong entrepreneurs launched brands Esprit and Bossini, purposefully choosing Western-sounding names. Contract manufacturers across mainland China and Taiwan followed, such as Giant and Merida in bicycles; Lenovo, Huawei, and Xiaomi in consumer electronics; and Haier and Midea in household appliances.

The motivation was simple: manufacturing delivered volume but thin margins. As factory owners scaled up, many wanted to capture more value. "We were core to these brands' supply chains, but they did the marketing and branding, and they kept most of the margin," says Fred Yau, second-generation owner of Dongguan-based Yen Sheng Factory Limited, a major leather handbag and accessories supplier to American and European multinationals. "Every few years one of our fellow industrialists would try launching a brand. Most failed. It's just not in our DNA."

Yet a handful succeeded, thanks to China's vast and fast-growing domestic market. As consumer demand grew, companies realized they could either brand what they built—or outsource production entirely and focus on marketing and distribution. Local brands proliferated: Kang Shi Fu in instant noodles; Baixiang and Jinmailang as fast followers; Snow, Tsingtao, and Yanjing in beer; Heilan Home in menswear; and later, digital-native beauty players like Perfect Diary and Florasis.

We call this China's shift from "hard" to "soft." Hard goods are measured in yield, efficiency, and cost per unit. Soft goods—design, stories, and cultural IP—carry emotional meaning and command pricing power. As Chinese firms moved upmarket, they began pairing performance with creativity and storytelling, following a path long popularized by global consumer brands such as Coca-Cola.

Proya is a vivid example, evolving from distributor to billion-dollar global beauty brand. Founder Juncheng Hou launched a distribution business with family members and soon became restless importing others' products. He moved to Hangzhou, launched Proya's first line twenty-three years ago, and came to root the brand's identity around themes of workplace equality and personal growth: "Gender isn't a boundary line—bias is," it advertised around International Women's Day on March 8, 2021. The company also invested heavily in R&D and highlighted technology innovation in its marketing: "41.12 percent reduction in 'smile line' depth after eight weeks of use," it claimed for one recent new product, alongside visuals of lab instruments. Another skincare line from a decade ago emerged from a partnership with Chinese-made manned submersibles tasked with collecting deep-sea extracts from Chinese coastal provinces. The result is a confident, innovation-driven, homegrown brand that resonates with contemporary Chinese women.

Branding in China, however, has distinctive characteristics compared with other mature markets. For years, Chinese consumers prioritized function over form: smartphones competed on camera specs, EVs on battery range, cosmetics on visible efficacy. This was branding, too—only rooted in performance rather than in emotional appeal. A client calls the Chinese way the "featurization" of marketing—fast, visual, and densely informative. International clients often wondered why Chinese apps felt cluttered: "Do the Chinese not want sleek, minimalist designs?" We explained that China's slow download speed in the early internet era made it crucial to load everything on the first page—mostly text descriptions and product specs—and that aesthetic simply stuck.

China's digital ecosystem accelerated the shift. Platforms like Douyin, RedNote, and Bilibili integrated discovery, validation, and purchase into a single loop, allowing brands to prototype, test, iterate, and scale in real time. Sprouting up alongside them was a vast "cultural supply chain" of livestreamers, creators, and mini-store operators—and a creative workforce producing digital assets for gaming, fashion, toys, and more.

Still, building a brand remains brutally hard. For every success, hundreds fail. Most manufacturers excel at operational rigor, not consumer insight or design. We often advise manufacturing clients to stick with what they're good at: discipline, efficiency, managing thousands of workers, and meeting punishing delivery schedules. Brand-building demands different muscles, such as marketing, product design, consumer insight, and relentless innovation.

That doesn't stop them from trying. Everyone wants to become "China's Nike" in sportswear—from Anta and Li-Ning to 361 Degrees and Xtep. In smartphones, Xiaomi, Oppo, and Vivo took on Apple and Samsung. China's huge domestic market made the fight irresistible. Of course, this rise has brought criticism: Chinese brands are often accused of mimicking Western designs; critics point to the Xiaomi sports car SU7's resemblance to Porsche's Taycan, for example. In the same vein, Xiaomi skipped the "16" series, branding its new flagship the Xiaomi 17 to align with and directly compete head-to-head with the iPhone 17.

The real differentiator is speed. China's market runs at a dizzying pace: millions of users cycle through promotions, gifting events, lucky draws, and livestream shopping every day; memes become product lines almost overnight. It's a high-metabolism environment where brands evolve in full public view. Those that endure learn to communicate and differentiate with humor, intimacy, and agility—capabilities that will matter even more as Chinese firms step onto the global stage.

The Soft Power Turn: Exporting Culture

Of course, many Chinese companies never set out to build global brands. They built category-killing products for 1.4 billion domestic consumers—and the world barged in.

Joe likes to tell a self-effacing story about his first brush with the concept of soft power, and it involves the late Harvard political scientist who coined the term. As a Harvard sophomore, Joe cold-called Jerry Cohen, the influential legal expert and China scholar, to invite him to speak at a student conference. Cohen heard the caller announced as "Joe Nye," assumed it was the legendary dean of Harvard's Kennedy School of Government rather than "Joe Ngai," and took the call immediately. "It was my first lesson," Joe recalls, "in the power of a good name."

Some of China's most visible soft-power successes were largely accidental. Douyin's domestic success became TikTok overseas, reshaping global media through short video. Pinduoduo's gamified, group-buying e-commerce model—so familiar to Chinese shoppers—is succeeding overseas as Temu. "As it turns out, Western consumers appreciate great-value-for-money goods and trust influencers on digital channels—just like the Chinese," says Michael, a partner in the consumer practice.

Increasingly, companies aren't just shipping goods—they're exporting elements of culture, whether gaming, film, bubble tea, fashion, or even design aesthetics. Much of this emerges bottom-up through China's cultural supply chain that links domestic creators with global distribution systems, often through serendipity—the right character or meme on the right distribution channel at the right time.

Perceptions have shifted accordingly. A decade ago, Chinese products were dismissed as cheap imitations; today they often rival global competitors, and by the time a product reaches Miami or Milan, it's typically been stress-tested by a vast ecosystem of users. Moreover, the lived experiences and desires of consumers in Shanghai, Tokyo, Johannesburg, LA, and London are converging.

Platforms like TikTok have accelerated this diffusion. Its pacing, humor, and rapid content cycles mirror cultural instincts honed in China, and a growing wave of Chinese consumer companies lean heavily on TikTok-native storytelling rather than traditional advertising. "We understand better than anyone else in the world how to market and monetize through TikTok. The global success of TikTok has given Chinese companies much more confidence to go abroad," notes one Chinese entrepreneur who has found success in the US and Latin America.

"China's scale gives companies permission to invest in global branding," says Daniel Zipser, a McKinsey senior partner and co-leader of the Asia consumer and retail practice. "Automotive is a great example. In performance, Chinese EVs are seen as technologically superior to some German models. That credibility creates the foundation for aspirational brands—and for competing through soft power."

Still, these are early days. We find ourselves repeating the same references, because there are only a handful of at-scale successes so far. China under-indexes sharply on global brand equity; on Interbrand's 2024 Top Global Brands, only two Chinese firms, Huawei and Xiaomi, rank among the top one hundred companies with 30 percent of revenue outside their home region. Kantar BrandZ, which paints a broader picture since it includes Chinese consumers' perception, counts twelve in their latest 2025 report. Soft power, after all, doesn't scale the way factories do—it takes longer to build.

Why Pop Mart Matters More than the Fanfare Suggests

Pop Mart matters not because it has captured the global imagination for however long, but because its trajectory hints at what may become more common as China's creative ecosystem matures.

Labubu emerged from the imagination of Hong Kong artist Kasing Lung, who grew up in the Netherlands sketching upstairs from his parents' Chinese restaurant. The character—part Nordic folklore, part childhood sketch—is a sharp-toothed rebel with a soft heart that first appeared in Kasing's book *The Story of Puca.*

At first, Labubus were produced in small batches for Hong Kong toy boutiques. When Pop Mart approached Kasing in 2019, scouting designers the way a record label might seek musicians, Kasing was wary that mass production might dilute his artistic roots. But Pop Mart founder Ning Wang offered a different model: a "blind-box" format combining chance, scarcity, and community.

The first Labubu release sold out instantly. The partnership would produce the first Chinese character IPs to break out internationally at this scale. Pop Mart handled global distribution and retail spectacle, turning queueing, dropping, and unboxing into a form of social performance. Labubu moved from niche collectible to global obsession, with fans lining up across Asia, Europe, and the United States.

The numbers were striking. Blind boxes typically retail for only $12 to $15 a pop, yet Pop Mart did $887 million in global sales in 2023, doubled that in 2024, and more than doubled that again in 2025 to roughly $4 billion. At its 2025 peak, Pop Mart's market cap briefly reached $49 billion, soaring beyond Hasbro, Mattel, and Sanrio combined. Since then, its stock performance has grown increasingly volatile—collectibles run on sentiment as much as loyalty—and its secondary market value has also fluctuated. But Chinese IP has created a bubble worth talking about.

Pop Mart's ambitions extend beyond any single character. Executives describe a Disney-style road map: a portfolio of IPs that can support content, entertainment, and experiences—a Chinese "house of characters." That path, however, demands sustained investment and deliberate storytelling, and masterful execution; Disney itself took more than a quarter century to expand Mickey Mouse from animated short film into a cast of characters and finally its first theme park.

Whether Labubu endures or fades, Pop Mart's cultural impact is already clear. It didn't just sell figurines; it reshaped consumer behavior through the blind-box format, a Japanese idea reimagined around a Chinese character IP. (The knockoffs—"Lafufus"—arrived quickly.) Cultural influence can move from China to the world—and this is likely to happen again.

Black Myth: Wukong: China's First Global Gaming Breakout

If Pop Mart shows how toys can travel, *Black Myth: Wukong* shows digital culture can, too.

Game Science—a mid-sized studio founded by veterans from Tencent Games—set out to reinterpret one of China's most familiar stories: *Journey to the West*, and its central figure, Monkey King, Sun Wukong. Long embedded in China's cultural imagination, the character was rendered for a global audience from the outset. Built for PlayStation and PC, it was designed to meet global expectations with top-tier production values in graphics, sound, world building, and animation. "The team wanted to introduce an international audience to a very Chinese story—with new and innovative design tools," says Shannon Cheung, founder and CEO of Averest Capital, one of the investors.

Early attention came in 2020, when Game Science released a thirteen-minute gameplay trailer on YouTube. It exploded, with over two million views on YouTube in the first twenty-four hours and more than ten million domestically. For many observers, it suggested the first time a Chinese studio could compete for global audiences at the level of established action-adventure franchises like Ubisoft's *Assassin's Creed* or FromSoftware's *Elden Ring*. "Wukong fought gods—giant titans—and the graphics were incredibly powerful and impactful," Shannon tells us.

In the month that the game launched, it drew over 2.4 million concurrent players—at the time the widest-reaching single-player title in video game distribution platform Steam's history. The game fulfilled the promise of that YouTube teaser: fluid, punishing combat, with a lush presentation that felt like stepping into a painting. Chinese mythology was deployed with confidence, and the game's re-imagined Monkey King felt ancient, uncanny, and intelligent—not campy.

Yicheng Qian, our colleague in Beijing, often plays the game with her husband and says experiencing it was "mind blowing." "The aesthetic of this game is just so beautiful—I haven't seen anything like it before," Yicheng tells us. "It reminded me of the first time I saw a Harry Potter movie when I was a young child."

The commercial results have been remarkable: ten million copies sold in the first three days; twenty million in a month, more than twenty-five million by early 2025. Despite a few controversies, including streamer guideline disputes and a delayed Xbox version, the game won major awards and was widely embraced. Many of the scenes drew from real-world places; for example, temples in Shanxi, Chengdu, and Xi'an were scanned into the game's engine with gigabytes of photorealistic data, videos, and photos. "The environments feel real because they literally *are* real," says Shannon. "We scanned original environments into the game—one of the game's first innovations."

Players responded to that authenticity. Tourists—both Chinese and foreign—began to seek out the real-life temples and mountains depicted in the game, prompting provincial government bureaus to begin recognizing the game's power as an engine: *Black Myth*'s soft power in action.

Chinese games had already been gaining traction internationally, but *Black Myth* is the first fully Chinese IP to break into global gamer culture at this level. "And there will be more companies trying to replicate its success," Shannon muses. "We'll have to see—it'll be very hard for another one to reach that type of international impact."

From Made in China to Created in China

This rise in commercial soft power shouldn't surprise anyone. Creation follows production, and after years of making everything from clothing and toys to mobile phones and home appliances, Chinese firms have developed strong design sensibilities, notes Derek Sulger, co-owner of luxury house Shanghai Tang. "After twenty years of building iPhones, why are people surprised that China can design a world-class smartphone or an EV or a high-end home appliance? If you've built a majority of what the world consumes, of course you get good at creating what people want."

As Chinese consumers become more sophisticated and demand more personalized goods, we predict the center of design gravity will begin to inch toward China, too. In digital retail, that transition is already visible: Temu and SHEIN are the world's two most downloaded retail apps, and TikTok, with 773 million downloads and counting, is slightly ahead of Instagram and far outpaces the rest of the field. We expect a similar pattern in autos: when a generation of global commuters from Australia to Israel to Norway drives its first EVs, they might be driving Chinese brands. In AI, Chinese large language models have emerged as an unexpected soft-power breakout—powerful, inexpensive, and often open-source. As US leaders pivot toward closed, premium systems, Chinese models have gained traction through utility: by early 2026, Chinese models accounted for over 60 percent of total token usage among the top ten models on the OpenRouter AI hub. With a vast domestic market, advanced supply chains, and powerful digital ecosystem, are Chinese firms poised to design as ambitiously as they manufacture?

To accelerate their global presence, some companies have acquired heritage where it already exists—Anta with FILA and Amer Sports; Geely with Volvo's Swedish legacy and London taxis; Shanghai investment group Fosun with Club Med's loyal customer base. "We can't create overnight the kind of brands that have honed their craft over centuries," says Daniel Tseung, founding partner of LionRock Capital, who acquired the British shoe brand Clarks and the Nordic outdoor performance company Haglöfs, both more than a century old. The Chinese companies likely to globalize fastest are those in categories where heritage matters less, such as consumer tech, EVs, mobile commerce, AI, and gaming.

As more Chinese brands prove they can connect with global audiences, a new generation will lean into storytelling, cultural relevance, and emotional resonance—amplified by China's strengths in AI and digital marketing. Not every brand will break out, and we expect many will thrive solely at home. We aren't holding our breath for Chinese music and movies to reach the impact of K-pop and K-drama anytime soon, but we do expect the number of global hits—some engineered, others unexpected—to begin to grow.

While the old label was "Made in China," we may soon start seeing more of "Created in China."

CHAPTER 11

Building AI the Chinese Way

In early 2025, a quiet evolution emerged out of Hangzhou—a city of thirteen million famed for its historic West Lake, misty mountains, and poets who depicted it as "Heaven on Earth." Yet it was here that a Chinese company—under-resourced by Silicon Valley standards—released a reasoning-focused large language model in January 2025 a few steps behind that era's ChatGPT 4-class models. DeepSeek had been trained, its parent company claimed, for only $6 million—pocket change compared to OpenAI or Google expenditures.

For a global industry convinced that US large language models (LLMs) were unassailable—built by companies with oceans of compute, elite talent, large capital infusions, and company valuations the size of small-nation GDP—DeepSeek upended assumptions. The Chinese model emerged at a time that China's AI sector seemed beleaguered by chip bans and a slowing economy and against a backdrop in which private sector investment into the US sector was twelve times China's and twenty-four times the UK's. Analysts found that DeepSeek's parent, High-Flyer, hadn't spent its way into contention; instead, it had been crafty: focusing on targeted domains, lean training, and aggressive energy efficiency. While critics whispered about secret Nvidia chips, covert ChatGPT usage, or hidden costs, the signal was clear: US companies wouldn't hold a monopoly on advanced LLMs.

This "DeepSeek moment" ignited a debate: "Are Chinese companies catching up in AI?" That framing misses the point. The AI stack is broad—spanning energy, infrastructure, chips, foundational research, and application deployment—and across that landscape the US and China possess different strengths. The real picture is that the world's two dominant AI markets aren't competing in the same race; they're running parallel ones shaped by different economic constraints, cost structures, and market demands—and that divergence will shape global AI over the next decade.

"If you look at the future of deep tech, it's clear that the US and China are like the two sides of [the traditional Chinese martial arts practice] tai chi, with its black-and-white yin and yang symbol—each with unique strengths, each pushing the other forward," says Soul Capital's Herry Han, "It's not just competition. It's a dynamic balance."

In the US, AI development follows a capital-intensive path: massive data centers, soaring talent costs, and billion-dollar frontier science bets. Well-funded US leaders will keep pushing toward artificial general intelligence (AGI) and increasingly sophisticated agentic systems designed to pursue goals through multi-step planning and self-directed action.

Chinese companies face a different competitive reality: relatively tighter capital, more limited access to high-end computing power, and a smaller domestic profit pool. Its companies respond by leaning hard into open-source, cost efficiency, fast application layer innovation, and global markets for monetization.

China's AI story isn't about catching up or winning the frontier model race but rather by industrializing the use of AI. Chinese AI firms are building an alternative ecosystem that's leaner by necessity, more open by design, and working to wire into the economy. This is prompting its adoption across start-ups, universities, and mid-market firms worldwide. As global industry leaders continue a preference for keeping their most capable models "closed-source"—which keeps source code proprietary or secret—Chinese models are diffusing through easy access and utility, quietly shaping global AI practices and creating a new, technical form of soft power.

One of China's Six Dragons

The Chinese spatial design firm Manycore Tech offers a close-up view of how China's AI dynamics play out inside a single company.

When Hang Chen and two friends at the University of Illinois Urbana-Champaign first started tinkering in the early 2010s with graphics processing units (GPUs) that excel at parallel computing, they explored gaming, film, and other applications before broadening out. "Almost no one realized they could be used for super-computing," Hang tells us. That hunch became the foundation for Manycore, a company built around rethinking how space is computed.

After returning to Hangzhou, the three engineers pursued the idea of moving multidimensional rendering entirely to the cloud. Instead of installing heavy software on powerful local machines, users could simply open a browser, sketch a layout, and watch it materialize in 3D. That vision became Kujiale in China and Coohom abroad, cheap to adopt and scalable, and now among the world's most widely used spatial design platforms.

Manycore's timing has been fortuitous. As China's home decoration and furniture industries went digital, its platform became their operating layer. Each object—every sofa, tile, or window frame—could be converted into production parameters sent directly to factories, enabling a whole-house customization boom that spawned companies big enough to go public.

E-commerce soon followed. Merchants needed product photos and videos: furniture staged in a Paris apartment, a kitchen gleaming under American Christmas lights. Manycore's rendering engine could generate thousands of virtual rooms and studios for merchants selling on Amazon, Shopify, and Shopee—a quiet global diffusion that emerges from practical AI tools.

Manycore's real advantage isn't software—it's data; after a decade of rendering, the company has accumulated a dataset of hundreds of millions of fully-labeled "3D scenes," or interiors with geometry, textures, lighting, and materials. These structured datasets help convert text or sketches into fully-realized 3D layouts, scenes, and videos, a foundation not just for design but also for research for robotics and AI agent developers. Tasks once requiring costly software can now be done by anyone.

The company relies on standard computing GPUs, which are sufficient for rendering, Hang says. And pragmatism, adaptation, and technical improvisation have kept the company scaling up even as competitors emerged. "Entrepreneurship is a 'nine-out-of-ten-ways-to-die process,'" he says. "If you're not stopped by one factor, you'll be stopped by another. Entrepreneurs operate in a highly dynamic state, constantly searching for a way."

The overseas business remains small, but Hang sees global expansion as essential for scale and monetization. Korea is now one of Manycore's fastest-growing markets. "It is easy for us given how GenAI (generative artificial intelligence) can help with localization," says Hang.

To understand how Manycore fits into China's broader AI landscape, we need to zoom out.

The Rise of China's AI Industry: A Natural Evolution

If you ask the Chinese when the country's "AI awakening" began, many will chuckle. AI? They've been living inside a digital and big-data society for years. Ping An Group digitized insurance claims and call centers a decade ago. McDonald's uses data analytics to run customer relationship programs. Alibaba and ByteDance rebuilt shopping and communication with recommendation engines, predictive logistics, and automated payments. Chinese firms learned early that surviving meant mastering data; by the time GenAI arrived, it didn't feel revolutionary—just the next logical step.

China's AI ecosystem has been expanding—pragmatic, open, and competitive—"letting a hundred flowers bloom," as the old metaphor goes. This was deliberate. Nearly a decade ago, Chinese leaders declared an ambition to lead the world in AI by 2030 and created scaffolding for research and commercialization; by 2021, the country was producing about one-third of global AI papers and drawing a fifth of global AI start-up investment.

When ChatGPT appeared in late 2022, Chinese entrepreneurs reacted instantly. As is often the case, the initial breakthrough came from Silicon Valley. In China, hundreds of teams piled into the space at once. Every major tech company—Baidu, Tencent, Alibaba, ByteDance— launched LLM programs, joined by an explosion of start-ups.

If this sounds chaotic, that's because it was. Entrepreneurs defaulted to the traditional digital playbook: copying, rapid itera- tion, free trials, and breakthrough or collapse. Out of the pileup, a few leaders emerged: Z.ai spun out of Tsinghua University labs; MiniMax and Moonshot AI raised hundreds of millions of RMB in their first year; Baichuan rivaled global models by mid-2024; iFlyTek's SparkDesk spread through classrooms and call centers.

By mid-2025, Chinese firms had released more than 1,500 large models—though most never gained traction—and built a full AI stack spanning chips, data centers, models, applications, and deployment. While a handful of players remain locked in a sprint at the model level, most have shifted into applications, building businesses on top of the models, from agents for design, commerce, logistics, medi- cal imaging, and education to a wide range of applied systems in between. The ecosystem now includes over five thousand AI firms, seventy-one unicorns, and more than three hundred listed companies generating roughly 70 percent of China's AI revenue. The intensity of experimentation has been unforgiving; several well-funded AI start-ups that launched competitive models in 2023–2024 failed to convert usage into revenue and shut down within eighteen months, their teams quietly absorbed into larger platforms or overseas labs.

Government support continues to accelerate in this strategic sector; several ministries have created plans to facilitate AI adoption and have even come up with key performance indicators (KPIs) to track progress. "AI is one of the ways the Chinese government intends to increase economic output—by making existing labor and capital more efficient," notes our former colleague Gordon Orr. The result is a nationwide race to build AI infrastructure, talent, and commercialization pathways.

US GPU export controls from 2022 introduced a new constraint, but instead of stalling progress, they forced further efficiencies and also compelled homegrown chip players such as Huawei to announce a road map to develop advanced chips. The government launched the third phase of its semiconductor fund in 2024—344 billion RMB (about $50 billion), the largest ever—to accelerate domestic chip capabilities.

The Chinese public is among the world's most optimistic about AI. Stanford University's 2025 AI Index Report found that 83 percent of Chinese respondents believe AI will improve their lives—more than double the share in the US or the Netherlands. That's helped bend adoption curves upward: platform companies like Alibaba, JD.com, and Pinduoduo have embedded AI end to end, while 80 percent of sellers on JD.com use AI-generated content tools. McDonald's China built "RGM Boss," a platform that codifies operations for two hundred thousand employees. It also offers a training agent: "Our restaurant managers can actually practice with an AI customer, so they feel more confident the next time they face a demanding guest," says Phyllis Cheung, McDonald's China CEO. "When you have the right infrastructure, a lot of new possibilities open up." According to the latest national policy plans, most state-owned enterprises have incorporated AI as an integral part of their upcoming strategy.

Chinese entrepreneurs are poised to lead in business-to-consumer (B2C) innovation, says GSR Ventures founder Allen Zhu, as competitive advantage shifts toward "AI+ scenarios"—such as gaming, education, and personalized content. "These are areas where Chinese teams excel," he says. He expects a major boom in AI applications with standout products emerging from platforms like TikTok alternative Kuaishou and RedNote.

According to a McKinsey survey of more than a thousand global companies, GenAI adoption across at least one business function in mainland China reached 84 percent in 2025, slightly ahead of the global average.

We'd like to highlight a few key dynamics that define China's AI sector.

China's AI Efficiency Machine: Low Costs and Constraints

An equivalent dollar in China goes farther—a fact that reframes the AI investment picture. While the US dominates total AI funding by a wide margin, Chinese firms often produce more output per unit of capital.

This efficiency begins with input costs. AI engineers earn about 400,000 RMB (about $57,000) per year, far below US salary norms. China also trains one-and-a-half to two times as many AI-relevant PhDs as the US, and many trained researchers are returning home, creating a large, affordable talent pipeline. Data centers benefit from cheaper electricity, discounted land, and aggressive local subsidies— reinforced by national policies that treat large-scale computing as strategic infrastructure. In some provinces, electricity costs are halved for facilities using chips.

These advantages are further sharpened by the constraints that characterize China's AI ecosystem. Foreign direct investment into China has fallen more than two-thirds since 2019, access to Western markets has tightened, high-end domestic GPUs lag behind imported ones, and regional grids are straining under data center loads. Moreover, China's business-to-business (B2B) market is characterized by a low willingness to pay for services; firms routinely build software tools in-house rather than buy them. The result is a domestic software market roughly one-quarter the size of the US's $237 billion industry, making it difficult for many AI start-ups to reach scale or charge premium prices. In addition, large corporation culture—especially state-owned enterprises—prizes headcount and incremental change, resists automation, and blunts AI's potential impact.

Angel investor Jun Xu captures a core monetization constraint: AI's total addressable market—the revenues available for a company's product or service—tracks the cost of white-collar labor. "And that pool is simply much larger in the US and other developed markets than in China because salaries are much higher," Jun says. "China's AI problem isn't chips or models or supply—it's demand. Demand is cheaper and smaller." These pressures have pushed Chinese firms toward efficiency and ingenuity.

Nvidia's Jensen Huang said in 2025 that restricting US chip sales to China would only accelerate China's domestic push. "Local companies are very, very talented and very determined," he said, "and the export control gave them the spirit, the energy, and the government support to accelerate their development." Altogether, the ecosystem has created a set of Chinese open-source LLMs operating along the "efficient frontier," delivering leaner architectures and stronger reasoning at modest compute levels. By late 2025, DeepSeek's parent announced that one million units of output could be had for about 3 RMB—that's about fifty cents and a twentieth the cost of ChatGPT at the time.

This combination of high efficiency, thin margins, and a smaller domestic monetization pool shapes how Chinese AI companies scale. Many are becoming what we call "skinny athletes"—lean, fast, and relentlessly efficient—which not only affects how they compete at home but also how and where they grow. For many, that increasingly means serving customers abroad, and the use of generative AI means that language, localization, and customer support are no longer decisive obstacles to global expansion.

"All AI start-ups have an international strategy from day one in China, and Southeast Asia is top of the list," says Cindy Chow, CEO of the Alibaba Hong Kong Entrepreneurs Fund, which recently launched a new fund dedicated to AI application start-ups. "In fact, many Southeast Asian conglomerates and financial institutions are keen to invest with us, as they believe that the region won't catch up in AI development on their own, and that accessing advancements from China is key to staying competitive."

The Chinese AI unicorn 01.AI shows what global expansion looks like when delivering value is the organizing principle. Founded by Kai-Fu Lee, an ex-Google China chief and president of leading tech

VC Sinovation Ventures, the company started as a pure LLM developer in 2023 but quickly shifted toward enterprise AI agents, or what they call "super-employees" designed for functions such as insurance brokering, procurement, and logistics optimization. "Monetization challenges force AI to accelerate faster," says Ning Ning, 01.AI's vice president of international business and AI consulting. "The future of enterprise AI is not about selling technology but rather making AI accountable for business outcomes."

In practice, delivering value means embedding "24/7 digital specialists" directly into enterprise operations. In one deployment with a Perth, Australia-based mining company, 01.AI's engineers positioned its AI agents as "teammates" alongside employees: a logistics scheduler to optimize rail and port traffic; a procurement agent that reads vendor emails and generates purchase orders; an operations planner to juggle trucks and crews. Each agent retrains itself as conditions change, says Ning, continuously improving its performance.

China's Open-Source Bet: Diffusion and Collaboration

China's open-source culture has become an accelerant. Hundreds of teams now openly release their model architectures and weights—the blueprints and parameters that a model acquires through training—creating a shared infrastructure anyone can examine, build upon, and improve.

Chinese AI firms are pragmatic, says Chloe Fang, a founder in the text-to-image/video space. They aim for AI that delivers value and often use open-source "as a global hook to attract global users," she says. "They start building brand equity and word of mouth—and then release better closed-source models later on." Chinese models now lead in several key generative media categories, accounting for five of the top ten image-to-video models globally and three of the top ten text-to-video and image-editing models.

This open-source approach aligns with national priorities emphasizing "open ecosystems," deep integration with all industries and sectors of the economy and society, and "increased global cooperation."

Chinese open-source LLMs—led by Qwen, MiniMax, and Deep-Seek—now account for one-third of global LLM usage, up from virtually nothing in late 2024.

Start-ups and companies from Silicon Valley to Africa and Southeast Asia now run Chinese models because they're accessible, transparent, and far cheaper to run than many US alternatives. "You can remove anything you want, add anything you need. That flexibility and openness actually gains trust," says Sinovation Ventures founder Kai-Fu Lee, an ex-Google China chief and an influential AI voice. He points out many US institutions, students, and researchers are using Chinese models "not because they're Chinese but because they're open."

Jian Wang, founder of Alibaba Cloud, argues that this moment in AI echoes the late 1990s: Netscape made its browser free and its code publicly available—an open-source "watershed" that helped catalyze the commercial internet. Today's AI parallel is similar, he says: foundational tools are now open and collectively improvable, so the constraint is no longer whether source code itself is accessible. Rather, the industry is shifting toward what Jian calls "'open resources,' especially model weights, data, and computing resources, which are indispensable to advancing this industry." As more of these resources become available, the more developers can skip over the massive costs of reproducing work already done by others—a key variable in accelerating the spread of AI, he says.

Involution (Surprise, Surprise)

Open-source cuts both ways: it not only quickens diffusion, but also brings on key features of involution: too many players chasing little to no margins.

We've seen multiple generations piling into China's AI race at once: industrialists in their sixties retrofitting legacy businesses and funding new start-ups; first-generation internet giants such as Alibaba and Tencent pivoting; second-generation digital natives such as ByteDance deploying AI across content and commerce; and a wave of AI-native start-ups alongside consumer electronics and even EV makers now calling themselves AI companies.

That deep bench matters. In the US, AI salaries remain sky high, but as we often say, California may attract the ecosystem's valedictorian and salutatorian while China might grab most of numbers three through one hundred. China's frenzied ecosystem can attempt many more low-cost prototypes, model variants, and application-driven experimentation.

Across China, large numbers of teams experiment simultaneously, open-sourcing models and chasing down practical applications. China's data-rich industries and dense digital infrastructure allow AI agents to plug into WeChat mini-apps, enterprise systems, and factory IoT networks with little friction. As one Shenzhen entrepreneur puts it, "We don't call them agents. We call them workers who don't need to eat or sleep."

AI literacy among young entrepreneurs is ubiquitous, fueling a competition that's ultimately Chinese versus Chinese. "Four generations of Chinese entrepreneurs are now thinking about AI, ten times as many engineers as in the West, working twice the hours—you can imagine the future," says Yibing Wu, China CEO of investment company Temasek.

We expect China's AI trajectory will unfold similarly to earlier digital revolutions in e-commerce, fintech, and mobile internet: application first, fiercely competitive with periods of involution, and propelled by rapid iteration rather than orderly planning.

Unidentical Twins: Partners and Rivals

Finally, while global commentary often frames US-China AI as a Sputnik-style race, this isn't a winner-take-all contest. The American approach remains the global benchmark for frontier model ambition, built on hyper-scale cloud computing, advanced semiconductors, enterprise software depth, and foundation models built on billion-dollar training runs. Chinese companies aren't trying to replicate that playbook; they couldn't afford to. Instead, political friction and firewalls are driving them to optimize for a different endgame, resulting in two parallel systems evolving side by side rather than together.

From inside the Chinese ecosystem, the dynamic feels even less like a geopolitical race. "Chinese companies aren't trying to beat the US—they're trying to outcompete each other and survive in a global market that's skeptical of them," says Hang of Manycore. "We didn't even call ourselves an AI company when we started—it wasn't in fashion yet."

If people like a space metaphor, a better one is two programs exploring different planets. They share some tools, occasionally glance sideways to check pacing and possibility, but operate in atmospheres shaped by different economics, regulatory pressures, markets, and industrial bases. The "competition" will feel fierce especially in model uptake, but their trajectories aren't directly comparable. At the same time, they're interdependent: "Each side pushes the other forward faster than it could move alone—unidentical twins with different strengths and headed for complementary futures," says Jason Chiu, co-founder of the spatial intelligence start-up Collectiv.

Despite geopolitical tensions, the US and Chinese AI ecosystem remains deeply intertwined. Nearly half of the world's AI researchers earned their undergraduate degrees in China, and many built their careers in US labs and companies before returning or founding new ventures. The lineage is braided: Kai-Fu Lee spent his formative years at Apple, Microsoft, and Google; Baidu founder Robin Li worked at Infoseek; ByteDance's Yiming Zhang had a stint at Microsoft. As Tsinghua University professor Yi Wu told a thousand-plus attendees and millions more watching online at a Shanghai AI conference, "I was mainly influenced by two places: Berkeley, where I did my PhD, and OpenAI . . . when the team was only a few dozen people."

That shared intellectual DNA shows up in daily practice. We've met founders in Shenzhen training models with open-source code from California. We know of start-ups in Boston fine-tuning on Chinese models. Every week, foreign groups arrive in Shenzhen and Hangzhou for immersion tours. Ideas, code, and talent continue to cross borders. In late 2025, Meta underscored that reality by announcing plans to acquire the Chinese-founded start-up Manus for more than $2 billion as part of its push into advanced AI agents. The Manus deal distilled the entire cross-border AI reality into a single transaction: Chinese entrepreneurs building the application layer of AI; funding from both Chinese and US venture capital; international monetization abroad; re-incorporation in Singapore to tap global customers; and an eventual exit to a US tech giant. And geopolitics shaped the transaction at every stage: the US Treasury reviewed the venture capital firm Benchmark's role, while Chinese regulators questioned Manus's overseas move and the loss of talent and technology to a foreign company. Meanwhile, some customers balked at Meta's data-privacy record. Though the deal closed in January 2026, uncertainty hangs overhead as regulatory bodies examine whether the acquisition violates export or national security rules.

Geopolitics draws borders more easily around companies than around ideas. For years, language was a barrier for Chinese companies expanding into overseas markets. That dynamic may be quietly changing. Joe Tsai, chairman of Alibaba, recounts seeing a social media post from a Meta employee that much of the informal idea exchange on his AI team now happens in Chinese—a language that employee didn't understand. "This is the first time . . . knowing Chinese has become an advantage in the AI world—that's very, very interesting," says Joe.

Channeled well, this intellectual cross-pollination could create a more resilient global ecosystem. As Nobel laureate Richard Sutton posited in Shanghai, centralized control is rooted in fear—an "us versus them" mindset. "Regarding the political aspects of AI, my conclusion is: the development of AI and the progress of human society can and should stem from decentralized cooperation."

It's an exciting dynamic, says Soul Capital's Herry, who argues that China's participation in the ecosystem "opens the door wider." "Without AI we're in kindergarten, and with AI we gain doctorate-level understanding. Previously only the US could provide it as a premium service, reaching a small percentage of humanity, and now the door's open wider with both providing this new electricity of AI."

We should expect more globally relevant AI companies to emerge from China, offering the global ecosystem a genuine alternative: more open-source models, lower training and inference costs, and an increasingly self-sufficient tech stack from hardware to tooling to LLMs.

The economic upside is substantial. McKinsey estimates AI could add $600 billion to China's GDP by 2030, while Goldman Sachs projects generative AI will lift annual growth by 0.2 to 0.3 percentage points by 2030—two to three times earlier estimates—driven by transport, autos, logistics, manufacturing, enterprise software, and healthcare.

Broadening out, China's AI trajectory fits a familiar historical pattern. Chinese firms entered the PC era nearly a decade behind Silicon Valley; by the internet era the gap had narrowed to a few years. With AI, the lag is now measured in months. As in every major industrial or technological wave, it will be competitive intensity—rather than outright dominance by either side—that will drive progress.

China will need that momentum. A shrinking population, low productivity relative to OECD standards, and swaths of low-margin, low-digitization industries raise the stakes for the country. That said, the barriers to AI adoption look the same everywhere. Whether in Hangzhou, Houston, or Hamburg, companies struggle to turn AI enthusiasm into real business impact—we often say that AI is everywhere except the bottom line.

The most significant barriers to adoption aren't technical but rather organizational: leadership, incentives, and re-designed workflow. Our colleagues see them all over the world, in developed and developing markets; we see them daily in China. Corporate structures anywhere can feel slow, hierarchical, and allergic to risk. And adoption, how quickly societies absorb and normalize a technology, is what drives impact. Frankly, in that context, "good enough" computing power matters more than absolute best. Ultimately, the biggest factor in AI-driven productivity won't be who taps the better models but which CEOs are willing to reinvent how their organizations operate. "At the end of the day, you don't keep score by looking at how good these large language models are. The score is being kept by the adoption rate," says Joe of Alibaba.

For now, AI's financial impact inside companies remains modest, even as its broader economic impact in China is likely to be enormous. As Unitree Robotics CEO Xingxing Wang—whose company is known for robot dogs and agile humanoids—humbly puts it, the industry is still in a "desert stage. Just a few blades of grass sprouting. The eve of large-scale explosive growth hasn't arrived yet."

We expect the next wave of momentum to emerge at the application layer, with gains to society realized only as organizations and individuals adapt how they work. The potential of AI is universal; the challenge of capturing it remains distinctly human.

CHAPTER 12

The Robots of Tomorrow

When Chunguang Gu tells the origin story of his robot company, Galaxis Technology, he sketches a "smile curve" in the air with his pointer finger: Nobel laureates on one side, scrappy builders on the other. "Those were the choices I faced," Gu jokes. "Become an academic heavyweight or try to create tangible value for society."

He chose the scrappy end. After completing his mechanical engineering PhD at MIT, he returned home to a China in 1999 that was full of industrial promise but short on infrastructure and technology. His story isn't just about a man building robots; it foreshadows an industry tailor-made for Chinese companies to flourish.

Convinced China would close its industrialization gap, Chunguang joined McKinsey in Shanghai to study business transformation and later moved to drug distributor Jiuzhoutong Pharmaceutical. There he encountered logistics chaos firsthand: costly manual labor, imported automation ill-suited to "China speed," systems designed for another era.

He built a five-hundred-person engineering team to design something better. "I was right at the intersection of the problem and the solution," he tells us. By 2009 he'd launched an internal R&D effort— backed by Tsinghua University alumni and corporate partners—that became the seed for Galaxis Technology. "There wasn't a single robot product that could manage tens of thousands, hundreds of thousands of boxes," he recalls.

By 2014, an exploding e-commerce sector made that need impossible to ignore. Logistics no longer moved in pallets but in boxes, and millions of them. German and Japanese mini-load systems couldn't keep pace with about 360 million Chinese consumers demanding delivery *now*. At JD.com, monthly deliveries jumped from 55 million in 2014 to 133 million two years later and eventually to almost 270 million in their last reported year in 2019. Yes, per *month*.

Local suppliers gave Chunguang fast access to motors and sensors, and rapid iteration with warehouse partners produced his breakthrough: a multi-directional shuttle robot that could move forward, sideways, and up and down racking systems. Part motorized dolly, part minimalist go-kart, it could move goods at two thousand units per hour—four times legacy systems—and it expanded warehouse capacity by 40 percent because it reached above human height. Another crucial feature was the technology's adaptability to changing demand: light or irregular workloads might require only a single robot, while higher or surging volumes could be handled by scaling up to a coordinated fleet of robots. Meanwhile, traditional German and Japanese systems struggled outside the "steady middle" of, say, five hundred boxes per hour.

When Galaxis robots launched in 2015, the marketplace was already fiercely competitive. Many start-ups in these strategic areas enjoyed speedy local government approvals and could launch with 1 to 2 million RMB (about $143,000 to $286,000). Competition forced rapid innovation. "Hard for us, but good for capability," Chunguang says. By the time Galaxis began selling overseas, its systems had been battled-tested in China's demanding marketplace.

Industrial robots aren't new—they've been used since the 1950s, and about 3.5 million units operate globally with 550,000 more deployed annually—but the emerging sector is finally poised for explosive deployment. Demand for automation is rising, robot hardware keeps getting cheaper, labor shortages are increasing, and new AI capabilities allow robots to learn tasks and adapt to environments that weren't possible before. China's landscape is crowded with firms racing to seize the opportunity.

Robotics sit squarely in China's sweet spot of strengths—and we mean the term "robot" broadly: not just industrial arms, shuttles, and warehouse automation, but the growing class of machines that sense, decide, and act in the physical world, from unmanned drones and vehicles to service robots in restaurants, hospitals, and homes. These are the physical embodiments of artificial intelligence. If top US companies lead in the foundational AI frontier, in the "embodied AI" world cup—where intelligence lives inside machines—Chinese companies have the edge in cost, scale, hardware supply chains, and deployment speed. And most of the factories that might deploy their products are right outside their doors.

The country has more than 450,000 "smart robots" enterprises—triple the number just four years ago—and accounts for roughly three-quarters of global production. The biggest industrial robot makers remain the global incumbents—ABB Robotics of Switzerland/Sweden and Japan's Epson and FANUC. But the center of gravity for the next generation of robots is shifting to China.

Most initiatives start with a use case in a sector the developers know well. From there, the broader ecosystem lifts them: booming demand, real-world testing grounds, supportive local governments, abundant engineers, fast prototyping, cheap AI, and foreign systems that remain world-class but costly and rigid. The result is a swarm of founders attacking every niche—heavy loads, tight spaces, high-speed throughput, food handling, pharmaceutical testing, e-commerce fulfillment, and more. "Of course, there's involution in robotics," says Chunguang, laughing. "Everyone's sprinting."

China is now, by far, the world's largest end market for robots, installing more than half of all industrial robots globally with demand continuing to accelerate at home and abroad. The global market, valued at roughly $50 billion in 2024, is projected to double by the end of the decade.

Increasingly, Chinese firms are designing and deploying robots not only for domestic use but for export markets—creating an ecosystem that both produces and absorbs automation at a large scale. As automation moves beyond cutting-edge factories and into ordinary industries, robots stop being productivity tools and start replacing labor outright, driven by rising costs and a shrinking workforce. In that world, automation isn't just a nice-to-have; it becomes core infrastructure. This scale may be both China's competitive advantage as well as a prerequisite for future growth.

An Early Glimpse of China's Sweet Spot

Nick caught an early hint of China's future robotics trajectory a decade ago in a Beijing electronics shop. On a shelf sat one of Xiaomi's first robot vacuums—a smooth white puck with an orange-rimmed laser sensor. At the time, iRobot dominated Western living rooms, but its Roombas were pricey, battery-hungry, and notorious for getting stuck under furniture. Xiaomi's version offered longer battery life, smarter navigation, and a friendly price tag—an early sign of how Chinese companies would compete: rapid cycles of improvement paired with cost discipline.

Nick bought a half dozen Mi Robots and carried them abroad. One landed in Switzerland, where his sister-in-law unboxed it. The device whirred to life, introduced itself in Mandarin, and began vacuuming the living room. Unfortunately, Nick's sister-in-law is fluent in Swiss German, High German, French, Italian, and English, while the Mi Robot could only make pronouncements in Mandarin. "She couldn't actually understand what it was saying," Nick recalls, "but she was determined to make it part of the family."

Her 2016 Mi wasn't perfect: once it got caught outside in the rain, but it dried itself out and was diligently working again the next day. Even then, while the US robot vacuum remained a luxury curiosity, the Chinese counterparts were smaller, fully functional, ubiquitous, and offered a price point most people could afford.

This story foreshadows what would come: Chinese companies using engineering efficiency to leapfrog incumbents before the rest of the world noticed. Xiaomi would soon apply its electronics expertise to phones, appliances, and eventually vehicles—essentially a four-wheeled robot. Today, Chinese home robots don't just clean; they pick up socks, climb stairs, and pluck tissues out of corners. What began as a glimpse of promise has grown into a vibrant, hypercompetitive robotics ecosystem with use cases across consumer, industrial, logistics, and healthcare.

Ten years ago, China's automation systems were built almost entirely on foreign components—ABB and FANUC robots powered by German controllers and Japanese cameras, recalls Cedric Leleu, a McKinsey partner who runs the digital manufacturing transformation practice. Today the landscape has flipped, he says, with Chinese suppliers now accounting for half of the world's top twenty automation-component makers, with three ranking in the top five. "These local players now offer fully integrated systems—robots, controls, and vision—that are reliable, high-performance, and dramatically cheaper."

China's robotics edge isn't just one advantage but the interplay of many.

The Supply Chain Next Door

To understand China's robotics advantage, you might start with Huaqiangbei Road in the southern city of Shenzhen. Often called "China's electronics street" or "the Silicon Valley of hardware," it's less a Sand Hill Road than a multi-block labyrinth of towers and alleys housing the world's largest electronics market. Thousands of tiny stalls sell everything a robot maker might need: actuators, torque sensors, reducers, control boards, casings, circuit boards, computer numerical control (CNC) machined parts.

Huaqiangbei is the kind of place where an engineer can walk in with an idea and walk out with the components—and even a consultant's expertise—to turn it into a working machine. Founders describe riding escalators through seven-story buildings—sometimes with a couple of engineering classmates—moving among more than three thousand vendors, negotiating part by part. The talks might soon shift to WeChat; regardless, custom pieces can be fabricated in hours, not weeks, at a fraction of Western prices.

One shop might harvest chips from discarded phones and laptops and sell them by the gram. Another offers server hardware at half of branded server prices and can assemble a team to build a robot prototype in under two weeks. Yet another can customize humanoids, teaching them to tap-dance or speak German. With a few hundred dollars, vendors can assemble a kid-sized robot prototype in a matter of days.

This ecosystem has launched dozens of hardware champions. RoboSense, headquartered nearby, became the world's largest lidar maker in under a decade. Founder Chunxin Qiu started with 800,000 RMB (about $114,000), an amount that in Silicon Valley might cover an office's annual coffee budget, he jokes. "Here a few hundred RMB gets me a hand-polished prototype in a day," he says.

In Huaqiangbei, Chunxin learned by doing. "I'd explain the torque requirements, and the seller would explain the parameters. I learned while sourcing from all the vendors—it's very convenient." For computer numerical control (CNC) parts, he'd revise drawings with a craftsman for "a few dozen RMB" ($5 to $6), and "wait downstairs" for the finished pieces. If they were complicated? He'd need to come back after lunch. "In this way, we could iterate through several generations in two to three months," Chunxin says.

This ecosystem allows founders to stay lean, as suppliers become extensions of the team. "The chain is so complete that two or three people can start a business," Chunxin says. "You don't need to master everything—you can outsource most tasks." Small factories can handle machining, printed circuit boards, and even final assembly, and a founder can order runs of ten or a hundred units—ideal for rapid demo and proof-of-concept validation.

When RoboSense scaled up, this supply chain expanded with it, partnering with companies that can mobilize any fraction of their technicians for cyclical production.

The World's Toughest "Robot Gym"

The same conditions that make this ecosystem so accessible have also pushed the system toward involution. Walk into any Chinese tech expo, and something is always whirring, blinking, staggering, or singing. Companies are building machines to teach children, deliver food, play music, patrol warehouses, clean kitchens, fold laundry; if humans do it, someone in China's robotics ecosystem is trying to automate it.

This isn't just start-ups; also crowding in are the mobility divisions of internet giants, logistics companies, and even EV makers. "The future world of mobility won't just be vehicles; it will be multiple mobility solutions," says Brian Gu, vice chairman and president of EV maker XPENG. "We're excited about the robotics space—especially humanoid robotics—where applications could be five times bigger than the automotive space." XPENG's leaders describe autonomous driving as "robotics on wheels"—perception, motion, decision—and recently unveiled a humanoid robot that can strut a fashion catwalk.

This sense of piling in is everywhere. "Is there excess competition? Maybe," one founder says, shrugging. "If you look at the start-ups and the robotics Olympics—there's certainly a lot of immature companies—and it's hard to see them all succeeding."

Capital isn't slowing down, either. Venture funding for general-purpose robotics globally has surged, tracking the bet that as AI improves, so will the robots built around the models. China has layered on top a $138 billion national innovation fund over the next twenty years for robotics and embodied AI. Private giants—from SF Express to BYD—are investing aggressively in their own robotics teams.

When Joe spoke at a Shanghai robotics and GenAI conference in winter 2025, the real action wasn't in the lecture halls—it was in the robotics exhibition pavilion. Bright, airy, and smelling faintly of warm plastic, the hall was packed with robots in various states of movement: some moving, some frozen. Start-ups squeezed in next to veterans like Unitree Robotics, whose robot dogs and humanoids are already in global university labs.

The scenes bordered on comical. A "dancing cowboy" wearing a red bandanna and blue vest stumbled through a hip-hop routine, then walked itself back to its recharging rack. A handler kept an orange rope looped around "John Wayne" the entire time, not trusting him to stay upright. Nearby, a gray robot head with lifelike eyes sat mute; "Sing," then "Sing NOW" produced nothing. A tall white humanoid raised its arms in surrender, again and again, but missed every third command. A motorcycle-sized velociraptor lurched forward, speakers along its spine booming synthetic roars—impressive if slightly terrifying. What's its use case? No one knew, though a sales rep gamely suggested "tourism . . . maybe movie sets." Teams studied competitors' ideas and coaxed passersby into offering feedback. To Western or Japanese eyes, it looks chaotic. To Chinese founders, this is how you learn: ship half-working robots, collect data, benchmark rivals, and iterate.

Talent keeps the flywheel spinning. China's robot builders range from scrappy hardware tinkerers to elite software engineers—many grew up fixing scooters or building drones in college and now prototype robots in forty-eight-hour sprints. As we've mentioned before, China's millions of STEM graduates create an engineering base larger than that of any other country, alongside the electricians, robot technicians, and senior experts who design core systems. "Layer on top the energy and adaptability of young engineers—willing to test, fail, and test again," says Chunguang of Galaxis Technology, "and you get an ecosystem built for massive acceleration."

Galaxis's early shuttle robots had no competitors, but rivals soon crowded in, forcing Chunguang to "launch faster, refine more, and cut costs." He likens China's robotics ecosystem to "rich soil that's given birth to a pack of wolves—small, fast, and combat-effective, with strong survival abilities." By contrast, robotics players in the US and Europe are more consolidated, with "a few large elephants."

The wolf-pack model has limits. Chinese firms file more robotics patents than any other country, but that's a metric for capacity, not quality. Many fundamental breakthroughs—tactile sensing, dexterous manipulation—still emerge from US, Japanese, or European labs. Of 450,000 registered "smart robot" enterprises, only a few thousand actually manufacture robots.

Moreover, the sheer proliferation of firms makes it difficult for Chinese robotics companies to scale. As Chunguang puts it, "Every robotics firm is chasing a very specific use case. For that context, they specialize and tailor-make the robot that is a perfect fit for purpose. They price aggressively, survive on thin margins, and in doing so make it hard for others to enter. That, in turn, forces competitors to seek out ever more niche applications." For all the dynamism in the sector, this fragmentation has real limits. Among the top ten robotics companies by revenue, none is Chinese—with the exception of Germany's KUKA, whose owner is the Chinese multinational Midea Group.

From Cheap Intelligence to the Embodied AI Advantage

As margins compress and intelligence becomes cheap and interchangeable, "we have the best model—pay us accordingly" becomes harder to defend. Thus, whatever durable payoff exists is more likely to shift into the hardware layer—where AI meets the physical world.

Already most Chinese firms have abandoned model development to focus on applications, echoing the internet browser era, when HTML commoditized and value migrated upward to apps and services.

Similarly, we expect the frontier to move beyond software and into "embodied AI"—robots, drones, agentic devices, smart sensors, and vehicles that use intelligence to act in the physical world.

This is where China's structural strengths matter most. The country produces roughly three-quarters of the world's lithium-ion batteries, and it accounts for roughly 90 percent of global rare-earth magnet production—including the neodymium magnets widely used in EV motors—components that underpin embodied AI by powering mobility and enabling precise, high-torque motion. China also maintains scale advantages in power electronics, embedded compute, and industrial automation.

"If intelligence is effectively free," says tech entrepreneur Jason Chiu, "the real competition shifts toward manufacturing excellence at scale—industrial robots on factory floors, machines that understand homes, drones that navigate dense cities, vehicles that coordinate with infrastructure. In that world, the embodied system becomes the differentiator." Intelligence alone is inert, say technology analysts such as Packy McCormick; value is created when it's paired with energy, infrastructure, and the ability to act in the physical world.

Ever-cheaper models are a gift to embodied AI entrepreneurs, who can plug into whichever foundation model best fits their needs. But for model providers, the economics turn harsh: overhead erodes margins faster than small capability gains can restore them.

Humanoids: Ambition Meets Physics

If China's robotics ambitions and constraints can be captured in one product, it might be humanoids: glamorous, policy-favored, technically challenging, and financially brutal. Hollywood has long imagined humanoids: C-3PO bumbling in gold, the Terminator stalking in leather, *Ex Machina*'s Ava gazing with eerie calm. People have always been obsessed with the human form, which has steered roboticists toward a humanoid look that unfortunately imposes constraints, making it the least effective form of robot. We haven't met a Chinese robot entrepreneur who hasn't thought about attempting one.

Humanoids promise versatility; shaped like us, they can, in theory, use our tools, fit through our doors, and operate in our world without costly re-designs of our physical environment. In an aging China facing mounting labor shortages, the appeal is obvious—machines that can lift patients in a nursing home or handle hazardous chemicals without needing lunch, sleep, or a salary. Policymakers tout humanoids as the next "disruptive product" after computers, smartphones, and new-energy vehicles, and investors are piling into the next sector with policy support, and global potential.

This fascination has hardened into an industry, but in 2012, creating one meant inventing the future with primitive technology.

UBTech Robotics founder Jian Zhou's earliest prototypes were palm-sized toys: "We created them at such an early stage that the Wright brothers had better technology when they started on planes. It was like wanting to make a car but starting with a bicycle." He scavenged parts in Shenzhen's electronics marketplace and waited for advances in flexible joints, sensors, and control software that would make possible stable movement.

At UBTech's Shenzhen headquarters, videos loop of robots marching up stairs, hiking uneven ground, swapping their own batteries, and working on Geely's assembly lines. The company now has more than two thousand employees, about half of them engineers, and its Tiangong robot won the world's first humanoid marathon—of course, this originated in China—its metallic stride going viral.

Costs are falling fast. Industry data show humanoid bill-of-materials costs falling about 20 percent annually between 2022 and 2024. With more than two hundred Chinese companies attempting humanoids, pricing pressure is fierce: a UBTech model once priced at $100,000 will sell for under $50,000; Unitree pushed prices even lower in 2025 with a $6,000 humanoid, down from $16,000 a year earlier, marketing it as a general-purpose platform for developers, researchers, and enthusiasts.

Still, humanoids carry deep structural disadvantages. Lots of motors and sensors make them power-hungry, limiting industrial runtime. How useful are legs if robots must stay plugged in? Wheels are simpler and stabler, and current wheeled versions already have the ability to climb stairs. Meanwhile, humanoid hands still struggle with the finger-bending range of motion and tactile sensing to reliably grip things.

Height adds risk: to see like humans, they must be tall, meaning heavy actuators that raise the center of gravity. In eldercare or childcare, a falling seventy-kilogram (155-pound) machine is no benign helper. Yet designing for safety limits strength. "They end up being able to lift what a twelve-year-old can," says Ani Kelkar, McKinsey Boston-based partner and advanced industries practice leader. Speed is another constraint: parkour they can do, but when it comes to "doing a useful task like picking up a screw, humanoids remain painfully slow—it's like watching paint dry," Ani says.

Economically, the trade-offs are stark: add power, speed, and dexterity, and costs rise. Dial them back, and usefulness suffers: "You might conclude you didn't need a humanoid—you just needed a dexterous arm on a wheeled platform," Ani says. It's not a surprise that humanoid and service robot firms routinely post the sector's worst losses, but it's early days, explains Ani. "We hope to see much more technical progress—only then will the hype be realized."

Humanoids struggle—as do most robots. Many manufacturing sectors, especially consumer electronics, still rely on human labor because product variation is high. Current robots lack the mechanical flexibility and adaptive control to switch from, say, assembling a MacBook Air and then a MacBook Pro without prohibitive changes, says Michael Chang, a McKinsey partner in the AI practice. "We're getting closer, but it's still three to four years away, and that timeline keeps shrinking. The hardest part is the mechanics. Software will move faster, because better foundation models make it easier to teach robots new assembly processes."

For most things, robots aren't better and cheaper than humans—yet.

China's Data Flywheel and Voracious Demand

China's robotics advantage is reinforced by a powerful data flywheel, created by pairing hardware with a vast factory base and deep engineering talent. Unlike large language models, robots can't be trained on text alone. They learn by entering the real world—failing, adjusting, improving, and trying again—reinforced by virtual simulation, human-guided control, and task demonstrations.

Companies that can tap into China's ecosystems can run this loop faster, cheaper, and at far greater scale than anywhere else. That uptake only creates more data, Ani explains. "The cheaper you are at the beginning, the earlier the foot in the door with deployment, the more data you collect, the better your models become," he says. "You're not going to get real-world data if your hardware costs $250,000."

In China, this cycle is turbocharged by proximity. Factories, logistics, and warehouses sit just outside roboticists' doors. Deployments remain small-scale, but they're growing in number, and they force technological leaps, says Shiquan Wang, co-founder and CEO of adaptive industrial robot company Flexiv Robotics, which made an early bet on using "force control"—programming robots to regulate and adapt during interactions with the world around them—over pre-planning rigid trajectories. "When we put our products in the field, we need engineers to use it, and partners to develop our applications—and we get a lot of insights and details," Shiquan tells us. Flexiv's office locations are strategic: R&D teams at its US headquarters carry out early-stage research, while engineers in Shanghai, Beijing, and Shenzhen work alongside manufacturing clients, says Shiquan. "Thousands of trivial things will make the product really different."

There are plenty of these fast-loop iterations available; in short, Chinese manufacturers, squeezed by labor shortages and fierce competition that push them to find cost efficiencies, are gobbling up robots. For twelve consecutive years, the country has been the world's largest industrial robot market, installing roughly 295,000 units in 2024—and the pace of installation growth is accelerating across China while rates in Europe and the Americas decline. Most new robots roll straight onto Chinese factory floors in the top five hungriest sectors for automation: automotive, electronics, metals and machinery, plastics, and chemicals and food.

More than two million robots already work the lines, and some factories are nearly fully automated, such as those that make power batteries—pushing the country's robot density past that of Germany, the longtime leader in industrial automation. Large logistics facilities increasingly operate with minimal human presence, and "dark warehouses" are no longer edge cases. If progress continues, the general-purpose robotics market could reach a value of $370 billion by 2040, with China accounting for about half.

Why is this demand snowballing so quickly? Scale. China generates one-third of the world's manufacturing economic value; more production means more potential places to deploy robots. At the same time, demographic change is turning robotics from novelty to necessity. Policy directives explicitly link automation to eldercare, healthcare, and agricultural modernization, among others, as China's workforce shrinks and its population ages. More than 310 million Chinese are over age sixty. A decade ago, a 30 percent pay bump might attract workers to hazardous jobs such as industrial glue application involving formaldehyde, says UBTech's CFO, Ju Zhang. "Now even a 300 percent increase won't attract workers, and young people might even sue the company. Robots aren't here to be more efficient than humans—they're here to fill labor gaps," says Ju. "Companies can't find workers."

Those labor gaps are already reshaping service and mobility sectors as well: coffee chains with no baristas; ride-hailing platforms deploying driverless robo-taxis; residential towers where robots bring packages from lobbies to apartment doors; hospitals where robots handle routine transport and sanitation; ports where cranes load ships with minimal human crews; and public spaces maintained by machines working through the night.

China's market structure accelerates uptake: compared with counterparts in Germany or the US, Chinese firms don't have to face unions or regulatory challenges; in fact, the government is actively encouraging the deployment of AI and robots. Chinese leaders are "much more open to innovation and new technology," says Cedric, who leads McKinsey's digital transformation services practice. "Sometimes ambition drives them to build fully automated factories, even if it's not justified financially short term. The vision is to be the most advanced."

*　　　*　　　*

China is poised to produce the next generation of global robotics leaders: its robotics ecosystem sits at the intersection of what Chinese companies do well. Whether and when the market reaches hundreds of billions or a trillion dollars is uncertain, but what's clear is that Chinese robots are going global.

That doesn't mean Chinese players will lead in every dimension. Some advanced components—especially sensors and semiconductors—come from German and Japanese champions, and the most advanced humanoid and mobility research remains concentrated in US labs such as Boston Dynamics, Tesla, Agility, and Figure. Further industry consolidation is also required for Chinese players to gain scale and financial muscle. This may take years. Further, Chinese robots might at some point face growing geopolitical and security headwinds—export controls, trust concerns in sensitive sectors, and the emergence of two partially split tech ecosystems built on different fundamentals—that limit how widely they can be adopted globally.

Yet for now, the Chinese industrial environment already contains most of the world's real end-use cases for robotics: factories, warehouses, logistics hubs, ports, and production lines where machines can be deployed at scale, instrumented continuously, and improved through repetition. These environments generate data, learning cycles, and economic payoff, allowing Chinese robotics firms to lower costs quickly and accelerate deployment. In practice, embedding AI inside structured production lines has proven far easier than applying it to white-collar work, where tasks are diffuse and outcomes harder to measure. In this domain, global companies risk playing catch-up.

For companies trying to understand our robotic future, there's no substitute for engaging with China's robotics cluster—in which its companies are increasingly eager to export, partner, and scale globally. In early 2026 in Las Vegas at CES, the world's largest and most influential technology trade show, about a thousand Chinese robot, drone, and consumer electronics players sought partners, customers, and routes to global scale. In panel discussions, we observed a growing consensus that the trajectory of "physical AI" will hinge less on technical possibility and more on economics. "In a match between the Chinese wolves and Western elephants, what will the future be like?" says Chunguang of Galaxis Technology—which, about a decade after launching its first shuttle robots, listed on the Hong Kong Stock Exchange in March 2026.

CHAPTER 13

The Chinese Enterprises Going Global

One winter in St. Moritz, Nick showed up in a Descente jacket—the sleek Japanese brand that outfits the Swiss national ski team and whose China joint venture is majority owned by the Chinese company Anta. He'd bought the jacket in China, complete with the embroidered Swiss team logos. In the café at the base, strangers assumed he skied for Switzerland and asked where he trained. "I love Anta," Nick recalls with a laugh, "but then they saw me ski and realized I certainly wasn't a member of the national team."

A mountain anecdote is fitting for a company that climbed from China's factory floor to the global summit of sportswear in just two decades. Anta exemplifies China's next era of globalization as Chinese companies move beyond exporting goods to operating globally—through acquisitions, partnerships, and global-first models—while also learning to govern, build legitimacy, and compete under unfamiliar rules and frictions.

Today Anta is $30 billion by market cap. In 1991, it was an ambitious shoe workshop in Jinjiang, Fujian province—one among hundreds of original equipment manufacturers (OEMs) competing on cost, volume, and reliability. Playing the classic "factory for the world" role, the workshop supplied others while building scale and process know-how. Then came the leap: in 1999, founder Shizhong Ding launched the Anta brand, signed Olympic table tennis champion Linghui Kong, and poured profits into a marketing blitz around the 2000 Sydney Games. Anta quickly became China's value alternative to Nike and adidas.

Over the next twenty years, Anta assembled a multi-brand empire, locking down China rights for FILA, Descente, and Kolon Sport. In 2019, it pulled off a landmark move by becoming majority shareholder of Finland's Amer Sports conglomerate; suddenly, Anta owned Arc'teryx, Salomon, Wilson, and more. "It was a marriage of brand heritage and product excellence, accelerated by Anta's execution capabilities in China," says Frank Tang, co-founder of Fountain-Vest, the investor partner of Anta in Amer Sports.

Anta now runs R&D centers on three continents, sponsors NBA stars and international athletes, and includes in its retail base more than thirteen thousand stores. It's now the third largest sportswear company by market cap—ten times Puma or Under Armour—and, combined with Amer, surpasses adidas. Anta's 2024 listing of Amer Sports on the New York Stock Exchange marked the first US IPO of a Chinese consumer company of its scale.

Anta's global reach has come with its share of comic moments. When Dominic Barton was invited to open Arc'teryx's Shanghai flagship in 2020, he was baffled: Why would the Canadian ambassador to China open a store for a Chinese company? Dominic sought out the PR manager to inquire. "There was fifteen seconds of silence," he recalls. "Finally, he told me, 'You're from Vancouver, right? Arc'teryx is a North Vancouver company.'" Dominic reflects, "It's amazing that it took a Chinese company to globalize a Canadian brand from my hometown."

Not every Chinese company's path abroad looks like Anta's. Some try acquisition; others try brand building, organic expansions, or partnerships; and still others try a combination. What's clear is the trend: slowing growth, intense competition, and thinning margins have pushed outward expansion from an option into a necessity across sectors—from medical devices and instruments to toys, home electronics, and e-commerce platforms. We call this *chuhai*—"going into the oceans." For most Chinese companies, a unit sold overseas generates significantly higher margins than an equivalent unit sold at home. Globalization is not just a growth strategy—it's a profitability strategy.

"The next twenty years will be about Chinese companies going international," says Wei Fu, the ever-energetic founder and CEO of CBC Group, the largest Asian healthcare private equity firm. "It doesn't matter whether you speak the language or whether you know these markets in North America, Europe, Africa, South America, and elsewhere. If you can, you do it. If you cannot, you will likely lose out. Find the right talents, the right experiences, assemble the right capabilities to get it done."

How do Chinese companies make the leap from local champion to true global multinational—not just selling worldwide but operating as global citizens? What new cultural, organizational, and strategic muscles are required? What can Chinese firms and established multinationals learn from the collisions ahead? This chapter explores the rise of China's global contenders, the obstacles they face abroad, and the lessons they must absorb. They will need to learn fast—and the world is already watching.

Where It All Started: The World's Factory Floor

The contours of China's rise as the world's factory are familiar. We now turn our focus to what that factory produced. China's first era of globalization forged capabilities far beyond low-cost manufacturing—robotics, data systems, and world-class production efficiency—introducing the deeply adaptive Chinese factory that reshaped global supply chains and became both the envy and the anxiety of the industrialized world. These capabilities were honed at home, but they weren't meant to stay there.

Yet the geopolitical context has also shifted. Free trade has given way to "strategic" trade, where managing critical dependencies and national competitiveness matters as much as efficiency. Tariffs and protectionist measures are surging worldwide. Globally, the number of restrictive trade actions rose from roughly six hundred to seven hundred before COVID to more than three thousand to four thousand today.

Yet reshoring—production returning home from overseas—hasn't materialized at a global scale. Instead what has gained traction is friendshoring, the practice of shifting production and trade toward politically aligned partners. Goods are traveling just as far, if not farther—they are just taking different paths. McKinsey finds that the average geopolitical distance of the global goods trade began compressing around 2018. From 2018 to 2024, total US imports grew by nearly a third, even as imports from China dropped about 20 percent. China's export engine adapted by redirecting more goods through new corridors such as Southeast Asia. In lower-tech categories, Chinese entrepreneurs are replicating their successes in Vietnam, Indonesia, and Cambodia.

China remains the backbone of global manufacturing, but the source of future growth is shifting. The next leap will come from tapping that accumulated "muscle memory"—engineering depth, process discipline, operational excellence—and transforming into global multinationals that innovate, brand, and lead worldwide.

Seeking a Shortcut: Globalization Through Mergers and Acquisitions

As Chinese firms grew richer and more ambitious, they faced a simple question: How do we expand faster? One client invokes the proverb of "crossing the river by feeling the stones" and then adds, "But if I can build a bridge, I will get across much quicker without the pain."

For outward-looking Chinese companies, mergers and acquisitions (M&A) became that bridge. As we've mentioned, most Chinese firms are only two to three decades old. "Even the biggest, most successful Chinese companies have just passed the survival line and are only now starting to think about culture, brand, and heritage," says Herry Han, a prominent tech investor and founder of Soul Capital.

What they've sometimes lacked—global brands, loyal customers, trusted relationships, seasoned management, and credibility—can take decades to build organically.

Outbound M&A offers a shortcut. When Lenovo bought IBM's Thinkpad PC division, it acquired factories as well as a worldview: labs, testing discipline, quality standards, and talent. In the best cases, Chinese owners can extract value in both directions, scaling the acquired brand in China while also tapping its know-how to upgrade the parent company's core.

Japanese companies are a particular source of fascination for many of our Chinese clients. The attraction? Decades of diligence and restraint, loyal customers, and steady revenues that represent almost the inverse of Chinese corporate culture. The folklore of sushi apprentices cleaning knives for years before cutting their first fish never fails to captivate; regardless, the most admired Japanese companies aren't for sale.

During the 2010s, Chinese outbound deals increasingly skewed opportunistic, driven by hubris and a fear of missing out. These stories are legendary: Anbang's $2 billion purchase of New York's Waldorf Astoria became emblematic—a trophy deal that later collapsed when regulators seized the company. "Anbang" is now shorthand for a Chinese buying spree gone wrong.

Outbound M&A peaked in 2016, when Chinese companies spent $227 billion on foreign acquisitions—six times what foreign companies spent on Chinese firms. Soon, regulators cracked down on speculative deals, domestic balance sheets tightened, and governments in Europe and North America grew more protective. We saw many Chinese CEOs infer "this is risky—better not do it." Indeed, many deals struggle under a mismatch of cultures, over-leveraging, weak post-merger integration, or sudden regulatory shifts.

Yet across markets, disciplined "serial acquirers" consistently outperform companies that stick to organic growth strategies. But M&A is a muscle, and value is created—or destroyed—in post-merger integration, requiring experienced teams and a repeatable playbook. That, in turn, requires a mindset shift on the part of Chinese

CEOs. Instead of "We can do it better," the logic should be "We can grow their brand in China better than they can—and they can help us expand globally better than we can alone." After a period of policy-driven retrenchment starting in 2017, there's been a measured rebound in interest in recent years.

The bridge to compressing a decade of progress into three years is there, though Chinese companies are still early on this curve. Consider the following examples.

Geely's acquisition of Volvo. This story traces back to the 2008 financial crisis, when Ford Motor Company, short on cash and shedding non-core assets, put Volvo up for sale. It was then, in 2010, that a two-decade-old Chinese automaker from Zhejiang province managed to acquire an eighty-year-old Swedish brand owned by one of America's most storied carmakers.

Founded in 1986 by Shufu Li, Geely began not as a carmaker but as a manufacturer of refrigerator components, later moving into motorcycles, before entering automobiles in the late 1990s. One of China's first private car companies, it had become a meaningful mass-market player by 2010 but with limited proprietary technology and virtually no global brand recognition. By 2009, Geely was generating only about $2 billion in revenue—roughly one-sixth of Volvo's—prompting some analysts to liken Geely's acquisition of Volvo to a "snake swallowing an elephant." Shufu was unruffled, pointing out that it's "too slow and not easy" to improve capabilities alone; Geely must "find a good partner and teacher, which is Volvo."

The $1.8 billion acquisition in 2010 was a landmark, and even today it remains a reference case of technology transfer and brand stewardship in Chinese outbound M&A. Volvo's strengths—world-class safety engineering, powertrain know-how, and premium brand equity—flowed back into Geely's domestic offerings. The compact modular architecture (CMA) co-developed with Volvo powered the Lynk & Co line and Geely's higher-end models, and also helped move a few others out of the low-end China market.

Equally important was what Geely *didn't* do. It resisted the urge to impose Chinese systems and left Volvo headquarters, factories, and senior leadership in Sweden intact: Volvo remained Volvo. The payoff came in China. Volvo gained one of its largest and most profitable markets, giving it a boost not possible under Ford leadership. Volvo's sales in China surged from thirty thousand units in 2010 to nearly two hundred thousand units in 2022, cementing China's position as its largest single market worldwide. Geely, meanwhile, gained credibility at home and abroad as a serious automotive player.

The deeper logic of a successful Chinese acquisition is clear: the Chinese owner supplies capital, speed, and access to China's scale; the acquired firm contributes technology, brand awareness, and institutional depth.

Midea's two-track acquisition strategy. Midea's origin story is emblematic of Chinese firms' rise as world-class process learners—and how they're turning those capabilities outward.

Its roots trace back to 1968, when villagers in Beijiao Shunde pooled 5,000 RMB ($714), roughly fifty times rural annual income, to mold plastic caps and glass-bottle parts. Among them was Midea's founder, Xiangjian He. From the company's humble beginnings, it would start producing fans in 1980, air conditioners in 1985, and eventually a full appliance lineup. A Fortune 500 destiny was nowhere yet in sight.

For decades, Midea remained largely invisible behind foreign brands as it optimized for scale rather than identity. By the mid-2010s, that model was running out of steam. Rising labor costs and tighter export conditions meant incremental efficiency gains were no longer enough; Midea needed a step change in capability. It responded by climbing the technology stack—automating production, developing proprietary compressors, building R&D laboratories, and completing more than a dozen strategic acquisitions.

This shift reflected a "two-track" consumer and industrial globalization strategy rooted in a vision Chairman Hongbo Fang traces back to the 1980s, when fierce competition in electric fans made clear that "We must go abroad to explore," he says. On the consumer side, Midea acquired established brands such as Toshiba's home appliances and Teka to gain recognition and distribution in mature markets. On the industrial side, it bought companies such as Israel's Servotronix Motion Control, Italy's Clivet, and Switzerland's Arbonia Climate—signaling its ambition to become a global technology company with worldwide R&D, localized manufacturing, and global talent.

An example of that ambition was Midea's €4.5 billion ($5.2 billion) acquisition of the century-old German robotics icon KUKA in 2016. KUKA was struggling, but its expertise in heavy-duty robotics and motion control offered Midea a fast track to digitalizing its own factories and expanding into industrial robotics—producing not just products but also the machines that make them.

Early integration was uneven. Midea initially tried exporting Chinese management practices to Europe and North America, then reversed course, rebuilding itself as a genuinely global organization with international HR systems, global governance frameworks, and a matrix structure that empowered local teams. "We retained the German management team and encouraged exchanges between German engineers and Chinese factories," says Hongbo.

Globalization also meant building "second-home markets"; after failed attempts to send Chinese managers abroad, Midea shifted to local teams, local decision-making, and local supply chains. Its long-term ambition is to move from contract manufacturing to original brands, targeting half of overseas revenue from self-owned labels. Brand building, Hongbo notes, "cannot be achieved overnight," but Midea now sees itself as a global operator with Chinese roots.

Although the company's many acquired businesses need "long-term nurturing," as Hongbo says, its overseas revenue share surpassed 40 percent in 2024. In sixty years, Midea has grown from a township-based fan maker into a global technology group spanning six major categories. It's also mastering organic expansion—growth from within—by observing and learning first.

Multinationals from China—for the World

The most successful Chinese companies are now growing globally by building for the long term—investing in local factories, logistics, teams, and governance. BYD anchors EV production near customers in Europe and emerging markets; Huawei has built one of the world's largest international R&D networks; TikTok has scaled through regional hubs and local hiring; and Haier has localized its manufacturing ecosystems and empowers local managers.

XPENG shows how this new wave of companies expanding abroad differs from the last. In 2014, founder, Xiaopeng He—fresh from selling mobile internet company UCWeb to Alibaba—saw that "legacy auto companies were being disrupted by software-defined, AI-defined vehicles." Inspired by driving a Tesla, he launched XPENG in Guangzhou to build cars as software on wheels from day one. Models like the G3 and P7 would earn praise for delivering Tesla-level features at lower prices—self-parking, real-time map updates, and in-car voice agents for every passenger.

Europe came next: Norway in 2020, then Denmark, Sweden, and the Netherlands. That path wasn't straightforward. "In the beginning, we wanted to go direct to customers in Europe, but this was really expensive," says vice chairman and president Brian Gu. XPENG pivoted to local partners and dealerships.

To earn trust, XPENG is adopting a "made in Europe, for Europe" model, partnering with Magna Steyr to assemble EVs in Austria and deepening ties with Volkswagen, which took a $700 million minority stake in the company. It also invested heavily in visibility and outreach, for example, supporting elite sporting competitions such as the cycling event Tour of Norway. "We learned the hard way that globalization isn't just logistics; it's legitimacy," Brian says.

We've never seen such urgency to go abroad. Global expansion now headlines nearly every client conversation, with founders increasingly designing for international customers from day one, including gaming, consumer electronics, and premium beverages such as Chagee. An executive from logistics company SF Express summed up the shift in fall 2025: "Three years ago, clients asked how to ship overseas cheaply; two years ago, they asked how to do so faster; today, most already have an overseas hub and ask how to use it to reach more countries."

The reality? Developed markets are lucrative but difficult, while developing markets are more price-sensitive. Southeast Asia feels geographically close but is fragmented, with consumers displaying low willingness to pay across many categories. "After years of trying to figure out Southeast Asian markets, a few have been very successful, but many Chinese players are thinking that only European and US markets will move the needle," says Hai Ye, a McKinsey senior partner leading the growth, marketing, and sales practice. That view, however, is sector-specific. Across categories from smartphones and mining equipment to mobility platforms and consumer apps, growth is coming from an increasingly diverse set of markets—including Southeast Asia, India, the Middle East, Africa, and Latin America.

When outbound companies enter mature markets, regulatory friction often follows, from anti-subsidy probes to strict data and environmental, social, and governance (ESG) regulations. European markets are highly regulated, says Jun Xu, a fintech entrepreneur who co-founded 360 Finance in China and is now building a global digital finance business in Italy. "That makes them tough to enter, which is why we're partnering. In China, we went from zero to IPO within three years. In Europe, it will probably take ten. The upside is, there's a natural barrier to entry, so once we're in, it's less competitive."

The welcome abroad is getting colder. Tariffs, export controls, and industrial policies now dominate trade. China's strength in high-value exports has triggered unease; Asia Society data show China's global favorability has dropped from 43 percent to 29 percent in the decade ending in 2024. Access increasingly depends on the inclinations of local politics, and sentiment can change rapidly.

Chinese firms also risk exporting a "winner-takes-all" mindset that alienates local communities. In solar, aggressive pricing accelerated the green transition but wiped out domestic producers in Europe; by 2025, Germany's Schott Solar, France's Saint-Gobain, and the last major player, Germany's GMB Glasmanufaktur, had all closed down. Similar frictions are surfacing in EVs, batteries, robotics, and e-commerce—where newcomers such as SHEIN and Temu have drawn pushback.

True global firms must invest in communities, hiring locally, reinvesting profits, and building goodwill. As McKinsey senior partner Sheng Hong puts it, "This next generation of Chinese companies has to position themselves as global companies—not simply Chinese ones. The day you're characterized as only a Chinese company you face an uphill battle." Increasingly, that legitimacy is built through highly visible global platforms. Chinese companies have become prominent sponsors of the FIFA World Cup, the Olympic Games, and Formula 1 teams, and are acquiring or stewarding globally recognized sports institutions. These investments signal permanence and partnership, helping Chinese firms embed themselves in local cultural ecosystems in ways that go far beyond advertising.

We've seen these strategies work. Companies such as Midea, Xiaomi, Huawei, Haier, Hisense, and a number of technology and media players have shown that disciplined organic expansion can succeed—if they're willing to adapt not just their products but their posture toward the world.

The Playbook for Chinese Companies Going Abroad

Simply exporting products doesn't make a company a global multinational. China now accounts for roughly 15 percent of global goods exports—up from about 4 percent in 2000—more than double Germany's share and roughly five times that of Japan or South Korea, three economies where export performance has been a major engine of growth. Yet China's corporate globalization has lagged behind its trade footprint: Chinese A-share listed firms generate only about 11 to 13 percent of their revenue overseas, compared with typically 30 to 60 percent for large German, Japanese, and Korean multinationals. This challenges a common assumption that Chinese firms have long been pure export machines; in reality, for most of the past three decades, domestic growth was large and lucrative enough to dominate strategic focus. Most Chinese firms remain homegrown giants that are dominant at home and tentative abroad.

Brand power lags even further. Global consumers everywhere buy "Made in China" yet struggle to name the companies behind the products. As we mentioned in an earlier chapter, China under-indexes on global brand value, with only two Chinese firms ranking among the top hundred companies with 30 percent of revenue outside their home region. The gap between China's trade footprint and its corporate footprint is both the opportunity and the challenge ahead.

There's no single formula for becoming a true multinational. Large companies expanding abroad face radically different demands than small "born-global" insurgents that simply need a killer product. Here are some lessons that will come in useful:

- Be a good corporate citizen. You don't need to win everything!
- Replace "China speed" with "global speed."
- Become a trusted partner.
- Hire great talent, both local and foreign, and embrace a multi-national culture.
- Build great governance.
- Consider a born-global model.

Be a Good Corporate Citizen— You Don't Need to Win Everything!

Imagine a Chinese guest arriving in a new neighborhood and being invited to a friendly game of tennis. Once on court, the guest turns up the intensity, wins the first set 6–0 and the second set 6–0, then declares victory. The host offers the obligatory handshake at the net, and both players pack their bags silently—a technically flawless win and a social disaster.

Many Chinese companies new to global markets have played this way. Driven by the same instincts that fueled their domestic rise, they compete aggressively, move fast, and grab share, handing out "bagels"—the "os" in a 6–0 score. This strategy might work in the short term: customers everywhere love value-for-money products. But rapid scaling and winner-takes-all strategies also trigger defensive reactions from competitors, regulators, and policymakers.

Global success isn't a zero-sum game. You're not just trying to win—you're trying to get invited back to the club. That requires restraint, partnership, and empathy. There has to be enough food on the table for everyone. Sometimes you need to lose a game. Success abroad requires more than technological superiority or operational excellence. It requires corporate citizenship.

Chinese companies will have to learn to be welcomed, not feared, and we're only in the first chapter of this journey. That journey involves investing in local talent, contributing to communities, and aligning with host countries' industrial priorities.

That's easier said than done. Many Chinese executives are competing just as fiercely overseas as they do at home—often against the same rivals—so why change? SHEIN and Temu are suing each other in US courts. Chinese solar suppliers are undercutting each other abroad. To bewildered local executives, it looks as if China's involution has simply been exported. As one Southeast Asian CEO puts it, "Margins are being destroyed, and then Chinese companies turn on each other—we're watching this happen live."

Still, there's hope. Soul Capital founding partner Herry Han sees signs of leading companies "learning to merge cultures, by supporting local hiring, adopting local practices, and even sponsoring the home football team. They're not just selling products."

We've observed tangible investments in local culture and systems, from Huawei-funded labs at German universities, Tencent's backing of European game studios, and experiential brand spaces like NIO House on a prime shopping street in Oslo. NIO's matcha latte went viral; locals came for the drink, then wandered upstairs and asked, "Wait—these cars are Chinese?" Global integration now means being part of the local scene, not just selling into it.

Replace "China Speed" with "Global Speed"

When asked what they wish they'd known before venturing abroad, Chinese executives rarely mention tariffs, hiring, or branding. It's much simpler: "To slow down."

We've discussed "China speed": quickness over precision, instinct over research, entrepreneurship over institutionalization. It works at home because executives negotiate with peers equally obsessed with growth. Experiments are cheap, failure is survivable, and iteration is constant.

Then companies land overseas and everything feels sticky as glue. A Chinese consumer electronics executive tells us, half joking, half exasperated, "We work harder than ever in Europe. Everyone is busy all the time. But nothing moves." Meetings are scheduled weeks out. Partners ask for certifications instead of prototypes. Lawyers replace engineers in early conversations. "In China," he says, "we argue about features. Here, we argue about process."

Outside China, ecosystems are thinner and more fragmented. Suppliers, labs, and distributors aren't clustered in one industrial park—they're spread across cities if not countries. Talent is scarcer, more expensive, and far less tolerant of China-style hours. Regulations aren't flexible guardrails; they're fixed rails. Speed is gated by proof: certifications, warranties, audits, references. This is where "China speed" stalls.

Global success requires a rhythm that is almost the opposite of China's: precision over speed, patience over brute-force iteration, trust-building over trial and error, and compliance as a capability. Why? Experimentation is more expensive. Legal bills pile up quickly. And not least, relationships and reputation matter. A failed pilot can close doors for years. We recommend that clients slow down—so they can ultimately travel faster and farther.

When speed truly matters, Chinese companies should apply it selectively—doubling down on areas of strength such as supply chain, manufacturing, and cost innovation, and targeting specific segments or sub-sectors in terms of sales and branding. Winning one segment first, building customer insight and a local team before expanding, may be less dramatic but far more durable. It shouldn't be a surprise that granularity of growth might be a winning strategy abroad, too.

Of course, when Chinese companies have overwhelming advantages such as digital distribution, massive scale, or network effects, speed still works. Temu in the US, SHEIN in Europe, or Tencent's games in Latin America all expanded rapidly in terms of customer acquisition and growth. Yet even there, success depended as much on earning legitimacy as on "China speed."

Some Chinese conglomerates learned early. WH Group, the world's largest pork producer, is leading in meat and food processing in North America. Early on, it recognized that Asian-style speed wouldn't translate overseas. Instead of pushing volume, WH emphasized patience, investing in local infrastructure, and placing senior Chinese managers at the No. 3 and No. 4 leadership levels into North American operations—not to dictate from the top but to absorb local norms and feed insights back to headquarters. The result was steady growth, operational credibility, and ultimately a successful IPO.

Become a Trusted Partner

There's irony in this phase of globalization. After China's WTO accession, foreign firms gained access to China largely on one condition: that they partner locally and share valuable know-how. In autos, insurance, and telecoms, those arrangements didn't just open the market, instead they upgraded China's industrial capabilities. Two decades later, the script has flipped. As Chinese companies export not just products but also intellectual property (IP), they're discovering what their former partners discovered years ago: access to foreign markets comes with expectations. In other words, Chinese companies have seen this play out before, only from the other side of the table. Now the question is whether they can become the kind of joint-venture partners they once learned from.

Early signs suggest a handful are doing just that. CATL's €1.8 billion ($2.1 billion) battery plant in Germany pairs manufacturing scale with commitments to local R&D, sustainable sourcing, and workforce development, which aligns neatly with EU industrial priorities. Tsingshan Holding Group, the world's largest nickel producer, has invested more than $10 billion alongside partners to build industrial parks that have created tens of thousands of local jobs and generated significant tax revenues for host governments. Haier's joint venture with Algeria's largest private industrial conglomerate focuses on technology transfer, workforce training, and expanded local production capacity.

Chinese companies are forging a new style abroad. Between 2012 and 2023, the share of local employees hired by Chinese firms overseas rose from less than half to more than 60 percent—a meaningful shift from "ship and sell" to "embed and build." Critically, these partnerships go beyond sharing intellectual property to sharing revenues, risk, and long-term responsibility for local ecosystems. Jason Zhu, CEO of Shanghai-based biotech company Henlius, remarks that the next billion-dollar drug company may well come out of China: "We're on track to introduce great products to the market. But once we do, we need to build overseas supply chains and find foreign partners. We can't let geopolitics get in the way; we have to share."

To achieve win-win outcomes abroad, Chinese firms must move beyond transactional market entry and earn trust as long-term partners—whether through joint ventures, co-development, or deeply integrated supply chain collaboration.

Hire Great Talent, Both Local and Foreign, and Embrace a Multinational Culture

It sounds obvious to say "hire great talent." Yet this is exactly where many Chinese companies stumble. The challenge isn't just attracting talent—it's deciding who leads. In theory, the best executives should run global expansion; in practice, they rarely do. Overseas growth is slow, risky, and often unprofitable for years. For high-performing executives running large domestic units, the trade-off rarely makes sense, especially since overseas businesses are typically tiny to start. "You can't be the hero when you're small," as one executive explains.

That leads to a controversial question: Should overseas businesses be led by Chinese executives or by locals? Many Chinese firms default to sending their own executives abroad. Cultural alignment—sending home-office employees to foreign posts—may feel safer. "We can always hire local executives in functional areas, but the top person must be Chinese," the chairman of a large consumer company insists. "Otherwise, communication and trust become difficult." But the sacrifice is market familiarity: local markets need local leaders. "We've seen multinationals struggle in China. Expatriate leaders just aren't adept at operating locally," says another client. The tension is real and unresolved.

What's clear is that many Chinese executives were never trained for this challenge. "A whole generation only knows how to land grab, Chinese style," says Lambert Bu, a McKinsey senior partner who's been helping Chinese companies in their overseas push. "But succeeding abroad requires a far more scientific understanding of segments and local insights, and different leadership capabilities. Most haven't developed the skills."

Execution failures predictably follow. "We've seen giant Chinese companies send very junior management teams abroad," says Mickey Rocha-Keys, who runs the sports marketing agency EMW Global. "They have great technical skills, but they just don't understand local culture and communities. It's hard for them to build sustainable relationships."

Lenovo remains a benchmark; it deliberately built a multinational leadership team made up of executives from Lenovo, IBM, and industry. Today at Lenovo, the working language is English and its senior leadership operates as a globally integrated team. As Ken Wong, executive vice president and president of its fastest-growing unit, Solutions & Services Group (SSG), puts it, "We are in 183 markets today. We're a true global team and that's what it takes to navigate the world."

In the long run, credibility abroad isn't built by exporting leaders any more than by exporting products. Trust and efficacy come from empowering local leadership, grooming multinational teams, and shedding the posture of a short-term visitor.

Build Great Governance

Going global forces Chinese companies to reckon with a concept that, at least in the Western sense, has never been their forte: governance. Top-down, first-generation-led Chinese companies are driven by an instinct for speed and competition. Building global structures, by contrast, is far harder. As one client in consumer electronics, long admired for rapid, iterative innovation, puts it, "Governance is not an entrepreneurial instinct. This is the hardest thing we've ever done." Management styles that work in China often fail abroad. "Many Chinese executives assume everything can be centrally decided," notes McKinsey's Lambert. "When things get tough, the answer at home is simply to work harder. That logic doesn't translate in most markets."

Successful globalizers have stopped treating local empowerment as a nice-to-have. TikTok adjusted early: it runs its business through five regional hubs—North America, Europe, the Middle East, Latin America, and Asia-Pacific—each with real decision rights. Lenovo also pushed decision-making closer to local markets. "When Chinese companies go abroad, they must find the right talent, the right strategy, understand the culture, deal with IP and data security. If you don't have strong corporate systems you can't change any of these factors," says Dai Feng, founder of CareCapital Group.

These challenges aren't uniquely Chinese. Many multinationals, after years of global operations, still oscillate between tighter central control and local autonomy. Chinese companies are still experimenting. Early signs suggest that a split structure with one CEO focused on China and another on international markets might feel most natural, as favored by many multinationals with a large domestic base and significant overseas operations. But no model works if it's copied blindly.

Luckin's overseas push shows how tricky the balance can be. After opening up in New York, the company quickly learned it couldn't just export its China playbook; supply chain, equipment, operations, marketing, consumer experience all required localization. "These are not 'ship-the-product' solutions," says David Li, the company's chairman. "We have significant local operations. We need robust oversight—past problems came from governance failures—but we don't want to become a slow-moving organization plagued by bureaucracy."

To balance speed and control, some firms are experimenting with "catfish teams"—small, fast, Chinese units embedded in overseas markets to inject urgency and challenge incumbents without destabilizing the core. "It's the 'catfish in a tank' concept," says Peng Xia, a McKinsey partner in China's digital practice—keeping the system alert, adaptive, and moving.

Consider a Born-Global Model

A new breed is emerging: Chinese firms born with a go-global mindset. Increasingly, Chinese entrepreneurs are building companies designed from the start for international markets. They form English-speaking multinational teams early, develop products with global users in mind, set up operations around the world, and attempt to understand their consumers deeply. Many are consumer-facing businesses with global appeal. Insta360, the action camera maker, and Bambu Lab, in 3D printing, are emblematic, as are China's leading gaming companies and a growing wave of AI start-ups targeting overseas customers from inception. Others, such as Transsion, followed a different but equally telling path; its mobile phones gained traction first in Africa and later in India, while remaining nearly absent from China itself—an inversion of the traditional home-first trajectory.

Structurally, these companies look different from earlier generations. Some even incorporate outside China, often in Singapore, and are attentive students of Western markets and culture. They work across borders naturally and design their organizations to navigate regulatory and geopolitical sensitivities. Consumers sometimes do not know that they are a Chinese company. For these firms, globalization isn't a pivot or a second act—it's the starting point.

Born-global firms internalize a higher baseline for process, documentation, compliance, and product reliability—because selling abroad requires it. They also have executives well-versed in international norms, who were educated overseas, or seasoned abroad. This knowledge of how it works "over there" tends to flow back into China operations. Of course, born-global firms still face the sensitivities of being Chinese companies operating abroad. For this cohort, learning to manage these tensions is a critical part of their operating manual from the start.

It's Kindergarten on the Global Playground

We tend to think of multinationals as companies from mature Western economies rather than from Asia—and certainly not from China. Yet every week, Chinese founders are asking about Latin America, the Middle East, Africa, and seeking to meet partners, investors, and regulators there. China Inc. is still early—in "kindergarten," as we like to joke—but learning fast.

The next decade will test whether Chinese firms can evolve from powerful domestic champions into true global citizens. Going global isn't only about scale: it requires cultural maturity, credibility, and a commitment to letting others win, too. Success will hinge on leveraging traditional strengths while building new capabilities to adapt to the slower, more complex dynamics of global markets. Some Chinese firms will remain world-class exporters, succeeding on value alone. But in industries where politics, standards, capital, trust, and narrative matter, value-for-money alone isn't enough. As we sometimes say: you may not be interested in geopolitics, but geopolitics is interested in you.

Ultimately, the question we pose is simple. Why should "multinationals" only describe Coca-Cola, Procter & Gamble, Apple, Volkswagen, LVMH, Sony, and McDonald's? We'd like to see more Chinese firms become true multinationals—global institutions that shape industries, communities, and norms everywhere.

For those who aspire to be global players, it's wise to avoid playing tennis with your new partners without letting them win a few games. Let them taste a little victory and leave everyone wanting to play again. Maybe even go out for a beer afterward and share tips that will raise their game. That's how you get invited back for the next game of tennis, and the one after, until your kids are playing with theirs.

Succession: The Founder's Dilemma

After three decades advising Chinese entrepreneurs, we've seen one theme rise steadily in importance: the next generation. Succession is the issue that often makes self-made Chinese founders who've exercised near-total control over their businesses feel powerless. It's a complex topic fraught with questions of longevity, family, and legacy—we've seen transition projects launched with urgency, only to stall or be quietly abandoned. As one entrepreneur who created a $10 billion retailing empire tells us, "With business matters, I can make decisions very quickly, often in minutes. I can rely on my years of pattern recognition. On succession, everything feels unclear."

And yet, paralysis isn't inevitable. Founders who confront leadership transitions early and put in place structures to professionalize and institutionalize companies that, for decades, have been driven by entrepreneurial instinct and personal relationships improve their odds of success. The stakes are rising, as the Chinese private sector faces a wave of similarly aged founders facing retirement amid rapid market change and cultural constraints. The companies that endure will be the ones that codify authority before they transfer it.

"Entrepreneurs naturally assume that their children will take over one day," says Roger King, a finance professor at the Hong Kong

University of Science and Technology and co-founder of its family business center, "but given how short business cycles are these days, it's never too early to plan ahead. Most Chinese entrepreneurs leave it until far too late."

One company that defied this pattern is the agribusiness giant New Hope, which managed a real handover. Founder Yonghao Liu built the company from scratch in 1982, eventually turning it into China's largest animal feed producer and pig farmer. He didn't cling to the wheel, and his heir didn't inherit an empty title. He planned early, arguing that succession was "not meant for just one person, but for a team and a system." The philosophy took shape early, even at home. Yonghao has said he deliberately gave his children responsibility through small but concrete tasks from a young age.

By thirty-three, his daughter, Chang Liu, had become CEO of New Hope Liuhe, the group's largest operating company. Yonghao imparted upon her real authority to prune underperforming executives, redirect investments, and professionalize the company—even when it unsettled long-standing relationships. When a prolonged crash in pork prices dragged the company into years of losses, Chang doubled down on systems, tightening governance and building management depth. "I'm not like the heroes of the founding generation . . . I am the result of a process," Chang has said.

These days Yonghao generally stays out of day-to-day management and focuses instead on other investments and larger strategic decisions for the overall group. The journey was far more complex than this account suggests, but the point stands: this transition was executed with foresight and discipline.

China is heading into a once-in-a-generation handover. Most A-share listed companies are private rather than state-owned, and a significant share are family-controlled, making family enterprises a core pillar of China's private sector. Further, among China's top five hundred private enterprises, just over half were founded during the Reform and Opening Up era, particularly during the 1980s and 1990s, and nearly 70 percent of their founders were born in the 1950s and 1960s. The result is a succession wave hitting China's private sector all at once.

Other economies have navigated similar moments: Japan's postwar conglomerates, Korea's chaebol, and Europe's family firms have undergone generational transitions. Those companies, many nearing or surpassing the century mark such as Toyota, Sony, Samsung, Hyundai, Bertelsmann, L'Oréal, IKEA, and ABB, endured not because every successive leader was exceptional, but because the businesses themselves were built to last across different leadership eras.

In China, succession challenges are as much structural as personal. The one-child policy, which ran from 1979 through 2015, narrows the pool of potential successors for some companies. Heirs often grow up in environments very different from those of their parents and may be reluctant to take over the business. Formal succession planning remains rare, and many aging founders have little desire to step aside. One founder in his sixties told us, "Today, all kinds of people come see me because I am the chairman. What would I do if I retire? I can't play golf every day!" Many entrepreneurs also believe medical advances will extend their working lives, and longevity has been a frequent topic of conversation with Chinese founders. The latest trend? Going to Tokyo to get stem cell treatment.

Compounding these challenges are the unprecedented domestic and global pressures facing Chinese businesses. Succession is often deferred and deemed important but not urgent, even though delay only magnifies the risk. "It is a high-stakes decision," says Acha Leke, a McKinsey senior partner leading the Firm's global work with family-owned businesses. "After studying more than six hundred family-owned businesses, it's clear that CEO transition is one of the most consequential decisions. It is also the one with the biggest upside, if done properly."

The long-term solution lies in building governance, systems, and leadership pipelines that outlast founders. These practices are well established in global management science, and more mainland Chinese companies are considering them as they scale and mature. Whether they move fast enough remains uncertain.

The Succession Crunch

As McKinsey approached its centenary in 2026, it marked the moment alongside a small peer group: other century-old enterprises. At the Firm's global partners' meeting in Chicago, messages streamed in from the CEOs of Delta Air Lines, United Parcel Service, Siemens, Tata Group, AIA, Bancolombia, and others—companies that, across the United States, Europe, India, Singapore, Colombia, and more, have endured multiple economic cycles and transitions.

What stood out wasn't who participated, but who didn't: no messages from mainland China. This isn't for a lack of longevity. China has roughly seven hundred nationally recognized "time-honored" brands with histories spanning more than a century; the oldest, Beijing's chicken-and-duck restaurant Bianyifang, dates back to the Ming dynasty.

What Chinese companies have largely found challenging was the ability to pair longevity with scale, modern corporate governance, and sustained performance—the combination that turned postwar Japanese and European companies into multinational icons. Almost all of China's modern large-scale private companies and the majority of our mainland clients are just twenty to forty years old. Many of their founders are in their sixties or seventies, yet remain firmly in control. That share of business originators still at the helm poses a challenge: more than 80 percent of mainland Chinese entrepreneurs say they wish to keep business in the family, but two-thirds lack a formal succession plan—one of the widest gaps anywhere between intention and preparation.

Handovers didn't happen earlier in part because founders were still young enough, and they found China's growth wave exhilarating to ride. The need for leadership transition is now arriving at an inconvenient moment, when firms must contend with slowing growth, demographic hurdles, regulatory and geopolitical challenges, and the disruption of generative AI.

It's not a good time to sell a business, but it's not a good time to hand one over, either. "These founders stayed in the kitchen and continued to work," says Bain Capital partner Michael Hui. "But as they ask their kids to step into the 'current kitchen' they're finding it's really hot now. The first-generation entrepreneurs know the kids might not make it."

The scale of this challenge is immense. Chinese family businesses account for roughly half of GDP and generate an even greater share of jobs. What happens when this cohort of founders finally steps back? Can companies built for speed during the golden boom era evolve into enduring institutions?

A generational cliff looms for these businesses. Globally, CEO successions in family-owned businesses tend to destroy value: in a study of more than two hundred transitions, McKinsey found that five-year post-handover performance lagged the prior five years by roughly 6 percentage points in total shareholder value, 2 points in revenue growth, and 3 points in EBITDA growth. In China, these risks are intensified by relationship-driven business norms, a capability gap between generations, institutions built around larger-than-life founders, and other factors.

We'll examine each in turn—and outline how transitions can be managed more effectively.

The Capability and Generational Mismatch

We've discussed before how sharply today's young Chinese differ in outlook and circumstances from their parents and their grandparents. "Two generations ago, no one in China had money," says Louis Cheung of Boyu Capital. "They grew up in completely different cultural contexts. The older generation also wants the younger kids to feel a bit hungry and unstable."

We draw this contrast through a mid-sized automotive parts maker. The founder, whom we'll call Wang, built the business in the 1990s with little capital, weak legal protection, and few rules. When policy windows opened—real estate, exports markets, infrastructure—he moved fast, borrowing heavily when needed. "If you hesitated, the chance was gone," Wang recalls. Decisions were informal, and relationships were central to how the business operated.

His son, Xiaocun, would inherit a larger, more regulated, and more exposed enterprise. Like other second-generation heirs—a majority of whom studied overseas—he speaks the language of governance, compliance, and capital markets fluently. "My generation was taught to reduce risk," Xiaocun says. "Our parents were taught to survive it." What he struggles with is the all-or-nothing decisions that defined the founder's rise.

This contrast can be jarring. Education in China back in the '70s and '80s was rudimentary and disparate. While some entrepreneurs in that earlier era may have had a university degree, many did not, and more than a handful were granted honorary doctoral degrees only after they achieved business success. They learned capitalism through improvisation, navigating the rapidly developing business ecosystems and institutions with intuition and personal networks. "Often, the first-generation entrepreneurs do not speak English, but they're obviously incredibly resourceful and resilient," observes Mingyu Guan, a McKinsey senior partner leading the Firm's succession work in China. "Meanwhile, their children have overseas experience. The challenge is figuring out how to use those global capabilities without losing the entrepreneurial instincts that built the company."

Founder Wang worries that his son lacks grit, political sensitivity, and the instinct to act decisively under pressure. Xiaocun, in turn, has questions: Are his father's business instincts, informal way of decision-making, and penchant for risk-taking still effective in a slower-growth, higher-risk environment?

It's not surprising that enthusiasm is mixed from both sides. Nearly half of Chinese entrepreneurs express concern about their children's ability or willingness to take over. The heirs pause, too, with about 45 percent ambivalent or uninterested in stepping into those shoes.

"I'm a one-in-a-million success story," says a successful tycoon who has given up the idea that one of his kids might take over. "In my generation, I was the winner out of millions of others like me and fought my way to the top. Why would my kids, just by virtue of their DNA, be worthy of being a one-in-a-million success? They're very likely going to underperform me."

The Founder as Institution

Many of China's private companies feel like extensions of the individuals who built them. It's hard to imagine a JD.com without Richard Liu, a Xiaomi without Lei Jun, or a Huawei without Ren Zhengfei. They might be founders or CEOs, but they're also much more: symbols of entrepreneurial success and even national pride. The same dynamic plays out across small- and mid-sized firms as well as provincial champions. The scale differs, but the pattern is the same. In this context, succession feels less like a true leadership transition, and in fact can erase the company's identity.

For outsized founder personalities, the shift to the next generation is both a theoretical and emotional test. The business is their life's work, with authority and legitimacy residing in the founder rather than in the institution. Stepping aside can feel existential, which is why many opt for half measures without fully letting go—for example, choosing to remain as a chairman or "senior adviser" while appointing co-CEOs, setting up a rotating leadership structure, or engaging in informal power sharing.

Even when a founder is ready to step back, customers, partners, and employees often take longer to adjust. At Suntar Environmental Technology, a fast-growing Chinese industrial technology company, Yihong Lan is preparing to succeed his father, Weiguang Lan, who built the business around membrane-based separation technologies now used from water treatment to lithium extraction.

But in the Chinese market, Weiguang's influence isn't easily transferred. "His skill set and his reputation are intertwined—you can't separate the two," says Yihong. "The way stakeholders deal with me is different precisely because he's the founder. I don't have the tools at my disposal that he has."

The larger the company, the harder it becomes to resolve this issue. Of course, the next generation might also be less likely to possess "the animal spirit, that entrepreneurial instinct" that engendered success in the first generation, says Sheng Hong, a McKinsey senior partner co-leading the global energy and materials practice. "Will the second generation work as hard? I have my doubts. They're less hungry than their fathers."

Another dynamic complicates succession: the divide between work and home. Many founders are absolute authorities inside their companies—"God" at work—yet struggle with the one audience they can't manage: their own children. When founders spend more time in offices and factories than at home, that distance only deepens the gap.

One-Child Considerations

For some businesses, the one-child policy has removed optionality. (Nevertheless, many entrepreneurs do have more than one child.) In Europe and the United States, leadership can sometimes pass to a second or third child; even when disputes arise, global business dynasties—from Bernard Arnault's five children at LVMH and Rupert Murdoch's family at News Corp to the Agnellis at Fiat and the Swires in Hong Kong—benefited from deeper benches. In China, that bench is often non-existent. When the sole heir is uninterested or unprepared, the dilemma becomes acute.

Under these conditions, succession shifts from choice to obligation. Emotional engagement is weak; only 21 percent of Chinese successors report feeling "excited" about taking over, and just 37 percent feel "motivated," both well below global averages. Heirs carry the full weight of expectation regardless of aptitude or interest. Many also are drawn to technology, global investing, or other non-business fields, rather than traditional sectors such as manufacturing or trading.

Hidden Rules and Ambiguities

China's business context is filled with a web of unspoken rules, and who will be next in the leadership role is one of the most sensitive. Indicating interest too directly can be seen as challenging authority— or tempting bad luck. Ambiguity also serves a strategic purpose:

when the successor is undefined, senior executives continue to orbit the founder. Siblings and cousins may compete quietly, but few dare to test the patriarch or matriarch openly.

And succession planning isn't sensitive only at the top. Oftentimes, we find that related discussions run directly against prevailing Chinese corporate culture, where executives are rewarded for emphasizing their uniqueness and irreplaceability. Most Chinese executives try to prove their unique contribution, rather than prepare the next generation to replace them. As one executive, while dismissing our succession project, tells us, "The day I leave, the company founders will see how valuable I am. That's my legacy—how much I meant to the company. Making myself irrelevant so someone else can take over is simply not a Chinese management virtue."

Over time, the result can be organizational fragility. Rumors replace clarity, loyalty is tested more than capability, and succession becomes a guessing game rather than a managed and structured process. When a health scare or external shock finally forces a transition, there is often no cohesive team ready to step in—only formal titles layered over unresolved tensions. Furthermore, the strengths Chinese founders most want to pass on are the most difficult to institutionalize: government ties, regulatory intuition, and deal-making skills built over decades.

Why Succession Planning Is Important— and What to Do About It

Leadership transitions are among the most consequential—and potentially destructive—events in the life of a family-owned business. McKinsey research has found that a transition to a family CEO is least likely to create value; only 29 percent generate positive returns, compared with 39 percent of transitions to non-family CEOs. The upside? When family successions do create value, they outperform: successful transitions to family CEOs generate an average 23 percentage point total shareholder return (TSR) uplift, compared with 15 points for non-family transitions.

In practice, the key questions facing Chinese founders are familiar worldwide. Who should succeed the CEO? Should that person be family or non-family? When should preparation begin, and how should success be measured? How can competing family aspirations be reconciled? As Acha, who leads McKinsey's global succession work, notes, these questions are universal—even if the context is not.

What often differs is how families approach the answer. Family business adviser Roger King argues that durable leadership depends less on bloodline than on what he calls "CCKP"—commitment, competence, knowledge, and passion from the next generation. When intrinsic motivation is absent, he warns, forcing transitions can destroy value, and sometimes the business itself. In such cases, preserving the "business family" may matter more than preserving the "family business." "Why force the next generation to run the company? It may be far better for the family to sell the business and manage the wealth," Roger explains. Some families respond by separating ownership from management or by creating family investment vehicles that allow the next generation to pursue entrepreneurial paths without being locked into predefined roles.

There's no one-size-fits-all answer. Instead, successful transitions rely on a multidimensional framework that treats succession not as a single event but as a long-term organizational capability involving disciplined execution of a small set of critical practices. At their core: a shift away from personality-driven leadership toward institutionalization that embeds continuity; professionalization that upgrades leadership capability; and governance that clearly defines power.

Institutionalization: Systems That Outlast the Founder

Marvin Bower, the Harvard-trained lawyer who shaped McKinsey into a professional institution in the mid-twentieth century, believed that leadership wasn't about personal power but rather building organizations that endure. A company is truly well led, Marvin often said, only if it continues to perform when the leader is no longer present.

For many Chinese founders, building systems, rules, operating logic, and processes that operate independently of the individual feels unfamiliar. Most grew their companies without exposure to large organizations with mature management infrastructure; hence what outsiders call "institutional discipline" can look like bureaucracy.

Yet institutionalization is precisely what allows companies to outlast their founders—and eventually to endure for decades. When a founder's knowledge and values are embedded into systems, employees' loyalty can then more easily shift from an individual to a mission, rules, and defined roles. Decision-making rights are made explicit. Regular management rhythms replace ad hoc directives. Critical relationships with regulators, customers, suppliers, and partners are transferred from personal networks to formal roles. The test is simple: If the founder disappears for six months, does the company still function?

Some Chinese leaders have embraced this concept. Lenovo founder Liu Chuanzhi made the principle explicit early on. "No matter how excellent executives' children are, they are uniformly not allowed into the company," he said in a 2012 interview, describing an effort to preserve fairness and motivation, even at personal cost. Haier founder Zhang Ruimin put it more starkly: "The greatest failure of a leader is to make himself irreplaceable."

Such ideas often clash with leaders' intuition. Over the years, our Chinese clients have always asked us about McKinsey's values. When we explain one of the Firm's core tenets—that leaders should leave the institution stronger than they found it and that senior roles rotate every few years—the reaction is usually disbelief. "Rotate—even if the leader is doing a great job?" one entrepreneur asks. "That doesn't make sense." That discomfort is the price of building something that lasts.

Professionalization: The Right People for the Right Roles

Professionalization, in turn, is about upgrading the quality and independence of the leadership team. It marks a shift from a world where "the boss knows everything" to one in which technocrats, functional specialists, and professional managers have real authority—a move from intuition to the science of management. In practice, that means clarifying performance expectations and incentives, strengthening boards and oversight, and empowering managers to make decisions that may diverge from the founder's instincts.

In a firm's early years, it's natural to rely on a small group of veterans who were "there from the beginning." Loyalty and shared hardship matter when firms are young. But as the complexity of the business grows and regulations tighten, leadership must be based on expertise, not tenure or personal relationships. In many cases, a transition needs to involve the entire leadership team—not just the top spot.

"It's hard to accomplish a good succession because we're often also talking about the first-generation founding team," says Leon Meng of Ascendant Capital Partners. "If you look at the head of procurement, head of manufacturing, head of this and that—all those are the 'battle brothers' who endured hardship together. How do you uproot this?"

"Company culture should treat leadership as a responsibility rather than a birthright or privilege," says Acha. "Then considering a broad pool of candidates becomes natural; whether a family member actually wants the responsibility should also be taken into account."

The ultimate test as to whether transition works is confidence beyond the founder: investors, employees, and customers believing in the company's prospects, with valuation and reputation no longer tethered to a single person.

None of that requires abandoning family ownership. Globally and in China, models range from full family control to hybrid structures in which families set strategy through boards while professionals run operations. New Hope and Lee Kum Kee sit at the family-led end; Lenovo, Alibaba, and Haier are professionally managed; Haidilao occupies the middle.

Choosing executives who can thrive within these structures can be tricky. Frank Tang, co-founder of FountainVest Partners, tells us, "We have tried to find professional managers to replace entrepreneurs, but it's really hard. You can find the best résumés—the multinational-trained executives, the foreign-educated returnees—but they may not have the entrepreneurial spirit to grow the company.

Further, the bench of successful professional executives in China is just not as deep as we would like to see." It is all relative. Alwin Poon, a former managing director of Carlyle, thinks China's professional talent pool is improving, with an "increasing rank of professional managers to choose from, many coming out of professional services and multinationals."

What Should Be Simple Is Often Complex

Even when the right candidates exist, bringing them in is rarely straightforward. First, recruiting top talent is costly: building leadership depth requires market-level pay, which can challenge cost-conscious founders. Progress often begins with making moves in finance and accounting—for example, through the early hiring of professional CFOs—while other functions such as HR and organizational development lag.

Longtime executives might represent barriers to this process. One client's CFO began as the accountant when the business was a ten-person restaurant in Guangdong. The company now exceeds $1 billion in revenue with more than fifty thousand employees, yet this now-CFO retains the founder's full trust. "If this person stays in the position, how can we recruit top finance talent?" the next generation asks, having lobbied for her retirement for years without success.

Companies should focus on a few core questions as decisions are made about personnel in the run-up to succession: Are roles matched to capability rather than lineages? Are successor candidates evaluated through disciplined, competitive processes that include family, internal, and external talent? Is there a deep, complementary leadership bench to support the next CEO and reduce reliance on any single individual?

Governance: Who Has Power and Accountability?

Governance is about who holds authority, how it's exercised, and how conflicts are resolved. Without it, neither institutionalization nor professionalization is durable. While the founder is present, ambiguity is often tolerated. Once the question of "who leads next?" arises, unresolved issues surface fast: who decides, who can veto, and whose interests prevail. As one entrepreneur put it, "Two brothers founded the company. Each has children. Now there are four potential successors. Who does what—and how do you keep the company intact?"

Most founders we know understand the need for rules, boards, and checks. The difficulty lies in making those mechanisms neutral and enforceable. This is where boards matter. In theory, they are neutral arbiters—overseeing the organization, setting its direction, and ensuring accountability while leaving day-to-day management to executives. In practice, many boards in Chinese private companies remain symbolic, dominated by family members or longtime loyalists with limited independence or authority. When boards lack real power, succession devolves into informal bargaining, driven more by relationships than by capability or long-term fit.

Effective stewardship requires clarity before it's needed. Decision rights must be explicit. Roles must be clearly demarcated. Mechanisms for resolving conflict—between siblings, branches of a family, or family and management—must exist in advance so leadership transitions are accepted as legitimate and final. Structure cannot guarantee harmony—but it can prevent chaos. As one adviser puts it: "If you don't fix governance, it doesn't matter how well you prepare for a transition; the whole thing can be overturned the next day should someone inherit power and decide to do things differently."

Chinese family businesses face an added dilemma: formal boards and governance structures are often seen more as Western imports than culturally-rooted solutions. They're also seen as overly rigid. The real challenge is finding that middle ground that will support succession and accountability without eroding cultural legitimacy or founder authority.

Already in Transition: From Founder's Instinct to Institutional Leadership

Elsewhere in the Chinese business world, this transition is further along. In Taiwan, family-controlled groups such as Fubon Financial,

CTBC Bank (formerly Chinatrust Commercial Bank), and Cathay Financial Holdings have navigated multi-generational transitions. In Hong Kong, firms like CK Hutchison Holdings have long operated with professionalized management and formal governance. Formed earlier, these companies have had decades to institutionalize.

For Elmer Cheng, who left Merrill Lynch in New York to become CEO of his Hong Kong family business, Polygroup, the early challenge wasn't competence but rather legitimacy in the eyes of his father's longtime lieutenants. Polygroup traces its roots back to his grandfather's 1960s Hong Kong workshop selling silk flowers by the stem; his father, Wai (Paul) Cheng, later transformed the business after watching his young sons beg for a "too expensive" artificial Christmas tree they'd seen at a Hudson's Bay store in Canada—prompting him to vow to make one himself. With the "one-man-show" instincts of a founder, Paul built Polygroup into the world's largest artificial Christmas tree manufacturer, driving explosive growth as he shifted production from Hong Kong to Thailand, Indonesia, Mexico, and mainland China, and also expanded into new product lines such as summer inflatables.

When Elmer became CEO at thirty-six, he felt like slinking out the very first time he stepped into the company boardroom. "Huge imposter syndrome," Elmer says. "Not knowing if I could lead, not knowing if my peers, all these older 'generals' who'd followed my dad for twenty, thirty years, would respect me." He also felt like he'd "lost a father and gained a boss—and family gatherings sometimes felt like I was having dinner with my shareholders."

Yet Elmer slowly put in place the structures to help guarantee the company thrives in his generation and beyond. He's already thinking about his fourth-generation son, hoping he'll have the freedom to choose his own path, but also trying to raise him with humility: "I tell my son, 'I had to wait until I was a teenager before I got real soccer cleats. I even slept with my first pair,'" Elmer says. His son now does the same.

Mainland firms are now beginning the same shift from founder-style leadership. In Shanghai, Kelvin Pan's path to leadership at AAC

Technologies—Apple's largest supplier of acoustic components, haptics, and precision mechanical parts—began with a call from his father, Zhengmin (Benjamin) Pan, to join the family business. In his twenties, Kelvin returned to China from Boston, where he'd studied math and computer science at Boston University and had planned to launch a start-up in the venture capital ecosystem there.

At AAC, Kelvin began in IT in 2014, went on to oversee a hundred engineers in R&D, and gradually moved into business operations, where he observed AAC sales teams repeatedly falling short in the smartphone business—their goal of achieving 30 billion RMB (about $4 billion) in annual sales often yielding only about 60 percent of the targets they'd set. It was an experience he found "deeply frustrating," he recalls. "That happened for a few years in a row. It wasn't a market issue—it was about how we operated." Kelvin pushed his father and internal advisers for changes in R&D, strategy, and organization. In parallel, he set AAC's Android motor business on a path to a fifty-fold expansion, reaching roughly 1 billion RMB ($143 million) in revenues today.

It was a milestone. "Once you start managing the business and getting results, you gain credibility," Kelvin says. By 2022, he was overseeing all business units and driving expansion into new products and markets. "There's no straightforward answer to succession," he admits. "It's about how you grow, and integrate, and take on more responsibility as you go."

The Opportunity: What the Next Generation Can Do Better

Succession in China is often framed as a liability. The stories in this chapter suggest a different way of seeing it—as a rare opportunity for second-generation leaders to bring new capabilities into businesses that saw success in a very different era. That shift matters as Chinese companies increasingly expand abroad, says Mingyu, who leads McKinsey's China succession work.

"The parents have proven themselves in China, but, given the business context now, it's impossible for their kids to be even more successful within China," he says. "The only way forward is to move the goalpost: 'what you did in China, I can do worldwide.' It's a mandate to go global." The prospect of globally-educated, next-generation CEOs transforming traditional Chinese corporates into the next multinationals from China is exciting.

That's exactly what Yihong, the second-generation leader at Suntar, is doing. Fluent in Mandarin and English and experienced across Asia and the United States, he is leading the company's push beyond China. "Culturally, it's easier for me than for my father to adapt to how business is done with clients outside China," he says. "I have fewer preconceptions in terms of how things should work; by contrast, in China, I'd never be as effective as my father."

Managing a successful transition, however, takes time. In a structure we expect will be increasingly common, Yihong sits on the board while a trusted management team runs day-to-day operations as part of a phased handover. He won't take the top role for another five to ten years.

For private equity firms and companies looking for consolidation opportunities, the coming succession wave presents an intriguing proposition. As founders age and families reassess their priorities, many businesses that were never intended for sale may come onto the market. "If the next generation has interest in other areas, which may have even higher potential, why do they have to stick with the old business?" says family-owned business adviser Roger King. "Why wouldn't selling the business at the right time, at the right price, be a good choice?" Increasingly, families may conclude that liquidity and diversification matter more than preserving direct control.

But for buyers of these businesses, the purchase decision is only the beginning. Private equity firms still face a hard question: Who runs the company next? In some cases, PE owners retain the founding team for a transition period, pairing them with professional managers to institutionalize operations, governance, and incentives. In other situations, founders exit entirely, forcing investors to recruit outside leadership—a tall order in markets with a scarcity of seasoned operators who can step into founder-led businesses.

Monetization remains the final hurdle. IPOs, trade sales, and secondary buyouts are all possible, but none is guaranteed. Investors are underwriting longer holding periods and prioritizing businesses that can survive leadership transitions, not just deliver near-term gains. In China's succession wave, private equity's advantage will rest not on capital alone but on its ability to supply governance, talent, and a credible path from founder-led growth to institution-led durability.

At this juncture in China's history, there are more questions than answers. Will this generation of family-owned businesses survive their founders? How many businesses will celebrate their one hundredth anniversary? In contrast, how many will follow the path of the Chinese proverb that asserts, "wealth doesn't last more than three generations?"

We are only beginning to see how the next era will unfold.

On the Cusp of the Next China

In early 2026, we found ourselves at the headquarters of a Chinese industrial components manufacturer. The founder, now in his sixties, had started the company in the mid-1990s with a single workshop on the outskirts of a coastal city, a few machines, and contracts he'd secured by personally visiting factories on his motorbike. Over the next thirty years, he expanded plant-by-plant, moved production inland as costs rose, automated aggressively in the 2010s, and built a business that now supplies global brands across Asia, Europe, and North America.

His story mirrors China's: years of growth, rising confidence, and the belief that scale would deliver progress. "I wake up earlier now," he tells us, "Not because I have more to build—but because everything is moving again." He wasn't describing collapse or crisis but a shift in rhythm. The instincts that he built his company upon still matter—but they're no longer enough.

China is once again passing through a period of technological and economic reordering. For some, the experience feels like loss. Growth has slowed. Property, once the unquestioned store of wealth, is being unwound. Debt is being confronted, though not yet resolved. Price wars are brutal. Margins are thin. For those exposed to these shifts, past strategies no longer make sense, and the future feels uncertain.

At the same time, others are experiencing the opposite. Chinese industrial and technological capabilities, refined over decades, are now genuinely world-class. Overseas markets are absorbing Chinese products and brands at scale. Chinese consumers remain among the world's fastest to try to adopt new products and services; any niche segment presents a potential mass-market opportunity. Capital markets in Hong Kong and on the mainland are again backing new IPOs. And a generation of entrepreneurs, enriched by successful earlier ventures, is recycling capital, experience, and ambition into new ones.

This coexistence of pressure and progress is why the moment is often misread. What we're witnessing is neither stagnation nor a break from the past. It's a reset. China is redefining how it grows, what success looks like, how companies are built and led, and how the country engages with the world.

In strategy, the hardest task is rarely analysis. It's letting go of assumptions forged during the last era of success. With that perspective, we offer a few closing observations.

Many Overlapping Agendas

Commentary often treats "China" as a single monolithic entity moving with one purpose. On the ground, the reality is far more complex and often surprisingly fragmented. As Harvard professor and China expert William Kirby has observed, "People think of China as one huge state actor, but in reality, there are thousands of provinces and districts competing with one another."

National directives may originate from the center, but outcomes are shaped locally—by a complex web of provincial governments, local municipalities, state-owned enterprises, and private firms, each with its own incentives and constraints. It's easy to declare, "Support advanced manufacturing." It's much harder to bring an end to involution, which requires allowing weaker players to fail. No one volunteers to take the loss.

This internal divergence is also geographic. China isn't Shanghai, Beijing, Shenzhen, or Hangzhou alone, nor is it just Xiaomi,

Huawei, or Geely. Travel inland to a third-tier city, and you'll find lower incomes, smaller firms, and businesses far from the technological frontier described in much of global commentary. Much of the economy remains closer to "catching up" than "cutting edge."

That gap explains both why China is under pressure—and why so much potential still exists. It's also why multinationals remain interested in China, particularly the opportunity to engage the vast middle of the economy, where productivity gains, upgrading, and diffusion of products and technology still have room to run.

Understanding China, therefore, requires recognizing this unevenness: not a single agenda but many, often overlapping, and pulling in different directions. Studying the most capable 1 percent tells you what's possible—but it shouldn't be confused with where the whole economy is headed. The "next China" should be read as a selective and uneven evolution.

What This Moment Is *Not*

In periods of transformation, it's natural to reach for analogies—and we've heard them all. China is variously compared to late-stage Soviet planning, wartime America, or an accelerated Industrial Revolution. Each captures something real, but most rely on outdated frameworks and ultimately fall short. Here are some of the most common misconceptions:

This is not Japan in the 1990s, headed for decades of stagnation. The parallels are familiar, but the comparison breaks down on scale and structure. Japan peaked as a fully urbanized, high-income society with one of the world's highest GDPs per capita. China has not reached that stage. Per capita remains low by developed-world standards, and both urbanization and middle-class expansion still have runway to grow. At the same time, the size of China's economy means that incremental progress unfolds on a vastly different scale.

Even modest growth produces outsized impact. China is confronting this moment as the world's dominant manufacturing platform and a leading R&D spender—that is still far from the global frontier in many technologies. Spending growth is slowing, but absolute spending remains well below US levels. Stagnation is possible; the base case is that China still has runway.

This is not decoupling. Supply chains are shifting, but they remain deeply intertwined. What is underway is not a clean economic separation—parallel systems, severed trade, and mutual irrelevance—but, instead, a reconfiguration: tighter boundaries around sensitive technologies, capital, and data, while leaving the majority of trade and production intact.

Some narratives frame this moment as a contest—*who* will win? Inside China, the fixation is different: adaptation, resilience, expanded ties with the global South, and reduced exposure to choke points such as semiconductors and other critical inputs. Within this framing, the United States and China are cast as the primary axes of competition for technology, markets, and strategic influence. Europe, by contrast, risks being at the margins of the conversation, grappling with how to position itself between the two as a partner, a counterpoint, or an autonomous actor.

The United States continues to exert a powerful pull, though no longer an exclusive one. Admiration among many Chinese persists, less as unquestioned aspiration than as a benchmark, much as a younger sibling might look to an older one for recognition of achievement rather than chastisement for shortcomings. Chinese entrepreneurs continue to cite American companies and founders. The ambition is to be the next Elon Musk or Mark Zuckerberg and to build the next Tesla or Meta; at the same time, China now has its own growing roster of icons and companies to emulate.

Indeed, American culture and institutions still matter. US sports leagues such as the NBA remain popular; and American firms are among the most sought-after employers. For many families, English fluency remains a priority, and Chinese migrants form a large, influential diaspora in North America. Educational ambitions, however, have diversified: while US universities remain a draw for many, more

Chinese students are looking to UK, European, Singaporean, and domestic universities, reflecting a broader recalibration. Mutual understanding and familiarity, however, are increasingly asymmetric. Even as numbers are down from pre-COVID peaks, tens of thousands of Chinese students still go to the United States each year, while fewer than two thousand Americans are studying in China. This gap will shape how future leaders and decision-makers will understand—or misunderstand—one another in an era of managed interdependence and geopolitical strain.

The Southeast Asia detour: the promise and the reality. This region plays a central role in global diversification strategies, offering competitive manufacturing bases, improving infrastructure, and meaningful long-term consumer growth. We've accompanied Chinese and foreign companies alike as they've expanded into India and Southeast Asia, particularly Thailand, Indonesia, and Vietnam—seeking to diversify from China and reach new consumers. What companies discover isn't a lack of opportunity, but a difference in structure. Consumer demand is distributed across multiple markets, which can make scaling slower and require more coordinated regional approaches than expected, with market sizes a fraction of China's.

In conversations with business leaders diversifying to Vietnam, Dominic Barton, chairman of Rio Tinto and Canada's former ambassador to China, has offered a pointed reminder: "That's great, but Vietnam's GDP is barely bigger than Chongqing's." The point is less a judgment than a reminder of how market size shapes expectations.

For many companies, this has clarified how different markets play different roles. Many Chinese executives now concede that "plus-one" markets are useful bases for manufacturing and diversification while recognizing that building consumer businesses there typically requires longer time horizons. By contrast, Europe and North America often provide more concentrated demand and clearer paths to near-term revenue scale. As one Chinese client puts it succinctly, "The next US is still the US." For many Chinese companies, no other market yet matches America's in scale, margins, or the global credibility that comes with winning over its consumers.

Looking Into the Next Decade

The question isn't whether China will continue to evolve, but rather when accumulated experiments will crystallize into lasting direction. Such turning points are seldom apparent at the time, and become visible only in hindsight.

Why the next few years will define the next decade. China has long moved in waves: extended periods of experimentation followed by shorter, decisive moments of consolidation. The next few years are likely to be one of those moments—not because the Chinese business landscape will suddenly transform, but because several macro-adjustments are converging at once: a tentative stabilization in the property sector; weakness in consumer demand; a transition from quantity to quality growth; the uneven but accelerating adoption of new technologies; and a tougher geopolitical landscape are no longer challenges that come sequentially—they're interacting in real time.

That convergence has compressed the margin for error. Companies are being forced to make structural decisions earlier, with less room for correction; adequacy, once sufficient in a fast-growing market, is no longer enough. Balance sheets, operating models, and competitive positioning are being tested simultaneously. The risks are substantial: policy missteps, external shocks, uneven technology adoption, organizational fatigue, and social strain could slow or derail progress. Some firms will fail. Some sectors will shrink. Many bets will prove wrong.

What makes this period decisive isn't its volatility but its irreversibility. Choices made now—about markets, technologies, partners, and risk tolerance—will shape operating norms and competitive positions for years to come.

Our clients are preparing for this next phase. In our minds we can see where this transition is headed: Nick and Joe meeting a next-generation

Chinese entrepreneur, not in Beijing or Shenzhen but in Riyadh, Istanbul, or Jakarta, building a company that feels truly global. The firm has Chinese origins, but its brands, manufacturing footprint, proprietary technology, talent, and capital span continents. This entrepreneur is fluent not only in engineering and cost control, but in governance, compliance, branding, and partnership—soft capabilities that were once peripheral and are now central. Competing globally is no longer about exporting efficiency; it is about credibility from day one.

Our multinational clients feel this moment just as acutely; they are being pushed not only to raise their own game in China—revisiting how they operate, localize, and justify their presence—but also to learn how to partner, co-develop, and innovate inside China. Increasingly, our meetings take place in R&D centers, joint labs, and regional hubs rather than headquarters, and we together focus less on market entry or scale than on where to collaborate, what to build together, and how to create value that can travel in both directions.

This is the next China taking shape—outward-facing, commercially sophisticated, and structurally embedded in the world economy. It's also the context in which the next generation will build their lives and careers. The paths ahead look different from the ones that shaped ours, with fewer obvious shortcuts and higher expectations at every turn. For us, this shift is no longer theoretical—it frames the questions we are now asking at home.

Our own next generation. We both have children now in their late teens and early twenties, and when we talk with them, our conversations often revolve around their future in the "next China." Their trajectories were very similar to ours: Joe's two sons were born and raised in Hong Kong before leaving to study and work in the US. Nick's four daughters grew up between Hong Kong, Beijing, and Europe and are now studying in the UK. Despite the geographical distance, their academic and extracurricular interests remain closely tied to China. As for us, like many "empty-nester" parents, we bemoan that we see them less than we once did—usually only during brief visits home.

During these visits, packed schedules and jet lag compress weeks of absence into a handful of shared meals. It's then that the conversation inevitably turns to familiar questions: where to find internships; whether to stay abroad after graduation; how long to build work experience before returning to Greater China; and whether coming back still makes sense at all.

It becomes clear to us during these discussions, as it does to our children, that the China upon which we built our careers is not the China they will inherit. When we started as young professionals traveling between Hong Kong and mainland China, the defining question centered around who might dare to take a chance on an emerging market whose future was uncertain. Opportunity lay in being early—in forging your own path and accepting risk. It was an era shaped by commercialization and institution-building, propelled by extraordinary macroeconomic tailwinds.

For the next generation, the challenge is fundamentally different. China is no longer a new frontier; it is one of the most competitive professional markets in the world. Every role attracts exceptional talent. Every advantage is contested, and simply showing up is no longer enough. Success now depends on distinctiveness—on identifying a niche, building real depth, and competing locally and globally from the outset.

Our dinner-table debate, therefore, is whether the opportunities ahead are greater or fewer than those we encountered over the last few decades. Your authors were beneficiaries of a historic era of growth—perhaps unmatched in modern business. Yet we are firmly convinced that China's golden era is not over—it has evolved. While narrower in margin, tougher in execution, and far more demanding of excellence, the possibilities today are also deeper and more sophisticated. They're rooted in technology, global integration, and the ability to shape markets both within China and beyond its borders.

*   *   *

In closing, China's story resists easy labels—neither unbroken triumph nor inevitable decline. Its business landscape is being reshaped by real structural constraints and equally significant structural strengths. This is not a zero-sum story; China's next phase will generate pressure far beyond China's borders while also creating new forms of opportunity. And whether the world chooses engagement or distance, it will feel the consequences all the same.

To understand—and thrive in—China's next chapter requires clarity, humility, and curiosity.

Acknowledgments

The idea for this book grew out of a long-running conversation between us that began years ago and never stopped—whether it was at the office, out on a client site, in a car to Shenzhen, on a flight to Lijiang, or while having a catch-up lunch at the China Club in the old Bank of China building in Hong Kong. "We should write a book!" was the constant refrain. We're thrilled *The Next China Is Still China* has finally come to life, helped along by colleagues, friends, and family members, as well as a few trusted advisers and mentors who guided us along the way.

First and foremost, we're indebted to the more than two hundred people who consented to have their perspectives included in this book, named or not. They spoke candidly about the challenges they face and the possibilities that excite them, and allowed us to surface thoughts from their boardrooms, conference rooms, factories, and strategy sessions alike. Without their stories—and most importantly, their trust—there would be little upon which to hang our insights.

For sharing in-depth accounts, we extend special thanks to: Joe Bao, Hang Chen, Elmer Cheng, Phyllis Cheung, Brian Gu, Chunguang Gu, David Ku, Yihong Lan, David Li, Kelvin Pan, Junjian Qian, Anne Tse, Haimeng Zhang, Mandy Zhang, and Jian Zhou. A special acknowledgment goes to Gordon Orr for both his stories and his detailed feedback on the manuscript, and for championing the project within our wider community.

For sharing their candid perspectives, we're also grateful to: Dominic Barton, John Cai, Louis Cheung, Shannon Cheung, Jason Chiu, Cindy Chow, Hong Chow, Asina de Branche, Chloe Fang, Hongbo Fang, Dai Feng, Wei Fu, Paul Gao, Alicia García-Herrero, Herry Han, Grace Hu, Michael Hui, Roger King, James Kralik, Franck Le Deu, Ethan Lin, Natalie Liu, Leon Meng, Alfons Mensdorff-Pouilly, Zoey Miao, Ning Ning, Alwin Poon, Xinghua Qin, Chunxin Qiu, Iskra Reic, Sha Sha, Junna Shi, Michael Straub, Derek Sulger, Frank Tang, Shiquan Wang, Xiaofan Wang, Alex Wong, Brian Wong, Yibing Wu, Yonglin Xie, Jun Xu, Xiaofeng Xu, Ervin Zaka, Michael Zang, Henry Zhang, and Ju Zhang.

From the outset, we knew that our ideas would need to be framed with rigor and unfolded along a compelling narrative. We owe our deepest thanks to Lenora Chu for her strategic and editorial leadership in shaping the empirical argument and keeping the team moving forward. Her influence is evident—we could not have done this without her. Jeongmin Seong, our lead Asia economist and partner at the McKinsey Global Institute, brought additional depth and perspective, and we owe a huge thank you for his leadership and orchestration.

Together, we were expertly guided by our editor Rick Horgan, his assistant editor Sophie Guimaraes, and their colleagues across the Scribner team. We thank Jenny Chan for encouraging us to bring this idea into the light; Lynn Johnston for finding a home for the book; and Raju Narisetti, the leader of McKinsey Global Publishing, for bringing the project together. Dozens of colleagues worked behind the scenes. From McKinsey's Greater China offices, our core project managers Yicheng Qian and Yannan Bu kept the effort on track. Others who have contributed include Meng Liu, Erik Rong, Jason Wang, Yaqiao Wang, and Chang Zhao. Chunxiao Yin oversaw the most detailed transcription work. Special thanks to our assistants Stephanie Leung and Jeanne Lee, who, as always, kept us organized so that the team could focus on the work.

We're thankful for our McKinsey Greater China partners who offered their thoughts, frameworks, data, and stories. A special call-out goes to the following for reading chapters or offering in-depth assistance: Daniel Birke, Tina Hou, Jin Wang, Kevin Wei Wang, Fangning Zhang, and Daniel Zipser. We're also thankful for the contributions of: Lambert Bu, Kevin Chan, Michael Chang, Michael Chi Chen, Fox Chu, Violet Chung, Karel Eloot, Derek Fu, Mingyu Guan, Sheng Hong, Xin Huang, Cedric Leleu, Jan Milark, Yermolai Solzhenitsyn, Antonio Sun, Mark Sun, Richard Wang, Sharon Wang, Stanley Wang, Peng Xia, Lingxiao Xiao, Minyu Xiao, Hai Ye, Wings Zhang, Liang Zhou, Tony Zhou, and Elsen Zhu.

We're also grateful to Ruth Heuss, Ani Kelkar, Acha Leke, and Andreas Tschiesner, who contributed expertise from across McKinsey's global network.

Most importantly, we'd like to thank our families, not only for spending winter holidays reading sections and discussing ideas, but for the decades of patience you've shown for the long absences that come with our demanding client work, global board duties, and other commitments. Our Firm responsibilities didn't let up at any point during this project, and neither did your support.

Joe would like especially to thank Angela, Matthew, and Michael, who put up with his nonstop Zoom calls and editing throughout their Christmas vacation. A special mention goes to Matthew, whose unwavering high bar, relentless editing, and insightful comments got us through the homestretch. Thanks for helping me with my homework!

Nick very much appreciates the patience and good humor of Lisina, Una, Binia, Lulu, and Tessa during their vacation, but especially Quintus and Emil—the canine family members—who kept him company as he holed up with the manuscript while the girls went skiing. The dogs were unable to help with any proofreading.

Lastly, to our children, this book is ultimately for you. It's about the choices you'll make, and the future you'll shape, and we're excited to see how it unfolds.

Notes

Except where specific citations are provided in this section, all statements, data, and factual references concerning companies or industries are based on McKinsey proprietary or client-supplied information.

For the purposes of clarity and comparability, all monetary values in this book use fixed exchange rates regardless of time period. The conversion rates applied are: RMB to USD at 7.00:1 and euro to USD at 1:1.16.

All web-based sources cited in the endnotes were accessed between October 2025 and March 2026.

Prologue

xiii *generating more than twenty-eight:* Media-monitoring analysis conducted by McKinsey, aggregating mentions of English- and Chinese-language press, broadcast, and online references, from 2023 to 2025.

xiv *At just 2 percent:* In 2024, China's GDP stands at $18.7 trillion, India's at $3.9 trillion, Japan's at $4.0 trillion, and Indonesia's at $1.4 trillion; at a 2 percent annual growth rate, the cumulative increase would amount to roughly $4.1 trillion over the next decade, whereas a 5 percent growth rate would yield an additional $11.8 trillion; World Bank Group, "GDP (Current US $)," n.d.

xiv *second biggest economy:* World Bank Group, "GDP, PPP (Current International $)—China," n.d.

xiv *China is the top trading partner:* MUFG Americas, *The United States & China: Volume 1—Assessing Trade, Investment, and Strategic Competition,* February 2024, p. 21.

xiv *and accounts for about 30 percent:* China contributed 33 percent of global real GDP growth in 2024 according to World Bank data.

xiv *Its companies are among the leaders in sixteen:* McKinsey Global Institute, *The Next Big Arenas of Competition,* October 23, 2024.

CHAPTER 1 McKinsey's Early Days in China

4 *home to 1.3 billion mobile users:* Ministry of Industry and Information Technology of the People's Republic of China, Bureau of Operation Monitoring and Coordination, *2015 Telecommunications Industry Statistical Bulletin,* January 21, 2016.

4 *population twenty-two million:* Beijing Municipal Bureau of Statistics and National Bureau of Statistics Beijing Survey Team, *Beijing Statistical Communique on National Economic and Social Development in 2024,* March 20, 2025.

4 *Beijing was a low-rise city of twelve million:* Beijing Municipal Bureau of Statistics, *Beijing Statistical Yearbook 2008,* "3–1 Population Status (1978–2008)." Accessed March 1, 2026.

7 *a $200 million Nestlé acquisition target:* McKinsey & Company, "History of Our Firm," company website, n.d.

7 *In the 1990s, "consulting" . . . of about $39 billion:* IBISWorld, Management Consulting in China Industry Data and Analysis, December 2024.

7 *private companies . . . half of total social investment:* Liu Zheng, "Non-Public Economy Becomes Main Channel for Employment," *China Youth Daily,* January 6, 2006.

7 *It moved about five million desktop PCs:* Sina Tech, "2005 China Desktop Computer Market: Lenovo Continues to Lead" [in Chinese], April 27, 2006.

8 *The $1.25 billion deal closed:* Lenovo, "Lenovo Completes Acquisition of IBM's Personal Computing Division," company website, May 1, 2005.

9 *In the 1990s, China's growth:* International Monetary Fund, "Real GDP Growth," n.d.

10 *foreign direct investment into China nearly tripled:* National Bureau of Statistics of China, *China Statistical Yearbook 2012,* "Foreign Direct Investment" [in Chinese].

10 *By the end of the decade:* Xi Jinping, "Keynote Speech at the Opening Ceremony of the Second World Investment Forum of UNCTAD," Xiamen, China, September 7, 2010.

10 *By 2002, Chinese buyers:* China Association of Automobile Manufacturers (CAAM), "2009 Automobile Production and Sales and Economic Operation Situation Information Release," CAAM.org.cn, January 11, 2010.

10 *more than 13.6 million vehicles . . . 10.4 million in the US:* China Daily, "China Becomes World's Largest Auto Market," January 9, 2010.

10 *3.8 million in Germany:* Verband der Automobilindustrie e.V. (VDA), "New Registrations: Annual Figures," August 4, 2025.

10 *by 2011, it had more restaurants:* Yum!, *2011 Yum! Brands Annual Customer Mania Report*, company website, February 20, 2012.

11 *Over the past fifteen years:* China pharma market size in terms of sales reached $112.8 billion in 2024, and the figure was $41.1 billion in 2010; IQVIA, *Top 10 Pharmaceutical Markets Worldwide, 2024*, May 2025; Patricia Van Arnum, "Tracking Pharmaceutical and API Growth in China," *Pharmaceutical Technology*, July 12, 2011.

11 *GM was selling more cars:* US Department of Energy, "Fact #669: GM Sells More Vehicles in China than in the US," April 4, 2011.

11 *Volkswagen:* Volkswagen Group, "Volkswagen Group Reports Delivery Record for 2009," company website, January 19, 2010.

11 *BMW crossed that threshold:* BMW Group, "BMW Group Posts Record Sales for 2013," company website, January 13, 2014.

11 *L'Oréal was booking:* L'Oréal, "Annual Results," company website, 2018–2020.

11 *Goldman's $2.5 billion stake:* Fiona Lau and Elzio Barreto, "Goldman Exits China's ICBC Seven Years and Billions Later," Reuters, May 15, 2013.

11 *more than forty Chinese firms went public in the US in 2010:* Bloomberg News, "Nasdaq Predicts 45 China IPOs in US in 2011, Topping Record," March 9, 2011.

12 *its share of GDP rose:* All-China Federation of Industry and Commerce (ACFIC), *Analysis Report on the Situation of Private Economy During the "Tenth Five-Year Plan" Period (with 2005 Data)*, 2006.

12 *to more than 60 percent:* State Taxation Administration, "Tax Burden on Private Enterprises Has Declined Significantly" [in Chinese], *China Tax News*, September 15, 2020.

13 Joe Ngai, The One Trillion Dollar Opportunity in Asset Management (Hong Kong: McKinsey & Company, 2005).

13 *is only around 1 percent:* Total assets of foreign-funded banks were 3.86 trillion RMB by the end of 2023, and the total industry size was 417.29 trillion RMB, equaling a 0.93 percent market share; People's Bank of China, "Total Assets of China's Banking Industry Reached 461.09 Trillion Yuan by the End of 2023" [in Chinese], March 20, 2024; China Banking Association, *Development Report on Foreign-Funded Banks in China 2023–2024*, September 13, 2024.

14 *its income from insurance premiums neared $32 billion: East Money*, "Ping An Insurance's Total Premium Income Reached 226.5 Billion Yuan in 2010," January 17, 2011.

14 *$1.9 trillion financial giant:* Ping An Insurance (Group), "Unaudited Interim Results Announcement for the Six Months Ended June 30, 2025" [in Chinese], August 26, 2025.

14 *mobile payments had reached 86 percent:* Xin Ping, "China in Digital Transformation: Fast and Furious," *China Daily*, October 23, 2025.

14 *Alibaba founder Jack Ma captured:* Jack Ma, "Speech at the World Economic Forum Annual Meeting 2019," Davos-Klosters, Switzerland, January 23, 2019.

15 *"It does everything":* Grace Kay, "Elon Musk Just Changed Twitter's Name to 'X.' His Old Text Messages Hint at What His Vision for an 'Everything App' Might Look Like," *Business Insider*, July 24, 2023.

15 *In the first seven months:* BYD Auto, "BYD Sold 344,296 Vehicles in July, with Cumulative Sales of 2,490,250 Vehicles from January to July 2025" [in Chinese], company website, August 5, 2025.

15 *70 percent of the world's new EVs:* Dongshu Cui, "Global New Energy Vehicle Sales Reached 16.03 Million Units in 2024, with 70.4 Percent Sold in China," *CNR Auto Channel*, February 13, 2025.

15 *Its express delivery volume:* CCTV, "Express Delivery Volume Ranks First in the World for 11 Consecutive Years, Exceeding 175 Billion Packages in 2024" [in Chinese], January 8, 2025.

15 *China installed half:* International Federation of Robotics (IFR), *World Robotics 2024 Report*, September 24, 2024.

15 *registered more World Health Organization–tracked:* World Health Organization, "Number of Clinical Trials by Year, Country, WHO Region and Income Group (1999–2024)."

16 *yet GDP per capita*: International Monetary Fund, "GDP per Capita, Current Prices (US Dollars per Capita); Real GDP Growth (Annual Percent Change)," n.d.

16 *A third of Chinese remain in rural areas*: National Bureau of Statistics of China, "National Two Sessions Service: National Economic Situation 2025," February 28, 2025.

CHAPTER 2 A Market Like No Other

18 *Antonio Stradivari emerged:* "How Many Stradivarius Violins Really Exist?," stradivarius.org, n.d.

18 *"only the wood of trees":* The Strad, "Great Violinists: Niccolò Paganini," July 17, 2024.

18 *Stradivari's violins command:* MyLuthier, "The 5 Most Expensive Violins in the World (updated 2024)," myluthier.co, n.d.

18 *factories produce almost 40 percent:* China Daily, "Town Becomes Instrumental in Global Violin Manufacturing," June 15, 2024.

18 *by 2007, a low-end:* Ziyi Huang, "Most of the Violins Favored by Middle-Class Families Come from this Small Town" [in Chinese], *Sanlian Lifeweek*, September 30, 2024.

18 *the town's largest producer:* Jiangsu Feng-Ling Company.

19 *Today, the Huangqiao industrial cluster:* Taixing Municipal Government, "China's Violin Industry Capital Shines with New Vitality," government website, August 31, 2025.

19 *Chinese violins have earned:* The Violin Channel, "Prizewinners Announced at the Violin Society of America's 2024 Competition," November 22, 2024.

19 *in 2024, Chinese luthier Liu Zhaojun: The Strad*, "One Gold Medal Awarded at 2024 Cremona Trikale Violin Making Competition," September 26, 2024.

19 *One Cremona luthier sold :* Author observation at Music China 2025, Shanghai New International Expo Centre; the luthier's name was Pasquale Sardone.

20 *with most economists expecting 4 to 5 percent:* International Monetary Fund, *World Economic Outlook*, October 2025; Goldman Sachs, "China's Economy Is Forecast to Grow Faster than Expected in 2026," November 21, 2025.

20 *China still adds:* World Bank Group, "GDP (Current US$)," n.d.

20 *and graduates more university students:* China: 14.5 million in 2024; Ministry of Education of the People's Republic of China, "Number of Students in Higher Education Institutions," n.d.

20 *Australia's total population:* twenty-seven million in 2024; World Bank Group, "Population," n.d.

20 *During its boom years, China poured:* Ana Swanson, "How China Used More Cement in Three Years than the US. Did in the Entire 20th Century," *Washington Post*, March 24, 2015.

20 *producing 5.2 billion cubic meters:* Cheng Zhou, "2024 Ready-Mixed Concrete Output Reaches 2.49 Billion Cubic Meters, Down 10.1 Percent Year-on-Year," China Cement Network Information Center, February 26, 2025.

20 *global output: Market Reports World*, "Concrete Market Size, Share, Growth, and Industry Analysis," January 26, 2026.

20 *China's 50,000 kilometers of high-speed: People's Daily*, "China's High-Speed Rail Network Now Exceeds 50,000 Kilometers" [in Chinese], December 27, 2025.

20 *its 190,700 kilometers of expressways:* Ministry of Transport of the People's Republic of China, 2024 *Statistical Bulletin on the Development of the Transport Industry in China* [in Chinese], June 12, 2025.

20 *exceed that in the US and EU together:* 108,485 kilometers for the United States and 76,509 kilometers for European Union; United Nations Economic Commission for Europe, "Total Length of Motorways," n.d.; Eurostat, "Length of Motorways and E-roads," n.d.

20　*263 airports built:* Civil Aviation Administration of China, 2024 *National Civil Transport Airport Operations Statistical Bulletin* [in Chinese], March 2025.

20　*you'll see that China Central Television's CCTV Chinese New Year show:* Chan Nan, "CCTV Spring Festival Gala 2024 Draws 679 Million Viewers, Up Nearly 13 Percent Year-on-Year," *China Daily*, February 10, 2024.

21　*more than five times Super Bowl 2025's viewership:* Nielsen, "Super Bowl LIX Makes TV History with over 127 Million Viewers," February 11, 2025.

21　*the sixth most frequented:* Themed Entertainment Association, Chimelong Ocean Kingdom, "TEA Global Experience Index™ 2024."

21　*more than 1,100 soccer fields:* Chimelong Safari Park . . . covers more than 2,000 acres, a standard FIFA soccer field is roughly 1.77 acres; Chimelong Group, "About Us," company website, n.d.

21　*a regional population:* Hong Kong SAR Government's Constitutional and Mainland Affairs Bureau, "Guangzhou Introduction" [in Chinese], bayarea.gov.hk, n.d.

22　*China already has:* McKinsey analysis; definition of upper-middle and above class is annual household disposable income greater than 180,000 RMB (about $26,000) (real income, in 2025 prices).

22　*a third-tier city can range:* Sanya News Network, "Permanent Population of Sanya Exceeds 1.11 Million by the End of 2024" [in Chinese], May 11, 2025.

22　*the population spread:* Nanyang Government, 2024 *Statistical Communiqué on National Economic and Social Development of Nanyang City*, April 8, 2025.

22　*there are about seventy:* Shanghai Media Group, "China Business News Releases '2025 New First-Tier Cities Charm Ranking,' Refreshing the Past and Rediscovering New Value" [in Chinese], n.d.

22　*five million STEM graduates:* General Office of the State Council of the People's Republic of China, "Over Five Million STEM Graduates Annually, Leading the World!—Understanding the New Advantages of China's Economy" [in Chinese], April 1, 2024.

22　*Apple CEO Tim Cook:* Fortune Global Forum, "Tim Cook Discusses Apple's Future in China," YouTube video, December 6, 2017.

23　*the Huajiang Gorge Bridge:* Xinhua, "Guizhou's Huajiang Gorge Bridge Officially Opens to Traffic" [in Chinese], September 28, 2025.

23　*accounting for roughly 70 percent:* According to the International Union of Railways, China has accounted for roughly 60 to 70 percent of newly operational high-speed rail since 2015 (≥250 km/h), rising to 75 to 80 percent if including lines ≥200 km/h, International Union of Railways, 2023 *Global Rail Sustainability Report*, 2023.

23　*it was scheduling 3.7 billion:* "China's Rail Sector Handles Record 3.68 Billion Trips in 2023," CGTN, January 10, 2024.

23 *In 2024, China's industrial enterprises:* Everbright Securities, "Non-Ferrous Metals Industry Dynamic Commentary Report" [in Chinese], *Sina Finance*, November 16, 2025.

23 *in the first half of 2025:* Renewable Energy Industry, "China Becomes the First Country in the World to Surpass One Thousand GW of Solar Power Capacity," August 25, 2025.

23 *more than the entire installed:* Solar Energy Industries Association, *Solar Market Insight Report Q4 2025*, December 8, 2025.

23 *and almost double that of Germany's:* PV Knowhow, "Germany Solar Installations: Impressive 920 MW Milestone," October 24, 2025.

23 *take note of purchasing power parity:* International Monetary Fund, "World Economic Outlook (WEO)—GDP at Purchasing Power Parity (PPP) Dataset," 2025.

24 *Services now account:* Wentao Wang, "Multiple Measures to Boost Service Consumption" [in Chinese], gov.cn, April 16, 2025.

27 *Meanwhile, 77 percent:* McKinsey & Company, "Chinese Consumption Amid the New Reality," May 7, 2025.

27 *Consumer confidence has been:* McKinsey & Company, "China Macro & Consumer Trends," China-Italy Chamber of Commerce discussion seminar, Shanghai, September 24, 2025.

28 *And the Chinese are sitting on a gross national savings rate around 44 percent:* World Population Review, "Gross National Savings Rate by Country 2025."

29 *Volkswagen Group CEO:* CGTN BIZ, "Volkswagen CEO: Driving Innovation with 'China Speed,'" YouTube, April 24, 2025.

29 *local manufacturers routinely complete:* McKinsey analysis.

30 *"Shenzhen speed":* China State Construction Engineering Corporation, "Shenzhen Speed" [in Chinese], December 13, 2018.

30 *with London Heathrow's runway expansion:* Heathrow Airport Limited, "Expanding Heathrow," 2025; "London Heathrow Airport Unveils £49 Billion Expansion Plan to Build a Third Runway" [in Chinese], *CNR News*, August 1, 2025.

31 *Roughly two-thirds of safety warnings:* US PIRG Education Fund, "Safe at Home in 2025?," March 24, 2025.

32 *building a plant in China . . . 20 percent of the time:* McKinsey analysis.

32 *companies see 50 percent lower capex . . . build times:* McKinsey analysis.

33 *Tesla has more than four hundred:* CnEV Post, "Tesla Now Has Over 400 Tier-1 Suppliers in China" [in Chinese], November 26, 2024.

33 *AAC can ramp up . . . at half the cost of comparable overseas production:* Kelvin Pan in discussion with McKinsey, September 12, 2025.

CHAPTER 3 The World's Toughest Gym

35 *"creative destruction":* Joseph A. Schumpeter, *Capitalism, Socialism and Democracy*, Routledge, 2003, 81.

36 *where five hundred million thrifty households:* National Bureau of Statistics of China, "2023 National Population Sample Survey: Household and Population Data" [in Chinese].

37 *early EV buyers could receive:* National Development and Reform Commission of China, "Notice on Continuing the Promotion and Application of New Energy Vehicles (Cai Jian [2013] No. 551)—Annex: 2013 New Energy Vehicle Promotion and Application Subsidy Standards" [in Chinese], September 13, 2013.

37 *but not before more than a hundred:* The Paper (*Pengpai News*), "China's NEV Market Sees Intensified Matthew Effect: Top 10 Carmakers Grab Over 74 percent of Market Share as Tail Brands Seek Restructuring" [in Chinese], January 23, 2026.

38 *From 2014 to 2024 . . . five times that of the United States:* McKinsey analysis based on data from National Bureau of Statistics of China, US Census Bureau, and S&P Global.

40 *Starbucks had 3,300 outlets:* Starbucks, "Starbucks Hosts First-Ever Global Investor Conference in China—Plans to Expand Mainland Store Count to 6,000 by End of FY2022" [in Chinese], company website, May 16, 2018.

40 *plans to open:* Nyshka Chandran, "Starbucks CEO: We're Going to Apply to the US What We Learned in China," CNBC, November 6, 2018.

40 *$20 billion industry:* Hongcan Think Tank, *Coffee Beverages Category Development Report 2025* [in Chinese], *Xinhua*, November 7, 2025.

40 *In 2020, the company divulged:* James Hatton, "Luckin Coffee Fires CEO, COO After RMB 2.2B in Sales Said Faked," *Mingtiandi*, May 13, 2020.

41 *nearly a hundred new products:* Luckin Coffee, "Luckin Coffee, Inc. Q4 and FY2023 Earnings Conference Call Transcript," February 23, 2024.

42 *more than thirty thousand nationwide:* Corporate Communications Team, Luckin, email message to authors, December 2025.

42 *surpassed Starbucks China:* Luckin Coffee, "Luckin Coffee Announces Third Quarter 2025 Financial Results," November 17, 2025; Starbucks, *Fiscal 2023 Annual Report*, November 17, 2023.

42 *it launched nine thousand:* David Li, in discussion with McKinsey, October 17, 2025.

43 *Starbucks expects the partnership:* Starbucks, "Starbucks and Boyu Announce Joint Venture for the Next Chapter of Growth in China," press release, company website, November 3, 2025.

43 *to about four hundred million: China Daily*, "Taking a Sip of New Coffee Culture in Nation's Northwest," April 11, 2025.

43 *offered a 3.9 RMB ($0.6):* Guo Jun, "Another Coffee Brand 'Suicidal Store Opening' in Shanghai: 2.9 RMB per Cup Breaks the Price Floor" [in Chinese], *Digitaling*, October 16, 2025.

44 *What left the deepest impression:* Luo Yonghao, "Interview with He Xiaopeng," *Crossroads with Luo Yonghao*, podcast episode, YouTube [in Chinese], August 26, 2025.

44 *fewer than four hundred thousand cars . . . more than four million:* BYD Company Limited, 2015 Annual Report and 2024 Annual Report, company website.

45 *at one point outselling:* Alan Martin, "This Electric Car Is Under $5,000— and It's Outselling Tesla Two to One," *Tom's Guide*, February 28, 2021.

45 *Chinese firms have built:* Zuosi Car Research, "Trends Through Patents: Three Major Directions for Smart Cockpits in 2025," *Zhihu*, July 31, 2025.

45 *Beijing expanded trials:* Transport of the People's Republic of China, "Four Ministries Announce the First Batch of Nine Consortiums Selected for the Intelligent Connected Vehicle Access and Road Operation Pilot Program, Covering Seven Cities," June 6, 2024.

46 *delivering over 1,300 kilometers:* One Shitong, "Quiet and Efficient: A Detailed Explanation of the Li L9's Fully Self-Developed Extended-Range Electric System" [in Chinese], Li Auto Community, July 13, 2022.

46 *just three years from announcing:* Zijie Wang, "Xiaomi's Carmaking Journey: From Zero to Mass Production in Just Three Years—Lei Jun: Xiaomi Officially Becomes an Automaker" [in Chinese], *Our China Story*, April 9, 2024.

46 *In 2024, Chinese carmakers produced nearly three-quarters:* International Energy Agency, *Global EV Outlook 2025: Expanding Sales in Diverse Markets*, May 14, 2025.

48 *Today, Chinese companies:* McKinsey analysis based on data from China Photovoltaic Industry Association.

48 *China installed nearly 60 percent:* Gaëtan Masson et al., *Snapshot 2025*, International Energy Agency, 2025.

48 *nearly 70 percent:* Ember, "Global Solar Installations Surge 64 Percent in First Half of 2025," September 2, 2025.

48 *Polysilicon prices surged:* from mid-2020 lows of around 60,000–70,000 RMB/ton to 310,000 RMB/ton in 2022; McKinsey analysis.

48 *advanced industry-wide cell efficiencies:* LONGi, "LONGi Publishes Its Annual Report for 2022 and 2023 Q1," company website, April 29, 2023.

48 *sending module prices plunging:* McKinsey analysis.

49 *From 2010 to 2025:* McKinsey analysis based on data from International Technology Roadmap for Photovoltaic and China Photovoltaic Industry Association.

49 *Gross margins collapsed:* McKinsey analysis.

49 *In some segments, production capacity:* China News Service, "PV Industry Must Avoid 'Losing Money to Gain Market Share,'" September 17, 2025.

49 *LONGi reported a $1.1 billion loss:* LONGi, "LONGi Publishes 2024 Annual Report: BC Tech Deployment Accelerates Across Industry," company website, April 30, 2025; Wei Zhongyuan, "Longi Is Last of China's Solar Panel Giants to Fall Below CNY100 Billion Market Cap," *Yicai Global*, July 9, 2024.

49 *home to both a billion:* Shanxi's annual coal production stood at 1.2–1.4 billion tons from 2021 to 2024 while global coal production is estimated to reach nine billion tons in 2024; *China Coal News*, "Shanxi Sets a Model for Smart and Green Coal Industry Development," *New Energy Era*, November 10, 2025; International Energy Agency, *Coal 2024 Report*, December 18, 2024.

49 *Wind and solar now . . . added annually:* Caroline Wang, "China Hit New Record of Solar and Wind Power Capacity Additions in 2024," *Climate Energy Finance*, February 18, 2025.

49 *with China building more than:* Ma Li and Charles Bourgault, "China's Renewable Energy Boom Has Its Own Challenges. Here's What We Can Learn," World Economic Forum, December 3, 2025.

50 *Chinese firms also:* From 2021 to 2024, China's share of global polysilicon output increased from 79 to 93 percent, while its market shares remained above 94 percent in wafers, roughly 98 percent in cells, and about 81 percent in modules; McKinsey analysis.

51 *China's return on invested capital:* McKinsey analysis.

53 *warning about the dangers:* Jin Sheping, "Achieve High-Quality Development by Breaking 'Involutionary' Competition," *People's Daily*, June 29, 2025.

53 *In vitamins, NHU now controls . . . net margin in 2024:* McKinsey analysis.

54 *Chinese producers collectively supply:* McKinsey analysis.

56 *Chinese steel sells at 30 to 50 percent:* McKinsey analysis.

56 *In advanced compressors . . . by only 10 to 15 percent:* McKinsey analysis.

56 *waste-to-energy plants:* Cinda Securities, "Environmental Industry Weekly Report (Week 51, 2025): Waste-to-Energy Companies Continue to Expand in Southeast Asian Market" [in Chinese], December 20, 2025.

CHAPTER 4 **The Price We Paid**

59 *China's urbanization surged:* World Bank Group, "Urban Population (Percent of Total Population)—China," n.d.

59 *The country now has 144 cities:* World Population Review, "China Cities by Population 2025."

59 *Europe's fifty-eight:* World Population Review, "Europe Cities by Population 2025."

59 *America's twelve:* World Population Review, "Largest US Cities by Population 2025."

59 *including eighteen mega-cities:* Hang Shi, "Four Cities Are Competing—Which One Will Become China's 19th Mega-City," *Tencent News*, December 29, 2025.

59 *This mass migration has fueled:* Daniel Zipser et al., "China's Consumption in the New Normal," McKinsey & Company, May 6, 2025.

60 *Corporate debt has climbed . . . two decades:* McKinsey Global Institute, "Out of Balance: What's Next for Growth, Wealth, and Debt," October 9, 2025.

61 *China's debt-to-GDP ratio:* Bank for International Settlements, "Comparative View of United States—Credit from All Sectors to Non-Financial Sector at Market Value, Percentage of GDP, Adjusted for Breaks," n.d.

62 *The collapse of Evergrande:* China Evergrande Group, "Announcement of Results for the Year Ended 31 December 2022," July 17, 2023.

63 *McKinsey's analysis suggests that without faster productivity growth:* McKinsey Global Institute, "Out of Balance: What's Next for Growth, Wealth, and Debt," October 9, 2025.

63 *China's household savings rate:* Longmei Zhang et al., "China's High Savings: Drivers, Prospects, and Policies," *IMF Working Papers 2018* (2018), no. 277.

63 *Japan and South Korea saw . . . never exceeded 10 percent:* McKinsey analysis based on OECD data.

63 *the country has invested tens of trillions worth of dollars:* National Bureau of Statistics.

63 *often more than 40 percent:* World Bank Group, "Gross Capital Formation (Percent of GDP)—China and United States," n.d.

64 *China's economy needed . . . to produce the same growth:* McKinsey analysis.

64 *where clearing existing inventory:* Shanghai E-House Real Estate Research Institute, 2025–2026 *National Real Estate Market Report* [in Chinese], WeChat Official Account, December 31, 2025.

64 *Household consumption . . . and South Korea:* World Bank Group, "Households and NPISHs Final Consumption Expenditure (Percent of GDP)"; Germany 50 percent in 2023, France 53 percent in 2023, Australia 51 percent in 2024, South Korea 48 percent in 2024.

64 *Families increasingly assumed:* Marcos Chamon and Eswar S. Prasad, "Why Are Saving Rates So High in China?," *IMF Working Paper* no. 08/145, 2008.

64 *Youth unemployment hovered just below 20 percent:* National Bureau of Statistics of China, "Unemployment Rate by Age Group" [in Chinese], 2025.

65 *Europe has grown at around 2 percent . . . 5 percent:* International Monetary Fund, *World Economic Outlook database*; McKinsey analysis.

65 *152 trillion RMB ($22 trillion):* National Bureau of Statistics of China, *2024 Statistical Communiqué on National Economic and Social Development.*

67 *Households devote a larger share:* Stanford Center on China's Economy and Institutions (SCCEI), Freeman Spogli Institute for International Studies (FSI), "The High Cost of Education in China," April 1, 2024.

67 *China had produced 260 million college graduates:* Ministry of Education of the People's Republic of China, "Education System Takes Multiple Measures to Promote Employment of College Graduates" [in Chinese], March 14, 2024.

68 *households earning 180,000 RMB (about $26,000):* McKinsey analysis; annual household disposable income >180,000 RMB (real, in 2025 price) is defined as the threshold for upper-middle-and-above class.

68 *with a carton of high-quality eggs:* Numbeo Cost of Living Data, "Prices by Country of Eggs (12, Large Size) (Markets)," accessed December 15, 2025.

68 *At the same time, the "4-2-1" burden:* China Social Security Research Center, Chinese Academy of Social Sciences, *China Pension Actuarial Report 2019–2050,* edited by Zheng Bingwen. (Beijing: China Labor and Social Security Publishing House, 2019).

68 *over three million applied:* BBC Chinese, "Observation: What Economic and Employment Changes Are Reflected by the Surge in China's 'National Civil Service Exam' Applicants Surpassing Postgraduate Entrance Exam Candidates?," 2023.

69 *Fertility has fallen to around 1.0:* National Bureau of Statistics, *China Population and Employment Statistical Yearbook 2025,* (Beijing: China Statistics Press, 2025).

69 *by mid-century the number of citizens over age sixty-five will rise from 15 to 31 percent:* United Nations Population Division, "Percentage of Total Population by Broad Age Group"; n.d.

70 *240 million rural migrants:* National Bureau of Statistics of China, *Statistical Communiqué of the People's Republic of China on the 2010 National Economic and Social Development* [in Chinese], February 28, 2011.

70 *The number of urban Chinese:* Pingping Wang, "Population Decline Narrowed, Population Quality Continued to Improve" [in Chinese], National Bureau of Statistics of China website, January 17, 2025.

70 *Yet the population peaked:* World Bank Group, "Population, Total—China," n.d.

70 *Western Europe is expected:* United Nations Population Division, "Percentage of Total Population by Broad Age Group," n.d.; by 2050, the share of

the population aged sixty-five and above is projected to reach 29 percent in Western Europe and 23 percent in the United States.

70   *with higher fertility rates:* United Nations Population Division, "Total Fertility Rate," n.d.; in 2025, fertility rate in China is 1.0 percent, 1.5 percent in Western Europe, and 1.6 percent in the United States.

70   *also higher rates of immigration: World Population Review,* "Immigration by Country," n.d.; Rockwool Foundation Berlin, *The Immigrant Population in the European Union,* December 4, 2025.

70   *Today, roughly five workers:* United Nations Conference on Trade and Development (UNCTAD), *UNCTADstat,* "Population Dependency Ratio," n.d. In 2025, China's old-age dependency ratio was about twenty-one (roughly five working-age adults per retiree); by 2050, it is projected to rise to around forty-five to fifty (about two workers per retiree).

70   *the shift from the two-child:* Communist Party of China Central Committee and State Council of the People's Republic of China, "Decision on Optimizing the Birth Policy to Promote Long-Term Balanced Population Development" [in Chinese], July 20, 2021.

70   *The overall fertility rate sits around 1.14 . . . are nearer 1.0:* National Bureau of Statistics, *China Population and Employment Statistical Yearbook 2025.* Beijing: China Statistics Press, 2025; He Yafu, "Latest Population Statistical Yearbook: TFR Stood at 1.14 in 2024, with the First-Birth Fertility Rate Rising Significantly" [in Chinese], *Zhihu,* January 27, 2026.

70   *fertility has fallen:* World Bank Group, "Fertility Rate, Total (Births per Woman)—China, Japan, Korea, Rep.," *World Bank Data,* n.d.

71   *Trip.com Group, announced: China Daily,* "Trip.com to Invest 1 Billion Yuan to Encourage Employees to Have Children, 50,000 Yuan Subsidy per Child" [in Chinese], July 3, 2023; Jane Sun, interview by McKinsey & Company, September 8, 2025.

71   *China still contributes:* Lanxu Zhou, "China to Remain Top Contributor to Global Growth in 2024: IMF," *China Daily,* February 3, 2024.

71   *The sharp drop in births:* World Bank Group, "Fertility Rate, Total (Births per Woman)—China," n.d.

73   *as Nick and his McKinsey Global Institute colleagues:* Sven Smit et al., *A Century of Plenty* (New York: McKinsey Global Institute, January 13, 2026).

73   *The arc of the past century is unmistakable . . . by more than seven:* Jutta Bolt et al, "Maddison Project Database 2023," Groningen Growth and Development Centre, 2023; World Bank, "Life Expectancy at Birth, Total (Years)," 2023; United Nations Development Programme, "Mean Years of Schooling (Adults)," 2023.

CHAPTER 5 Waking Up in China's Next Chapter

81 *China is still growing*: World Bank Group, "GDP Growth (Annual Percent)—China, European Union, Japan," *World Bank Data*, n.d.

83 *Shuanghui, for example:* McKinsey analysis.

84 *McKinsey colleagues published the book*: Patrick Viguerie, Sven Smit, and Mehrdad Baghai, *The Granularity of Growth: How to Identify the Sources of Growth and Drive Enduring Company Performance* (Hoboken, NJ: John Wiley & Sons, 2008).

84 *China's express delivery sector:* National Postal Service of the People's Republic of China (State Post Bureau), "Express Delivery Volume Exceeds 170 Billion Pieces, 'Smooth Flow of Goods' Vision Further Realized" [in Chinese], January 10, 2025.

CHAPTER 6 Unleashing the Entrepreneur's Advantage

88 *6.4 RMB ($0.9) for a hamburger*: Xiaofeipai (Consumer Group), "McDonald's: The Disappearing Sense of Ritual," *Foodaily*, January 4, 2024.

88 *more than half a day's:* Ministry of Human Resources and Social Security of the People's Republic of China, *Communiqué on the Development of Labor Undertakings in 1992*, July 23, 2011; the national average annual wage for workers in 1992 was 2,711 RMB; calculated based on 250 working days per year (excluding weekends and holidays), the average daily wage was approximately 10.84 RMB.

88 *A Big Mac purchased in the US:* Brianna Ruback and Meghan De Maria, "What a McDonald's Big Mac Cost the Year You Were Born," *Eat This, Not That!*, May 23, 2024; in the 1990s a Big Mac cost $2.45–2.50 in the United States.

88 *but the average worker:* US Bureau of Labor Statistics, "Historical News Release: Annual Pay Statistics, 1992," September 16, 1993; the average annual pay in the US was $25,903 in 1992; using 260 working days (fifty-two weeks) and eight working hours every day, average hourly wage was $12.

88 *A Big Mac in China today:* National Bureau of Statistics of China, *2025 Report on Residents' Income and Consumption Expenditure*, January 19, 2026; Big Mac price in China approximately 28.5 RMB ($4.01) as of January 2026. Based on per capita annual income of 24,555 RMB (2,046 RMB per month), a Big Mac represents roughly 1.4 percent of the average monthly income.

88 *Chinese wages have surged: Trading Economics*, "China Average Yearly Wages," n.d.

89 *By 2015:* McDonald's Corporation, *Annual Report on Form 10-K for the Fiscal Year Ended December 31, 2015*, US Securities and Exchange Commission, February 25, 2016.

89 *The company sold 80 percent: Foodservice Equipment Reports*, "McDonald's Sells 80 Percent Stake in Chinese Business," January 17, 2017.

89 *a proprietary digital backbone: PitchBook*, "McDonald's China Overview," n.d.

90 *McDonald's China*: Duowei Zou et al., "'Our Restaurants Always Surprise Overseas Peers': Zhang Jiayin, CEO of McDonald's China, Talks About the Road to Localization." *Xinhua News Agency*, July 19, 2025. Reported interview at the Third China International Supply Chain Promotion Expo.

90 *McDonald's agreed to buy out Carlyle's stake:* McDonald's Corporation, "McDonald's to Acquire Carlyle's Stake in McDonald's China," company website, November 20, 2023.

92 *Inovance—a rising Chinese:* Inovance, company website, n.d.

92 *The EV maker:* BYD, "How an Electric Vehicle Company Became the World's Largest PPE Mask Manufacturer," company website, n.d.

95 *local players such as Master Kong:* Zhuoqiong Wang, "Nissin Snaps Ties with Instant Noodle Maker Jinmailang," *China Daily*, December 1, 2015.

95 *In the following days:* McKinsey analysis.

96 *the original ByteDance video app:* Total views accumulated on TikTok by the end of 2025.

96 *recorded 3 billion RMB (about $430 million) in annual sales:* McKinsey analysis.

97 *This helped compress:* McKinsey analysis.

99 *It engineered a lower:* Straumann Group, "Straumann Group Delivers Strong Organic Growth and Confirms Full-Year Outlook," company website, October 29, 2024.

99 *China accounts for more than 15 percent:* Straumann Holding AG, "Straumann to Invest in Villeret While Localizing Production for China in Shanghai," EQS-News, June 6, 2025.

99 *which is already 24 percent:* Straumann Group, "Strong Start in an Environment Marked by Macroeconomic Uncertainties," n.d.

99 *the company says it can cut:* Vikas, "Volkswagen Shifts EV Development to China to Cut Costs by Up to 50 Percent," *EV Talks*, November 27, 2025.

100 *From industrialist Henry Ford's "Whether you think":* "Quote Origin: Whether You Believe You Can Do a Thing or Not, You Are Right," *Quote Investigator*, February 3, 2025.

100 *Jeff Bezos's "The biggest obstacle":* New York Times Events, "The Interview: From Amazon to Space—Jeff Bezos Talks Innovation, Progress and What's Next," December 5, 2024.

100 *Much of this intensity:* Future Start-Up Team, "The Origin of Huawei: When Desperation Becomes Strategy," October 26, 2025.

102 *WeBank had served:* Ziqi Liu, "Digital Finance Top 10 Smart Banks Revealed! WeBank Ranks First, ICBC's Tech Investment Exceeds 20 Billion Yuan" [in Chinese], *Stockstar*, September 25, 2025.

CHAPTER 7 **The Chinese Land Grab: How Scale Becomes Power**

105 *a nation once short of rebar:* IISS, *China's Steel Slowdown and the Global Iron-Ore and Emissions Outlook*, November 2025.

105 *As China urbanized:* IISS, *China's Steel Slowdown and the Global Iron-Ore and Emissions Outlook*, November 2025.

105 *In the winter of 2015:* 21st Century Business Herald, "Steel Prices Plummet to 'Cabbage-Level Lows' with Five-Year Supply Glut," October 8, 2015.

105 *At its peak in 2016, China's steel sector:* Ministry of Industry and Information Technology of the People's Republic of China, *Performance of the Steel Industry in 2016 and Outlook for 2017* [in Chinese], March 1, 2017.

105 *enough to build the Burj Khalifa:* The Burj Khalifa used about 39,000 tons of steel, and the Golden Gate Bridge about 83,000 tons; Moses, "Structural Details of Burj Khalifa," *Building and Construction*, August 17, 2025; *Design and Construction Stats*, Golden Gate Bridge Highway and Transportation District, n.d.

106 *yet capacity had surged:* Ministry of Industry and Information Technology of the People's Republic of China, *Performance of the Steel Industry in 2016 and Outlook for 2017* [in Chinese].

106 *More than five hundred producers:* McKinsey analysis.

106 *As the number of mills nationwide:* McKinsey analysis.

106 *in 2002, the company famously completed:* China Steel News Network, "Yonggang Group," June 15, 2021.

106 *Yonggang emerged not as the biggest:* Dagong Global credit reports on Jiangsu Yonggang Group Co., Ltd. (2017; 2020) [in Chinese]. Net income as a percentage of revenue rose from 3 percent in 2015 to 13 percent just two years later.

107 *GDP growth has slowed:* World Bank Group, "GDP Growth (Annual Percent)," n.d.

107 *Customer acquisition costs online: Digitaling,* "Platform Ecosystem Helps Build Private Domains, and Brands Launch a 'Protracted War'" [in Chinese], May 17, 2021; acquisition costs have risen from 37.2 RMB ($5.24) in 2010 to 486.7 RMB ($68.55) in 2019.

108 *China's total debt:* National Institution for Finance & Development (NIFD), *2025 Q1 Macro Leverage Ratio Report* (July 13, 2025) [in Chinese]; China Center for National Balance Sheets (total debt >300 percent of GDP; non-

financial corporate debt >170 percent by Q3 2025, about 2.5 times and 2.0 times 2000 levels); McKinsey Global Institute, *Out of Balance: What's Next for Growth, Wealth, and Debt?* (2025) (total debt about 3.1 times GDP; corporate debt about 1.8 times GDP).

109 *By 2015, China Life:* China Life, *2015 Annual Results Announcement* [in Chinese], company website, March 23, 2016.

109 *Ping An nearly nine hundred thousand:* Ping An, *2015 Annual Report*, company website, March 29, 2016.

109 *and CPIC four hundred thousand:* CPIC Life, *2015 Annual Report*, company website, April 27, 2016.

109 *By 2017, China Life's market cap:* CompaniesMarketCap, "Market Capitalization of China Life Insurance," n.d.

109 *Ping An's $150 billion:* Ping An, *2017 Annual Report*, company website, March 28, 2018.

109 *and CPIC $54 billion:* CompaniesMarketCap, "Market Capitalization of China Pacific Insurance," n.d.

110 *by the late 2010s:* China Evergrande Group, "Unaudited Operating Statistics of the Group for 2019 and Contracted Sales Target for 2020," company website, January 2, 2020.

110 *with Chinese e-commerce platforms:* 100EC (NetEase Commerce Research Center), "SYNTUN Releases Double 11 'First Round Report': Total Online Sales Exceed 845 Billion RMB as of October 30" [in Chinese], November 1, 2024; Adobe Analytics, "Black Friday 2024 US Ecommerce Sales Hit $10.8 Billion, Up 10.2 Percent Year-Over-Year," *Digital Commerce 360*, November 29, 2024.

110 *"That's nothing, you need":* Lie Jun, "Xu Xin: The Main Reason to Invest in JD.com" [in Chinese], *Bilibili*, February 7, 2025.

110 *"Seventy-five million isn't even enough":* Guoqi N. Singer, "Why Most Smart People Can't Make Big Money? Because They Lack Intellectual Honesty" [in Chinese], *Toutiao*, December 3, 2025.

110 *Kathy's early stake had grown:* Laoer Lu, "An In-Depth Look at China's Most Mysterious Investor" [in Chinese], *Tencent News*, August 28, 2021.

111 *with more than twenty million shared bicycles:* China Academy of Information and Communications Technology (CAICT), Policy and Economics Research Institute, and Mobike, *China Shared Bicycle Industry Development Report 2018*, (Beijing: China Academy of Information and Communications Technology, March 2018).

111 *in an industry expected to expand:* iResearch Consulting Group, *2024 China Shared Power Bank Industry Research Report*.

111 *more than nine hundred million fintech users:* HROne, "How Is Fintech's Size in China? Unveiling the Impressive Scale of a Booming Industry," August 8,

2025; *China Daily*, "China's Mobile-Payment Users Reach 583m in 2018," March 3, 2019.

111 *more than 350 million Gen Z Chinese . . . the size of the US:* Quest Mobile, "Bilibili Remains the No. 1 App Favored by Generation Z" [in Chinese], *China Daily*, January 25, 2019.

111 *forming a base five times the size of the US:* Statista, "US Generation Z Population Estimates 2025"; Rebecca C. Slepian et al., "Social Media, Wearables, Telemedicine and Digital Health—A Gen Y and Z Perspective," *Comprehensive Precision Medicine*, ed. Kenneth S. Ramos, vol. 1 (Elsevier, 2024).

111 *Alipay and WeChat Pay processed:* Barry Elad and Kathleen Kinder, "Alipay vs. WeChat Pay Statistics 2025: Market Share, Innovation & Digital Yuan Impact," *CoinLaw*, August 3, 2025.

111 *mobile payments hitting 332 trillion RMB:* People's Bank of China, "The People's Bank of China (PBOC) Releases Payment System Report (2024)" [in Chinese], February 18, 2025.

112 *Mobile users jumped:* WeBank, "Tencent's WeBank Turns Five," *China's Digital Economy*, December 19, 2019.

113 *Between 2010 and 2024:* National Bureau of Statistics of China, "Profits of Major Industrial Enterprises in 2024 Declined by 3.3 Percent" [in Chinese], January 27, 2025; National Bureau of Statistics of China, "National Data" [in Chinese], n.d.

113 *Nearly one in eight firms:* National Bureau of Statistics of China, "Profits of Major Industrial Enterprises in 2010 Rose by 5.7 Percent" [in Chinese], January 27, 2011; Zhiyan Consulting, "Loss-Making Enterprises Accounting for 25.42 Percent of the Total January to November 2024" [in Chinese], January 12, 2025.

113 *Ping An has cut:* Ping An Insurance (Group), "Expertise Makes Life Simple," 2022; Ping An, "Announcement of Unaudited Results for the Nine Months Ended September 30, 2025," company website, October 28, 2025.

113 *At its peak, it owed:* China Evergrande Group, "Announcement of Results for the Year Ended 31 December 2022," Hong Kong Exchanges and Clearing Limited (HKEX), July 17, 2023.

113 *has since become Chinese corporate history's largest bankruptcy:* Renhui Fu and Yaqi Shi, *Evergrande Group: The Largest Bankruptcy in Corporate China* (Ivey Publishing, Harvard Business Review Store, 2025).

114 *only to produce five years:* Simply Wall St, "Perfect Corp (PERF): Exploring Valuation as Shares Lose Momentum," *Yahoo! Finance*, October 21, 2025.

116 *three times the size of its nearest rival:* "Data Report: 2024 Q4 Instant Food Market Review" [in Chinese], *36kr*, February 10, 2025.

119 *by July 2025, combined daily orders:* AAStocks, "Taobao Flash Sale Recorded Over Ninety Million Orders on Each of the Two Consecutive Weekends," *Futubull*, July 27, 2025.

120 *Luckin launches more than a hundred:* Luckin, "Luckin Coffee, Inc. Q4 and FY2023 Earnings Conference Call Transcript," company website, February 23, 2024.

120 *Menu switchovers:* Luckin, confirmation by corporate communications team, email correspondence with McKinsey, March 12, 2026.

120 *Even with weekly menu updates:* Woshipm.com, "Luckin Coffee: How It Surpassed Starbucks to Become China's No. 1 Coffee Brand by Store Count" [in Chinese], November 21, 2025.

CHAPTER 8 **Seeking Granularity for Growth**

123 *China became:* William Johnson, "Leading in a New Phase in China," KONE, September 28, 2016; KONE, "KONE Corporation's Annual Review and Remuneration Report 2020 Have Been Published," company website, January 28, 2021.

123 *granularity of growth:* Mehrdad Baghi et al., *The Granularity of Growth: How to Identify the Sources of Growth and Drive Enduring Company Performance* (Wiley, 2008).

123 *Its economy:* World Bank, "GDP Growth (Annual Percent), China," 2024.

124 *many times the $1.8 billion:* Blackstone, "Blackstone's Fourth Quarter and Full Year 2015 Earnings," company website, January 28, 2016.

124 *In China:* Zhejiang Provincial Institute of Architectural Design and Research, Hengzun Group Co., Ltd., "Standard for Design of Office Buildings (GB 50370–2013, Revised Edition)" [in Chinese], State Council Government Information Office, April 3, 2020.

125 *Housing starts fell:* Wang Jing and Denise Jia, "China's Housing Construction Slumps to Lowest Level in Two Decades," *Caixin Global*, December 17, 2025.

125 *China's eleven million installed elevators: Elevator Magazine*, "A Look at the World—Part 4: The 'Giant' of the Global Elevator Industry," November 29, 2024.

125 *its twenty thousand technicians:* KONE, "Salesforce Helps KONE Strengthen Customer Service," company website, n.d.

125 *For one coffee client:* McKinsey analysis.

126 *Nearly 75 percent of millennials:* Daniel Hui et al., "Chinese Consumption Amid the New Reality," McKinsey & Company, May 7, 2025.

127 *ANE Global Logistics grew:* ANE, "Announcement of Annual Results for the Year Ended December 31, 2024," company website, May 20, 2025.

128 *That realization prompted:* Bingyan Shao, "ANE Logistics' First-Half Net Profit Rises by 10 Percent: Transportation Service Unit Price Falls, Says Anti-Involution Signal Spreads to Express Logistics" [in Chinese], *The Paper*, August 20, 2025.

129   *which ANE reduced by 95 percent:* McKinsey analysis.

129   *the bottom line swung:* ANE, "Announcement of Annual Results for the Year Ended December 31, 2024," company website, May 20, 2025; McKinsey analysis.

129   *Depot productivity . . . profitability strengthened:* McKinsey analysis.

130   *roughly 700 billion RMB ($100 billion):* Keju Wang, "Baijiu Makers in High Spirits on Foreign Sales," *China Daily*, September 20, 2023.

130   *For decades, growth was:* Shenwan Hongyuan Securities, "Liquor Industry 2024 Annual Report—25 Q1 Quarterly Report Summary," May 14, 2025; China.com.cn, "Liquor Industry 2015 Annual Report & 2016 Q1 Quarterly Report Summary," *Sohu*, May 4, 2016.

130   *State-owned Kweichow:* Justin Ko, "The Mystery of Moutai: State-Owned Enterprises in China's Alcohol Industry," *SSRN*, February 27, 2025.

131   *Kouzijiao, a 6 billion RMB ($857 million):* Yahoo! Finance, "Anhui Kouzi Distillery Co., Ltd.," n.d.

131   *With 80 percent of its revenue:* Anhui Kouzijiao Distillery Co., Ltd., "2024 Third Quarter Report," Shanghai Stock Exchange, October 29, 2024.

131   *Its debut product was:* Shenzhen Municipal Archives, "The Shenzhen Story: The First Fortune Global 500 Company to Invest in Shenzhen," gov.cn, December 17, 2022.

131   *five times the cost: China Daily*, "Tickets Pricey, Movie Buffs Stay Away," January 19, 2007; Gao Bo, "Subway Ticket Price Changes," *China Daily*, October 29, 2014.

132   *In savory snacks:* Iris Wang, "Steadily Moving Forward amid Challenges: PepsiCo's Resilience and Agility," *FoodTalks*, June 9, 2025.

133   *In peak years, LVMH drew:* LVMH Moët Hennessy Louis Vuitton SE, "Annual Report 2024," company website, 2025.

133   *Chinese consumers:* LVMH Moët Hennessy Louis Vuitton SE, "2024 Annual Report," company website, 2025.

133   *But as consumers grow:* Cherry Chen et al., "China Luxury Report 2019: How Young Chinese Consumers Are Reshaping Global Luxury," McKinsey & Company, April 2019.

134   *#TheLouis had clocked:* RedNote and Douyin; McKinsey analysis.

135   *Moncler's 2024 "City of Genius":* Thomas Durin, "On October 19, Moncler Unveiled a Spectacular Event at Shanghai Fashion Week: 'The City of Genius,'" *Acumen*, December 22, 2024.

135   *Tiffany & Co.:* Xiaoqing Huang, "Zhangyuan's Nightscape Renewed! Tiffany Light Show Lands in Jing'an, Brand Links with Light to Unlock New Night Consumption Scenarios" [in Chinese], *Shanghai Observer*, October 29, 2025.

135   *a category in which spending is still rising 7 to 9 percent a year:* McKinsey analysis.

136 *yet KONE has steadily flipped its China mix:* KONE, confirmation by corporate communications team, email correspondence with McKinsey, January 20, 2026.

137 *China's household consumption . . . 55 to 60 percent:* World Bank Group, "Households and NPISHs Final Consumption Expenditure (Percent of GDP)," n.d.

137 *contributing roughly 10 to 15 percent:* Jeongming Seong et al., "Five Consumer Trends Shaping the Next Decade of Growth in China," McKinsey & Company, November 11, 2021.

138 *Auto sales reached:* Xinhua, "China's Auto Output, Sales Both Reach New Heights in 2024," gov.cn, January 14, 2025.

138 *Per capita coffee consumption rose:* Xinhua, "Taking a Sip of New Coffee Culture in Nation's Northwest," *China Daily*, April 11, 2025.

CHAPTER 9 From Factory to Innovation Lab

141 *His Twelve Landscape Screens sold:* Eileen Kinsella, "Qi Baishi Just Became the First Chinese Artist to Break the $100 Million Mark at Auction," *Artnet News*, December 19, 2017.

142 *China has narrowly become the world's top R&D spender:* Davide Bonaglia et al., "End of Year Edition—Despite the Odds, Global R&D Spending Grew Again in 2024, Inching Closer to the USD 3 Trillion Mark," World Intellectual Property Organization (WIPO), December, 23, 2025; numbers are as of 2024 (in constant 2015 PPP dollars).

142 *China's ecosystem also now generates:* World Intellectual Property Organization, "World Intellectual Property Indicators 2025," 2025.

142 *The Chinese are:* Eric Schmidt and Selina Xu, "DeepSeek, Temu, TikTok: China Tech Is Starting to Pull Ahead," *New York Times*, May 5, 2025.

143 *Elon Musk said in 2022:* Arjun Kharpal, "Elon Musk's Twitter Plans May Take Inspiration from Chinese Super Apps," CNBC, October 5, 2022.

143 *China leads in total granted:* World Intellectual Property Organization, "Patent Landscape Report: Generative Artificial Intelligence (GenAI)," WIPO, 2024.

143 *but ranks only fifth in average citations:* Brian Buntz, "Quality vs. Quantity: US and China Chart Different Paths in Global AI Patent Race in 2024," *R&D World*, November 3, 2024.

144 *Nearly half a billion Chinese live:* CEC Capital Group, "2025 CEC Capital Group Chronic Disease in China Report" [in Chinese], May 2025.

144 *more than eight million die each year:* National Bureau of Statistics of China, "Mortality Data 2024–2025" [in Chinese], February 28, 2025; People's Network, "Mortality Data 2024–2025" [in Chinese], September 12,

2024. Deaths from chronic diseases account for over 80 percent of total resident deaths.

144 *In 2015, Chinese pharmaceutical firms contributed:* Kiki Han et al., "The Dawn of China Biopharma Innovation," McKinsey & Company, October 29, 2021.

144 *the country's top five pharmaceutical companies:* "Building the Bridge to Global Innovation," McKinsey & Company report at Biocentury China Healthcare Summit 2025, Shanghai, October 2025; top five pharma companies are defined as the top five companies focusing on innovative drug and having highest market cap in October 2025.

144 *Fewer than six hundred hospitals:* National Medical Products Administration, "Announcement No. 172 of 2015 Issued by the State Food and Drug Administration Regarding the Clinical Trials Conducted by Drug Clinical Trial Institutions and Contract Research Organizations" [in Chinese], September 9, 2015. There were 82 clinical trial sites for bioequivalence and Phase I studies, 383 for Phase II/III, and 126 CROs, totaling 591 organizations.

146 *China's large talent pool . . . half the cost of global peers:* McKinsey analysis.

146 *The top five firms:* McKinsey analysis.

146 *a third of the global pipeline of drugs:* Xinhua, "China's Pharmaceutical Industry Now 2nd Largest in the World: Official," gov.cn, August 22, 2025.

146 *In the first quarter of 2025, about 32 percent:* Gabrielle Masson, "China Biotechs 'Reshaping' US Biopharma as Outlicensing Deals Rise 11 Percent: Jefferies Report," *Fierce Biotech*, July 14, 2025.

146 *roughly 1,700 hospitals:* YaoYanShe Intelligence Data Center, "2024 National Report on the Filing Status of Drug Clinical Trial Institutions in China," March 11, 2025; based on data from the National Medical Products Administration (NMPA) drug clinical trial institution filing system, 2024.

146 *In biopharma, China's:* Albert Bourla, "Remarks at the National Committee on US–China Relations 2025 Annual Gala Dinner," New York, October 14, 2025.

146 *Shanghai alone hosts:* Shanghai Municipal Commission of Commerce, "Joint Opinions on the Handling of Proposal No. 1162 of the Third Session of the 14th Municipal Committee of the Chinese People's Political Consultative Conference" [in Chinese], gov.cn, July 23, 2025.

146 *Bosch employs over ten thousand:* Xinhua, "Bosch Executive Highlights China's Role in Company's Global Strategy," August 4, 2025.

146 *BASF has opened:* Holger Kapp, "BASF Further Expands Its Innovation Campus Shanghai," company website, June 28, 2023.

147 *Airbus designs next-generation components in Shenzhen:* CGTN, "Airbus Launches Innovation Center in Shenzhen," February 22, 2019.

147 *Tesla's decision to manufacture:* BBC, "Tesla's China Manufacturing Decision 2019," December 30, 2019.

147 *Chinese vehicle development cycles:* McKinsey analysis.

148 *And with more than five million STEM graduates: People's Daily,* "With Over Five Million STEM Graduates Annually, China Leads the World! Understanding China's New Economic Advantages" [in Chinese], April 1, 2024.

149 *CATL's condensed battery technology has demonstrated energy densities around 500 watt-hours per kilogram which could push into aviation territory:* CATL, "CATL Launches Condensed Battery with an Energy Density of up to 500 Wh/Kg, Enables Electrification of Passenger Aircraft," company website, April 19, 2023.

150 *In global pharmaceuticals, no Chinese firm: Drug Discovery & Development,* "Pharma 50: The Top Pharma Companies in the World for 2025," n.d.

150 *Only about 7 percent:* National Bureau of Statistics of China, "China R&D Expenditure Surpasses 3.6 Trillion Yuan in 2024," January 23, 2025.

150 *compared with 12 to 15 percent in advanced economies:* Basic research R&D expenditure accounts for 12 percent of total R&D expenditure in Japan and 15 percent in the United States and Korea, according to OECD data.

150 *IP imports are still 4.5 times larger than exports:* In 2024, charges for the use of intellectual property, payments was reported at $45.8 billion in China and receipts were reported at $10.1 billion, according to World Bank data.

151 *China now accounts for roughly half:* World Intellectual Property Organization, "Global Patent Filings Report," 2025.

151 *the majority of AI patent:* World Intellectual Property Organization, "Patent Landscape Report: Generative Artificial Intelligence (GenAI)," 2024.

151 *backed by a national-level IP tribunal:* Supreme People's Court of the People's Republic of China, "Establishment of Intellectual Property Court of Supreme People's Court as Historic Breakthrough of China's Intellectual Property Litigation System," gov.cn, December 30, 2018.

151 *Rising IP enforcement:* Aaron Wininger, "China's Supreme People's Court Releases 'Status of Judicial Protection of Intellectual Property Rights in Chinese Courts (2024),'" *China IP Law Update,* April 21, 2025.

151 *In the top court:* Supreme People's Court of the People's Republic of China, "Chinese Court Increasingly Favored for IP Disputes," gov.cn, July 1, 2024.

152 *with low success rates of 10 percent:* Biotechnology Innovation Organization, "Clinical Development Success Rates and Contributing Factors 2011–2020," February 2021.

152 *Disney, Universal, and Warner Bros. sued:* Harshita Mary Varghese and Dawn Chmielewski, "Disney, Universal, Warner Bros Discovery Sue China's MiniMax for Copyright Infringement," Reuters, September 16, 2025.

153 *Then it reinvented itself:* Porter's Five Forces, "What Is Brief History of Jiangsu Hengrui Medicine Company?," December 14, 2025.

153 *Merck, the 358-year-old:* Merck Group, "Where We Come From . . ." company website, n.d.

153 *China accounts for €3 billion:* Merck Group, "2024 Annual Financial Statement," company website, January 7, 2025.

153 *It started at a 2023:* ASCO 2023 Oncology Conference, American Society of Clinical Oncology, 2023.

154 *a $2 billion licensing partnership:* Jiangsu Hengrui Pharmaceuticals Co., Ltd., "Hengrui Pharma and Merck Reach Collaboration to Advance Innovative Cancer Therapies" [in Chinese], company website, October 30, 2023.

154 *a new $2.5 billion:* Adrian Kemp, "AstraZeneca Invests $2.5 Billion in Beijing R&D Campus," AstraZeneca, March 21, 2025.

154 *China now plays a central role:* AstraZeneca China, "Focusing on Early-Stage Research and Collaboration in the Field of Chronic Rare Diseases, AstraZeneca China R&D Day 2025 Was Successfully Held in Shanghai" [in Chinese], company website, September 23, 2025.

154 *and contributing to approximately 15 to 20 percent:* AstraZeneca China, "AstraZeneca China R&D Day Held in Beijing for the First Time, Strengthening Cooperation in China's R&D and Innovation Ecosystem" [in Chinese], company website, March 31, 2025.

154 *supporting more than two dozen:* Yicai, "AstraZeneca China 'Dual Centers' to Support Global R&D, $2.5 Billion Investment to Boost AI and Translational Research" [in Chinese], China International Import Expo, October 27, 2025.

155 *Geely's three million-vehicle supply chain:* Zhejiang Geely Holding Group, "2024 Sales by Geely Holding Brands Rise 22 Percent to 3.337M Units, Targets 5M Units by 2027," company website, January 8, 2025.

156 *Volkswagen Group has:* Volkswagen Group China, "Forty Years of Volkswagen in China: Group Accelerates Its Realignment with 'In China, for China' Strategy," company website, April 11, 2024.

156 *Tesla shipped roughly:* Phate Zhang, "Tesla Sells Record 82,927 Cars in China in Dec. Exports 10,839 from Shanghai Plant," *CnEVPost*, January 9, 2025.

157 *Foreign direct investment:* McKinsey Global Institute, "The FDI Shake-Up: How Foreign Direct Investment Today May Shape Industry and Trade Tomorrow," September 22, 2025.

158 *Bosch Mobility's Suzhou factory:* Forest Hou, "Global Lighthouse Voices: A Talk with Bosch Mobility China COO Norman Roth," McKinsey & Company, April 18, 2025.

160 *we're referring to the frontier edge:* International Monetary Fund, "GDP Based on PPP, Share of World," n.d.

CHAPTER 10 **From Hard Goods to Soft Power**

165   *nearly $2 billion in revenue in the first half of 2025:* Pop Mart International Group Limited, "Interim Results Announcement for the Six Months Ended 30 June 2025," company website, August 19, 2025.

166   *China may still be:* "The State Council Information Office Held a Series of Press Conferences on 'The Achievements of High-Quality Economic Development in China,' Introducing the Import and Export Situation for the Whole of 2024 (Transcript Included)," [in Chinese], State Council Information Office of the People's Republic of China, January 13, 2025; in 2024, China's export volume exceeded 25.45 trillion RMB ($3.6 trillion) for the first time.

166   *attraction rather than coercion:* Joseph S. Nye, *Soft Power: The Means to Success in World Politics*, Public Affairs, 2004.

168   *Founder Juncheng Hou . . . Chinese women:* Corporate communications team, Proya, email to authors, February 2026.

171   *only two Chinese firms:* Interbrand, "Best Global Brands 2024," n.d.

171   *Kantar BrandZ, which paints:* Kantar Group, "Kantar BrandZ Most Valuable Global Brands 2025," n.d.

171   *When Pop Mart approached Kasing:* Zeyi Yang, "A Journey into the Heart of Labubu," *Wired*, October 1, 2025.

172   *yet Pop Mart did $887 million:* Pop Mart International Group Limited, "2024 Annual Report," company website, March 26, 2025.

172   *and more than doubled that again in 2025 to roughly $4 billion:* Niamh Rowe, "Labubu Maker Pop Mart Predicts $4 Billion in 2025 Revenue," *Yahoo! Finance*, August 20, 2025 n.d. "Equities: 9992:HKG—Summary." *Financial Times Markets*.

172   *At its 2025 peak: Financial Times*, "Pop Mart International Group Ltd," n.d.

172   *Pop Mart's ambitions:* Casey Hall et al., "Exclusive: Labubu-Maker Pop Mart Learns from Disney to Capitalise on Toy's Viral Success," Reuters, October 1, 2025.

173   *over two million views on YouTube in the first twenty-four hours:* Yao Li, "Black Myth: Wukong and the Rise of China's Playable Soft Power," *US–China Today*, July 16, 2025.

173   *it drew over 2.4 million concurrent players:* Corporate communications team, Valve Software, email to authors, December 2025.

173   *ten million copies sold in the first three days: Statista*, "Lifetime Unit Sales of Black Myth: Wukong Worldwide as of January 2025," January 2025.

174   *Temu and SHEIN are:* SCAYLE Commerce Engine, "Temu & SHEIN: The Science of Disrupting eCommerce," November 19, 2024.

175   *by early 2026, chinese models accounted for over 60 percent:* Kerem Gülen, "Chinese AI Models Hit 61% Market Share on OpenRouter," *Dataconomy*, February 25, 2026

CHAPTER 11 **Building AI the Chinese Way**

177 *released a reasoning-focused large language model:* DeepSeek's R1 is often compared with OpenAI's GPT-4o/o1.

177 *DeepSeek had been trained:* DeepSeek Team, "DeepSeek-V3 Technical Report," *arXiv*, December 26, 2024.

177 *in which private sector investment:* Stanford Institute for Human-Centered Artificial Intelligence (HAI), "2025 AI Index Report: Economy Chapter," 2025.

179 *Manycore's real advantage:* Manycore Tech Inc., "Manycore Tech Unveils Next-Gen Spatial AI Models: SpatialLM 1.5 and SpatialGen, Accelerating Open-Source Ecosystem for 3D Scene Understanding and Generation," PR Newswire, August 27, 2025.

180 *Nearly a decade ago:* State Council, "2017 New Generation Artificial Intelligence Development Plan," gov.cn, July 20, 2017.

180 *the country was producing about one-third of global AI papers:* Stanford Institute for Human-Centered Artificial Intelligence (HAI), "The 2022 AI Index Report: Measuring Trends in Artificial Intelligence," March 16, 2022.

181 *Chinese firms had released more than 1,500 large models:* China Economic Net, "The Number of Chinese Large Models Exceeds 1,500, Ranking First Worldwide," July 28, 2025.

181 *The ecosystem now includes . . . 70 percent of China's AI revenue:* China Academy of Information and Communications Technology (CAICT), "Outcomes Released at the 2025 AI Industry and Enabling New Industrialization Conference" [in Chinese], September 23, 2025.

181 *several well-funded AI start-ups . . . within eighteen months: Fortune,* "Big AI Thins Out the Competition as Start-Ups Quit the Race to Build Large Language Models," December 9, 2024; *Fortune,* "Stability AI CEO Emad Mostaque Steps Down as Investors Pressure Over Finances," March 23, 2024.

182 *The result is a nationwide race:* State Council, "Opinions on Further Implementing the 'Artificial Intelligence +' Action," August 28, 2025.

182 *The government launched:* Beijing newsroom, "China Sets Up $47.5B State Fund to Boost Semiconductor Industry," Reuters, May 27, 2024.

182 *83 percent of Chinese respondents believe:* Stanford Institute for Human-Centered Artificial Intelligence (HAI), "The 2025 AI Index Report: Public Opinion on AI," July 2025.

182 *while 80 percent of sellers on JD.com: AIbase,* "Releases 10 Major AI Marketing Tools, with Model Sizes Up to 81 Billion Parameters," December 6, 2024.

182 *According to the latest national policy plans:* State-Owned Assets Supervision and Administration Commission of the State Council (SASAC),

"SASAC Deepens Central Enterprises' 'AI+' Special Action—Prioritizing AI in the 15th Five-Year Plan," March 1, 2025.

182 *He expects a major boom:* Allen Zhu, comments at Shanghai 2025 Inclusion Conference, September 2025.

182 *reached 84 percent in 2025—slightly ahead of the global average:* McKinsey & Company, "McKinsey Global Survey on the State of AI," June 25–29, 2025.

183 *AI engineers earn:* SalaryExpert, "Artificial Intelligence Engineer," n.d.

183 *China also trains one-and-a-half to two times:* Remco Zwetsloot et al., "China Is Fast Outpacing US STEM PhD Growth," Center for Security and Emerging Technology, Georgetown University, August 2021.

183 *Foreign direct investment:* McKinsey Global Institute, "The FDI Shake-Up: How Foreign Direct Investment Today May Shape Industry and Trade Tomorrow," September 22, 2025; calculated between the 2015–2019 period and the post-2022 period (on an annualized basis).

184 *Nvidia's Jensen Huang said in 2025:* Helen Davidson, "US Chip Export Controls a 'Failure' to Spur Chinese Development, Nvidia Boss Says," *The Guardian*, May 21, 2025.

184 *the ecosystem has created:* Such as DeepSeek-V3, Kimi-K2, and Qwen-72B-Instruct.

184 *DeepSeek's parent announced:* DeepSeek, "Model & Pricing" [in Chinese], DeepSeek API Docs, 2025.

185 *accounting for five of the top ten image-to-video:* Arena AI, "Image-to-Video Leaderboard," n.d.; Artificial Analysis, "Artificial Analysis Image Editing Leaderboard," n.d.

186 *Chinese open-source:* Malika Aubakirova et al., "State of AI: An Empirical 100 Trillion Token Study with OpenRouter," *OpenRouter*, December 1, 2025.

186 *"You can remove anything you want, add anything you need":* Yuexin Kong, "Kai-Fu Lee Leads Charge into B2B Market: I Am My Own Best Salesman" [in Chinese], *China Entrepreneur,* August 5, 2025.

186 *Jian Wang, the founder of Alibaba Cloud:* Jian Wang, appearance at Shanghai 2025 Inclusion Conference, Shanghai, September 2025.

189 *The deal closed in January 2026:* Bloomberg, "China Deepens Review of Meta's Landmark $2 Billion Manus Buyout," January 23, 2026.

189 *Joe Tsai, chairman of Alibaba . . . that's very, very interesting:* Joe Tsai's lecture on "Technological Drivers of China's Economic Growth" at HKU Business School Edward K Y Chen, November 7, 2025.

189 *As Nobel laureate Richard Sutton said in Shanghai:* Richard Sutton, appearance at Shanghai 2025 Inclusion Conference, Shanghai, September 2025.

190 *McKinsey estimates AI could add:* Kai Shen et al., "The Next Frontier for AI in China Could Add $600 Billion to Its Economy," McKinsey & Company, June 7, 2022.

190 *while Goldman Sachs projects generative AI will lift:* Goldman Sachs, "What Advanced AI Means for China's Economic Outlook," May 6, 2025.

CHAPTER 12 **Building the Robots of Tomorrow**

194 *with about 360 million Chinese consumers demanding delivery now:* China Internet Network Information Center (CNNIC), "CNNIC Released 2014 China Online Shopping Market Research Report," September 14, 2015; exact number is 361 million.

194 *At JD.com, monthly deliveries jumped from:* Annual Reports (2014–2019), published April 7, 2015; April 19, 2016; May 1, 2017; April 27, 2018; April 15, 2019; and April 15, 2020; company website.

194 *it could move goods at two thousand units per hour . . . five hundred boxes per hour:* Chunguang Gu, in discussion with McKinsey, September 9, 2025.

194 *Industrial robots aren't new:* Federico Berruti et al., "The Robot Renaissance: How Human-Like Machines Are Reshaping Business," McKinsey & Company, March 22, 2024.

195 *The country has more than 450,000:* Lili Lin, "China Has Over 450,000 Smart Robot Industry Enterprises," *People's Daily Overseas Edition*, February 10, 2025.

195 *and accounts for roughly three-quarters:* "Across China: Robot Dogs Being Tested in Quest to Keep Mount Tai Clean," *Xinhua*, October 27, 2024.

195 *The biggest industrial robot makers remain the global incumbents:* Bruno Venditti, "The World's Top Industrial Robotics Companies by Market Share," *Visual Capitalist*, September 1, 2025.

195 *China is now, by far:* International Federation of Robotics, "Global Robot Demand in Factories Doubles Over Ten Years," September 25, 2025.

195 *The global market:* George Chowdhury, "The Global Robotics Market Outlook," *ABI Research*, July 31, 2025.

197 *Chinese home robots don't just clean; they pick up socks, climb stairs, and pluck tissues out of corners:* Choi Ji-hui, "Mova Unveils Zeus 60 Robotic Vacuum That Climbs Stairs and Enhances Cleaning Efficiency," *Chosun Biz*, September 6, 2025; Evelyn Cheng, "Chinese Robot Vacuum Cleaner Company Reveals Model with an AI-Powered Arm," CNBC, January 5, 2025.

197 *Chinese suppliers now accounting:* McKinsey analysis based on data from the Manufacturing Intelligence Repository (MIR) Databank, 2025.

198 *became the world's largest lidar maker:* RoboSense Technology Co., Ltd., "RoboSense Releases 2024 Annual Results: Leading LiDAR Market Share and Paving the Way for AI Robotics Growth," company website, April 2, 2025.

199 *Venture funding for general-purpose: Founders Network*, "$4.2 Billion Invested: Robotics Start-Ups See Funding Surge," n.d.; Chris Metinko, "Robotics Funding Remains Robust as Start-Ups Seek to Expand Robots' Skills," *Crunchbase News*, November 12, 2024.

199 *China has layered on top:* Announcement by China National Development and Reform Commission at press conference for the third session of the 14th National People's Congress, March 6, 2025.

200 *Chinese firms file more robotics patents than any other country: People's Daily*, "China Leads in Robotics Patents, Applications," December 24, 2024.

201 *Of 450,000 registered "smart robot" enterprises: Qianzhan*, "Analysis of China's Robotics Industry Supply Market in 2024: Supply Levels Continue to Grow [Infographics]" [in Chinese], January 31, 2025.

201 *Among the top ten robotics companies:* Bruno Venditti, "The World's Top Industrial Robotics Companies by Market Share," *Visual Capitalist*, September 1, 2025.

201 *Similarly, we expect the frontier:* Clayton M. Christensen, *The Innovator's Dilemma: When New Technologies Cause Great Firms to Fail* (Brighton, Harvard Business Review Press, 2016).

201 *The country produces roughly three-quarters:* Byeongku Lee, "CATL, BYD . . . The Secret to China's Twenty-Year Dominance in EV Batteries," DongAScience.com, November 14, 2025.

201 *and it accounts for roughly 90 percent: IDTechEx*, "Routes for EV Motors to Reduce Their Chinese Rare Earth Reliance," November 19, 2025.

202 *Intelligence alone is inert . . . the ability to act in the physical world:* Packy McCormick and Sam D'Amico, "The Electric Slide," *Not Boring by Packy McCormick* (blog), August 26, 2025.

202 *Policymakers tout humanoids:* Ministry of Industry and Information Technology of China, "Interpretation of the 'Guiding Opinions on the Innovative Development of Humanoid Robots'" [in Chinese], November 2, 2023.

203 *The company now has more:* 10jqka.com, "UBTech Robotics Corp Ltd (HK9880) Company Profile" [in Chinese], n.d.

203 *Industry data show humanoid:* Gaogong Robotics, 2022–2024 humanoid BOM cost CAGR –21.3 percent.

203 *more than two hundred Chinese companies attempting humanoids*: China Mobile Robot Alliance, "China Now Has Over Two Hundred Humanoid Robot Manufacturers!," November 28, 2025.

203 *a UBTech model once priced:* Weixin Zhu, "Securing the World's Largest Humanoid Robot Order Worth Nearly 100 Million Yuan: Why Is Guangdong-Based UBTech Selected?" [in Chinese], *Nandu Government Affairs*, July 23, 2025.

203 *Unitree pushed prices even lower in 2025 with a $6,000 humanoid, down from $16,000 a year earlier:* Brian Heater, "Unitree's Fifty-Five-Pound Humanoid Costs $6,000, Can Cartwheel," A3 Association for Advanced Automation, July 25, 2025.

205 *For twelve consecutive years, the country has been the world's largest industrial robot market:* People's Daily, "China Has Maintained Its Position as the World's Largest Industrial Robot Market for Twelve Consecutive Years," gov.cn, August 3, 2025.

205 *installing roughly 295,000 units:* International Federation of Robotics, "World Robotics 2025: Industrial Robots," 2025.

205 *Most new robots roll straight onto:* Yanting Han, "2024 China Robotics Industry Demand Market Analysis: Accelerated Penetration in Various Fields [Infographics]" [in Chinese], *Qianzhan*, February 10, 2025.

205 *More than two million:* International Federation of Robotics, *World Robotics 2025 Industrial Robots: Executive Summary* (Frankfurt: International Federation of Robotics, 2025).

205 *pushing the country's robot density:* International Federation of Robotics, "World Robotics Report 2024: China's Robot Density Surpasses Germany and Japan" [in Chinese], November 20, 2024.

205 *general-purpose robotics market could reach:* Michael Chui et al., "Will Embodied AI Create Robotic Coworkers?," McKinsey & Company, June 30, 2025.

206 *China generates one-third:* World Bank Group, "Manufacturing, Value Added (Current US$)—China, World," n.d.

206 *More than 310 million Chinese:* Ministry of Civil Affairs and China National Committee on Aging, "2024 National Aging Cause Development Communique," July 24, 2025.

206 *China's workforce shrinks:* National Bureau of Statistics of China, "2024 National Economic and Social Development Statistical Bulletin" [in Chinese], February 28, 2025.

CHAPTER 13 The Chinese Enterprises Going Global

209 *Today Anta is $30 billion by market cap:* Yahoo! Finance, "ANTA Sports Products Limited (ANPDY)," n.d.

210 *Anta now runs R&D centers:* Anta Sports Products Limited, "2024 Annual Report" [in Chinese], Hong Kong Stock Exchange, March 19, 2025.

210 *and includes in its retail base:* Anta Sports Products Limited, "2025 Interim Report," company website, August 27, 2025.

210 *It's now the third largest:* CompaniesMarketCap, "Largest Sporting Goods Companies by Market Cap," n.d.

212   *restrictive trade actions:* Simon J. Everett et al., "Annual Report 2024: The State of Global Trade Policy," *Global Trade Alert*, 2024.

212   *From 2018 to 2024:* McKinsey Global Institute, "The Great Trade Rearrangement," June 25, 2025.

212   *China's export engine adapted:* McKinsey Global Institute, "Geopolitics and the Geometry of Global Trade," January 17, 2024.

213   *Anbang's $2 billion purchase:* Jack Freifelder, "Chinese Insurer Buys NYC's Waldorf Astoria Hotel," *China Daily USA*, October 17, 2014.

213   *Chinese companies spending $227 billion:* David Cogman et al., "Making Sense of Chinese Outbound M&A," McKinsey & Company, July 3, 2017.

214   *Geely was generating:* Geely Automobile Holdings Limited, "Financial Statement 2009" [in Chinese], company website, April 12, 2010.

214   *roughly one-sixth of Volvo's:* Volvo Cars recorded revenue of $12.4 billion in 2009; Ford Motor, "Ford Motor Annual Report 2010," company website, February 25, 2010.

214   *Geely must "find a good partner":* Geely Holding Group, "Li Shufu on Why Geely Acquired Volvo: Self-Exploration Is Too Slow and Unlikely to Succeed" [in Chinese], *Tencent News*, March 28, 2024.

214   *The $1.8 billion acquisition:* Victoria Klesty, "Geely Signs $1.8 Billion Deal for Volvo," Reuters, March 29, 2010.

215   *Volvo's sales in China surged: Business Review Digest*, "A Fifteen-Year Review of Geely's Acquisition of Volvo: A 'Snake Swallowing Elephant' Revaluation" [in Chinese], *Dongchedi*, April 9, 2025.

215   *pooled 5,000 RMB ($714), roughly fifty times rural annual income:* National Bureau of Statistics of China, "Fourth in a Series of Reports: Urban and Rural Residents' Lives Are Moving from Poverty to a Moderately Prosperous Society" [in Chinese], September 10, 2009; China's rural annual income per capita is recorded as 73 RMB in 1949 and 134 RMB in 1978

216   *Midea's €4.5 billion ($5.2 billion) acquisition:* FreshFields, "Chinese Acquisition of German Technology," December 24, 2024.

216   *its overseas revenue:* Midea Group, "Midea Group 2024 Annual Report, Delivers Unprecedented Shareholder Returns," company website, 2025.

217   *Inspired by driving a Tesla:* Launched in 2018 and 2022, respectively.

217   *Models like the G3 and P7 would earn praise:* Ben Sullins, "Does the XPENG P7 Leave the Tesla Model 3 in the Rearview?," YouTube video, May 19, 2020.

217   *which took a $700 million minority stake:* Mark Rainford, "XPENG and Volkswagen to Merge Super-Fast Charging Networks," *Inside China Auto*, January 7, 2025.

217   *It also invested heavily:* Ganglie Xu, "XPENG and AutoNavi Join Forces to Ignite the Billion-Dollar Robotaxi Market: Three Driverless Cars Are

Expected to Enter Mass Production by 2026" [in Chinese], *Toutiao*, November 5, 2025.

217 *An executive from logistics company SF Express summed up:* At a Forbes China conference in fall 2025.

218 *Asia Society data show:* Asia Society Policy Institute, "Global Public Opinion on China," n.d.

219 *China now accounts for roughly 15 percent of global goods exports:* World Trade Organization, "International Trade Statistics Database," 2024.

219 *Chinese A-share listed firms generate :* The China Academy, "Hits 8 Trillion Overseas Revenue in 2023, How Did Chinese Enterprises Make It?," June 17, 2024.

219 *compared with typically 30 to 60 percent for large German, Japanese, and Korean multinationals:* McKinsey analysis based on top 50 largest companies (by 2021 revenue) globally across example sectors including life sciences, chemicals, consumer, and auto.

220 *with only two Chinese firms:* Interbrand, "Best Global Brands 2024," n.d.

221 *NIO House on a prime shopping street:* Li Zhang, "If You Don't Go to Sea, You're Out of the Game; a Chinese Car Was Driven into the Vicinity of the Arctic Circle" [in Chinese], Tou Zhong Web, August 27, 2025.

223 *CATL's €1.8B ($2.1 billion) battery plant:* CATL, "CATL's German Plant Kicks Off Cell Production," company website, December 21, 2022.

224 *Tsingshan Holding Group:* Aseanbiz.News, "Indonesia's Tsingshan Industrial Park: A Model for Chinese Enterprises Going Global" [in Chinese], May 24, 2025.

224 *Haier's joint ventures:* Haier, "Haier Cooperates with Samha in Algeria," company website, October 29, 2024.

224 *Between 2012 and 2023:* Ministry of Commerce of People's Republic of China et al., *2012 Statistical Bulletin on China's Outward Foreign Direct Investment* [in Chinese], (China Statistics Press, 2013); Ministry of Commerce of the People's Republic of China et al., "2023 Statistical Bulletin on China's Outward Foreign Direct Investment" [in Chinese], CCT Press, September 1, 2024.

224 *Jason Zhu:* Jason Zhu, speech at the 2025 Forbes China Horizon Summit, Shanghai, November 7, 2025.

CHAPTER 14 Succession: The Founder's Dilemma

232 *"not meant for just one person":* China Youth, "Liu Yonghao on Second-Generation Succession: It Is Not Meant for Just One Person, but for a Team and a System" [in Chinese], March 10, 2019.

232 *"I'm not like the heroes":* Yaning Li, "Liu Chang: The Reluctant Heiress Who Saved Her Father's Agriculture Empire," *Think China*, November 27, 2025.

232 *Most A-share listed companies:* China Stock Market & Accounting Research Database (CSMAR). Shenzhen: GTA Information Technology Co., Ltd., n.d.

232 *and a significant share are family businesses*: Kanghong Li, "Promote or Inhibit: State-Owned Equity Participation and Family Firms' Innovation Investment," *Journal of Innovation & Knowledge*, April–June 2023.

232 *just over half were founded . . . nearly 70 percent of their founders were born in the 1950s and 1960s:* McKinsey analysis based on Hurun Report, "2025 Hurun China Top 500" [in Chinese], accessed February 5, 2025.

234 *China has roughly seven hundred: People's Daily*, "Five Departments Jointly Issued a Document to Promote the Innovative Development of Time-Honored Chinese Brands: Century-Old Shops Polish Their 'Golden Signboards'" [in Chinese], February 19, 2023.

234 *Many of their founders are:* McKinsey analysis.

234 *more than 80 percent of . . . lack a formal succession plan:* HSBC, "Family-Owned Businesses in Asia: Harmony Through Succession Planning 2025," April 2025.

235 *Chinese family businesses account:* IE Foundation et al., "Understanding Family Businesses in China: The Path, the Trend, and the Future," November 23, 2020.

235 *generate an even greater share of jobs:* C. Bin-Feng, "Family Control and Corporate Risk-Taking in China: Does Working Capital Strategy Matter?" *Economic Research-Ekonomska Istraživanja*, December 10, 2021.

235 *in a study of more than two hundred transitions:* Acha Leke et al., "Passing the Baton: Creating Value Through CEO Succession at Family Businesses," McKinsey & Company, February 3, 2026.

236 *a majority: People's Daily*, "Second-Generation Entrepreneurs Bring New Life to Family Businesses" [in Chinese], March 20, 2025.

236 *Nearly half of Chinese entrepreneurs . . . into those shoes:* Hurun Report and CITIC-Prudential Life, "China High Net Worth Family Succession 2022" [in Chinese], December 12, 2022.

238 *only 21 percent of Chinese successors:* HSBC, "Family-Owned Businesses in Asia: Harmony Through Succession Planning 2025," May 12, 2025.

239 *only 29 percent generate . . . 15 points for non-family transitions:* Acha Leke et al., "Passing the Baton: Creating Value Through CEO Succession at Family Businesses," McKinsey & Company, February 3, 2026.

241 *"No matter how excellent": Xinhua*, "Liu Chuanzhi's Iron-Fisted Approach to Corporate Governance: Children of Senior Executives Banned from Joining Lenovo" [in Chinese], *Sina*, April 16, 2012.

241 *"The greatest failure of a leader":* Zhang Ruimin, *Haier Is the Sea* (Beijing: China Machine Press, 2015).

246 *their goal of achieving:* Kelvin Pan in discussion with McKinsey, September 12, 2025.

246 *a fifty-fold expansion:* From 20 million RMB ($2.9 million) to 1 billion RMB ($142.9 million); Kelvin Pan, in discussion with McKinsey, September 12, 2025.

EPILOGUE On the Cusp of the Next China

253 *tens of thousands of Chinese students:* Institute of International Education (IIE), "International Students," Open Doors Data, n.d.; there were 277,398 students from the Chinese mainland enrolled in US higher education institutions during the 2023–24 academic year and 265,919 during 2024–25, a figure that has been dropping annually since peaking at 372,532 in the 2019–20 academic year.

253 *while fewer than two thousand:* Institute of International Education (IIE), "US Students Abroad," Open Doors Data, November 2024; there were 1,749 US students studying abroad in China in 2023–24.

Index

RAISING READERS

Books Build Bright Futures

Dear Reader,

We'd love your attention for one more page to tell you about the crisis in children's reading, and what we can all do.

Studies have shown that reading for fun is the **single biggest predictor of a child's future life chances** – more than family circumstance, parents' educational background or income. It improves academic results, mental health, wealth, communication skills, ambition and happiness.[1]

The number of children reading for fun is in rapid decline. Young people have a lot of competition for their time. In 2024, 1 in 10 children and young people in the UK aged 5 to 18 did not own a single book at home.[2]

Hachette works extensively with schools, libraries and literacy charities, but here are some ways we can all raise more readers:

- Reading to children for just 10 minutes a day makes a difference
- Don't give up if children aren't regular readers – there will be books for them!
- Visit bookshops and libraries to get recommendations
- Encourage them to listen to audiobooks
- Support school libraries
- Give books as gifts

There's a lot more information about how to encourage children to read on our website: **www.RaisingReaders.co.uk**

Thank you for reading.

hachette UK

---

[1] OECD, '21st-Century Readers: Developing Literacy Skills in a Digital World', 2021, https://www.oecd.org/en/publications/21st-century-readers_a83d84cb-en.html

[2] National Literacy Trust, 'Book Ownership in 2024', November 2024, https://literacytrust.org.uk/research-services/research-reports/book-ownership-in-2024